The Myth of Social Action is a powerful critique of contemporary sociology and a call to reject the prevailing orthodoxy. Arguing that current sociological theory has lost its way, Colin Campbell presents a case for a new 'dynamic interpretivism', a perspective on human conduct which is more in keeping with the spirit of traditional Weberian action theory. Discussing and dismissing one by one the main arguments deployed against individualistic action theory, he demonstrates that this has been wrongly rejected in favour of the interactional social situationalist approach now dominating sociological thought.

Colin Campbell is Reader in Sociology at the University of York. He has written widely on sociological theory, culture and cultural change, religion, and the sociology of consumption. He is the author of *Toward a Sociology of Irreligion* (1971) and *The Romantic Ethic and the Spirit of Modern Consumerism* (1987).

D1352378

The myth of social action

Colin Campbell

University of York

CAMBRIDGE
UNIVERSITY PRESS

PUBLISHED BY THE PRESS SYNDICATE OF THE UNIVERSITY OF CAMBRIDGE
The Pitt Building, Trumpington Street, Cambridge CB2 1RP, United Kingdom

CAMBRIDGE UNIVERSITY PRESS
The Edinburgh Building, Cambridge, CB2 2RU, United Kingdom http://www.cup.cam.ac.uk
40 West 20th Street, New York, NY 10011–4211, USA http://www.cup.org
10 Stamford Road, Oakleigh, Melbourne 3166, Australia

Printed in the United Kingdom at the University Press, Cambridge

Typeset in Plantin

A catalogue record for this book is available from the British Library

Library of Congress Cataloguing in Publication data

Campbell, Colin, 1940–
The myth of social action / Colin Campbell.
     p.   cm.
Includes bibliographical references and index.
ISBN 0 521 55079 3
1. Action theory. 2. Sociology – Philosophy. I. Title.
HM24.C229 1996
301'.01-dc20 95–9288   CIP

ISBN 0 521 55079 3 hardback
ISBN 0 521 64636 7 paperback

WD

For Verna

Contents

1 Introduction

This book is a critique of a critique. In other words, it is a defence. It defends that form of action theory with which Weber's name has traditionally been associated; one which presumes that action refers to behaviour possessed of a subjective meaning. It follows that the object of my attack is that critique of this position which has been mounted over the past twenty to thirty years by the proponents of a newer, 'social', form of action theory. One that has come to the fore as a result of what has been called the micro-sociological revolution of the 1970s and early 1980s (although this phrase is rather misleading as those perspectives that rose to prominence at this time were actually less specifically 'micro' than 'interactional' in character). For it was generally proponents of these perspectives who took it upon themselves to launch an attack on the traditional idea of action, aided in large part by certain post-Wittgensteinian linguistic philosophers and philosophers of action. The critique that they launched can now be judged, from the standpoint of the 1990s, to have been successful. For one can say that most contemporary sociologists, at least in Britain, now accept this critique as valid. This would appear to be just as true of those sociologists who do not adopt a micro or interactional perspective as of those who do. Consequently to reject this critique and defend the traditional theory of action is, in effect, to attack contemporary sociology in general.

Now I have long believed that sociology should be a broad church discipline, one which permits its members to study any aspect of any social phenomena in any manner they wish; so long, that is, as the rights of subjects are respected. Consequently I do not approve of those sectarian disputes that regularly break out between those who hold to differing versions of the 'one and only true faith' that is sociology. Not only do I see little point in telling my fellow professionals that they are wrong to be doing whatever it is they are doing (even if I should think it), but I expect fellow sociologists to be tolerant of my own preferred interpretations and practices. However, unfortunately, sociology is not always (or even often) animated by such a liberal and tolerant spirit. Those who wish to promote their own approach to the study of social life often find it convenient to do so by exaggerating, or even inventing, deficiencies in those schools of thought or perspectives that currently prevail. This, it seems to me, was the situation in the 1970s and early 1980s, when advocates of the new micro-sociologies frequently matched some of their harshest critics in the degree to which they manifested intolerance. More crucial, however, was the way in which they represented their specific understanding of the nature of sociology as one which was *necessitated*, and indeed largely *justified*, by what they identified as incoherences and inadequacies in the premises that had long guided action theory. Hence the case commonly presented for doing various forms of ethnomethodology, phenomenology, Goffman-style dramaturgical analysis, and even some forms of symbolic interactionism, was, at the same time, represented as the case against the traditional form of Weberian action theory.

As a Weberian myself naturally I found such negative claims extremely disturbing – so much so that I was stung into formulating my own response. This book is the result of that response, and I feel it important to stress that my primary intention in writing it was to defend my own position, not to attack that of others. However, in practice, such a distinction is hard to make and especially in the latter part of the book, defence slips easily into attack.

The origins of a critique

In fact most of the arguments deployed in the book pre-date my irritation with the micro-sociological critique, and have their origins in the research undertaken for *The Romantic Ethic and the Spirit of Modern Consumerism*. As the title implies, that work was modelled on Weber's famous essay on Protestantism and capitalism, and followed a period in which I studied Weber's work very closely. This was not only an interesting and rewarding exercise but one that led me to develop some ideas of my own concerning the study of action. It was therefore with the principal intention of working out the full implications of these that I began work on this book in the early 1980s. However, I quickly realised that the Weberian vision of sociology which I was intent on developing was no longer one which I shared with my colleagues in the discipline. For although most of them still professed to hold him in high esteem – often claiming to find his work a source of inspiration – in practice they no longer adopted Weber's programme for the discipline. Indeed, they no longer held to his definition of its subject-matter; nor, as he did, regarded 'motivational understanding' of human conduct as central to the discipline.

Consequently I was forced to turn my attention to the beliefs of my fellow sociologists and to their strange abandonment of what were, to me, central features of the interpretive action tradition. Two developments in particular concerned me since they seemed to undermine this tradition completely. These were the widespread belief that actors' reports of their conduct could not be employed as a resource with which to understand their actions, and the abandonment of the study of motive for the study of motive talk. Hence I began to gather material concerning the arguments advanced to justify abandoning the classic action theory position on these two critical issues. Gradually, after devoting a good deal of time to studying the writings of a variety of sociologists, I became aware that I was encountering the same arguments over and over again, no matter from which micro-sociological perspective these tenets were being attacked. Not only that, but each writer appeared to share the same underlying assumptions and premises concerning action, accounts, meaning and, indeed, the discipline as a whole. This was somewhat surprising as I was reading material by sociologists who belonged to such different theoretical traditions as phenomenology, symbolic interactionism, and ethnomethodology. However, it did appear that there was a single common position – in effect, a paradigm – underlying all the current micro-sociologies, one which provided the basic rationale for rejecting the classic action theory position. This realisation led me to shift my focus of attention from the specific arguments with which I had started to the more general position which, it now appeared, underlay them all.

The dogma of social situationalism

It was not easy to study this paradigm, however, for although what one might call its negative features (that is, the case against Weberian action theory) were readily apparent, its more positive ones were less obvious. Thus, whilst the representatives of each known, named, micro-sociology, were usually eager enough to outline what made their particular tradition of inquiry unique, they were, perhaps understandably, less concerned to identify what it was that they all had in common. Indeed, it was not clear that such spokespersons were necessarily fully aware of what this might be, for this shared paradigm appeared to consist of mainly taken-for-granted assumptions. Faced with this difficulty I decided to try and stand back from my material, in order if possible to see this larger picture more clearly. To help me in this I turned to an examination of sociology textbooks and dictionaries. By studying these, and in particular by comparing their contents over time, I believed that I could discern more clearly just what these taken-for-granted assumptions might be. Textbooks and dictionaries are, I believe, very useful in this respect as they tend to reveal a discipline's prevailing dogmas (as well as some of the contradictions and ambiguities to which they give rise) more clearly than any other form of writing. The result of this exercise was that I was able to give 'my enemy' – that is to say, the positive form of the critique of Weberianism – a name. I was able to identify it as 'social situationalism'.

In the pages that follow the principal tenets of social situationalism are identified as the definition of the subject-matter of sociology as 'social action' (which is, in turn, taken to mean conduct which has 'a social meaning'), whilst such meanings are presumed to be constituted and defined by social situations. These are tenets which have the effect of defining the subject-matter of sociology as situated conduct rather than action in the conventional sense, and hence serve to explain why Weber's position is rejected. Now, as indicated, these tenets would appear to be so widely accepted by contemporary sociologists that most of them do not see them as contentious. Rather, they simply take them for granted, such that these beliefs have the status of dogma.

Indeed, it is revealing to consider what the most taken-for-granted premise in contemporary sociology might be. For I would propose that it is the claim that 'social action' constitutes its principal subject-matter. Certainly a perusal of textbooks would provide strong support for such a claim (see the discussion in chapter 3). Of course, one can find other definitions; ones in which alternatives such as 'society' or even 'social structure' are mentioned. Yet these are exceptions. There is little doubt that social action is the most favoured term. However, it is also the case that this central, defining, concept is not the subject of much discussion. Indeed, it is rarely defined. Rather its status as the term best suited to define the subject-matter of the discipline is simply taken-for-granted. Most sociologists would appear to regard the statement as entirely self-evident; obviously *sociology* consists of the study of *social* action – what could be more obvious? One imagines that sociologists of most theoretical persuasions (or indeed, of none) would probably have little difficulty agreeing with it. Perhaps the fact that such a high degree of consensus exists in a discipline otherwise noted for its intellectual discord, schismatic tendencies and widespread theoretical eclecticism, should be taken as grounds for celebration. Unfortunately, it is far more likely that agreement in this respect stems from the extensive latitude with which this term is, in practice, interpreted. Something which in turn stems from the remarkable lack of discussion over its actual meaning.

Indeed, there is a certain irony here which non-sociologists especially might well appreciate. It is that whilst sociologists are among the most vociferous advocates of 'reflexivity' on the part of academics and researchers, and hence among the first to criticise practitioners of other academic disciplines for failing in this respect, they seem largely to have failed to follow their own advice in this case. For, with a very few exceptions, sociologists in general rarely appear to reflect on the precise meaning and hence suitability of the very concept which is used to define the subject-matter of their own discipline. Not surprisingly, a climate in which there is such a widespread lack of reflection and hence discussion is also one in which taken-for-granted assumptions become entrenched as dogmas. It is the central thesis of this book that such dogmas now constitute a major obstacle to further progress.

An outline of the book

The book commences with a brief survey of the current state of 'action theory' within the discipline, together with evidence of how the classic Weberian conceptual trichotomy of action, behaviour and social action has been replaced by the modern dichotomy of behaviour and social action. Then the rise of social situationalism is charted, prior to outlining and then confronting each of the principal arguments which situationalists employ in order to try and exclude the study of subjective meaning from the discipline. These are identified as first, the argument by denial; second, the argument through exclusion; and third, the argument through incorporation. In addition, specific chapters are devoted to such critical issues in the confrontation between the action and social action perspectives as: actions and accounts (especially motives); the claim that individuals learn everything from others; and the significance accorded to language and communicative acts. Finally, although this book is largely critical in tone some comments are made in the last chapter concerning the direction which a revived, and 'de-situationalised', action theory might take.

The author's position

The general support which is manifest here for the traditional form of action theory should not be taken as implying that my own position is identical with Weber's or, indeed, for that matter, with any of the other main exponents of this tradition. My own understanding of this form of analysis differs in certain critical respects from that outlined by such theorists as Talcott Parsons or Alfred Schutz, or at least from the positions which are usually attributed to them. This is true in two crucial respects. First, in the treatment of rational action as the norm (if not also as the ideal), against which all other forms of action are to be judged; and secondly, in the exclusion of any concern with behaviour. My own view of action theory is that it is necessarily only part of a wider theory of conduct, and hence must embrace the study of behaviour, whilst I consider that there are no good grounds for according rational action a privileged place in any conceptual scheme. However, it is my contention that, despite these caveats, my position is still 'Weberian' in essence.

This does not mean that I endorse Weber's view of sociology unreservedly. In fact, some criticisms of his conceptual distinctions are made in the course of the discussion that follows, and my own position differs from his in at least one crucial respect. This is that I consider 'social action' to be a redundant concept. This is not, however, to my mind, a matter of great moment, since I do not believe that this concept is as central to Weber's conceptual and theoretical scheme as sociologists commonly imply. But then sociologists are noted for their ability to differ with each other over the correct interpretation of Weber's writings and hence this contention should surprise no one. This is not the place to provide all the details which I believe justify this claim, so I shall content myself with observing that whenever I have been at a loss to know how best to resolve those ambiguities which all readers encounter in Weber's work, I have generally tried to resolve them by paying more attention to what might be called his 'applied' work (especially perhaps, *The Protestant Ethic and the Spirit of Capitalism*), than to his rather cryptic observations on the nature of sociology. It is my belief that if one approaches Weber's work in this way, one will arrive at the conclusion that 'action', and not 'social action', is the more significant concept.

A final caveat

Arguments concerning theories of action – together with those conceptions of the individual actor which these theories contain – constitute the principal subject-matter of this book. However, the fact that it is limited to these topics should not be taken as implying that I consider the subject-matter of sociology to comprise no more than this. Thus, although I criticise contemporary sociologists for defining the subject-matter of the discipline as social action, and argue strongly that it should be action, this does not mean that I would be content with a definition which stated that sociology is merely the study of action. On the contrary, although grounded in such a study, I believe that the discipline should include investigation of social interaction, social institutions, social structures, in addition, critically, to cultural systems. How precisely the study of these phenomena should be related to the study of action (especially as envisaged in the final chapter) is a question I hope to answer in a subsequent work.

2 Action reported missing in action theory

It has become a commonplace for sociologists to observe that there is no action in Parsons' famous voluntaristic theory of action or action schema. Either they argue that his elaborate and analytic model never did actually find room for action as such, or else they argue that whatever merit it might have had in this respect was only contained in *The Structure of Social Action* (first published in 1937) and that this early promise was not fulfilled in his later work. But perhaps this view embodies a judgement which is unfair to Talcott Parsons; not because, as some have claimed, that his is indeed a genuine theory of action, but rather because there is no action in *any* of the existing, designated 'theories of action' in the discipline of sociology.[1] Parsons is certainly not the only theorist against whom such an accusation can be levelled. It can equally be argued, for example, that Alfred Schutz's phenomenologically inspired 'theory of action' is really only a theory of meaning, whilst symbolic interactionism is merely concerned with individuals who 'name' objects, people and events or 'negotiate meaning' with others rather than with people who 'act'. In a similar vein one can argue that the actor in Goffman's dramaturgical model is portrayed as 'impressing others' through the manner of their action rather than accomplishing the action itself. Finally, what are commonly described as 'rational actor' and 'rational choice' theories can be seen to be little more than perspectives for studying forms of decision-making rather than frameworks for the analysis of action. Indeed, the judgement that the majority of 'action theories' do not, in practice, really address the phenomenon of 'action' is one which it is hard to avoid no matter which perspective is under examination. Perhaps, therefore, sociologists should no longer single out Parsonian action theory for special comment in the way they do, but report instead that action is missing in action theory as a whole.

It will be argued in the pages that follow that this is not an entirely unreasonable conclusion, even if it is does require some qualification. For it would appear that the action theory tradition within sociology has lost its way, with sociologists straying far from both the spirit and the form of Weber's original enterprise. The promise contained in that early programme has, like Parsons', simply not been fulfilled. What is more, it will be argued that there is little likelihood that this promise will be fulfilled in the near future so long as sociologists strive to develop 'action theories' which have little connection with Weber's original concept of action. For the essence of his vision was the belief that the key to explaining human conduct lay in adopting the actor's point of view and hence in focusing on that subjective perspective which was the very defining feature of action. However, despite the general impression given in sociology textbooks that Weber's action theory relates closely to current theories, together with the widespread approval which many sociologists still accord to his work, few, if any, contemporary sociologists actually adopt his approach to the study of action.

What is action theory?

But before developing this gloomy diagnosis any further it might be sensible to outline what the term 'action theory' conventionally covers, as it would be unwise to treat its meaning as self-evident. In fact the term is used to cover a diverse and far from coherent tradition of work, not just in sociology but also in the social and behavioural sciences more generally. Yet apart from a readiness to accord prominence to the concept of action it is not always obvious what these different strands of theorising have in common. On the surface what appears to unite them is an acknowledgement that their approach has been influenced by the work of earlier action theorists, with Weber (closely followed by Parsons) most commonly nominated as the principal source of inspiration. Indeed if we consult sociology textbooks we can discover that characteristically its pedigree is traced from the early work of Weber and, to a lesser extent, Pareto and Simmel, through to that of Parsons and Schutz. But it is Weber and Parsons who are the two sociologists most commonly identified as action theorists, although among those identified at one time or another as contributors to this tradition have been F. von Mises, Karl Marx, George Herbert Mead, W. I. Thomas, Vilfredo Pareto, Georg Simmel, Alfred Schutz, Herbert Blumer, George C. Homans, Harold Garfinkel and even Erving Goffman. Among contemporary sociologists Jürgen Habermas and Anthony Giddens are those most commonly described as action theorists. Usually commentators are content to observe that action theory is identified by its distinctive subject-matter, which is 'action' or meaningful, voluntary behaviour, as distinct from mere (and therefore 'meaningless' and involuntary) behaviour. Sometimes, however, this theoretical tradition is identified less by its distinctive subject-matter than by what Weber regarded as its distinctive method, that of *verstehen*.[2] It is thus in this guise that it is identified with 'the actor's standpoint', or 'taking the actor's point of view'; although rather confusingly, the terms 'the action frame of reference', or 'the action schema' can also refer to Parsons' highly analytic theoretical system.

Not surprisingly, such a broad general theoretical tradition – one which has been developing for over sixty years – is bound to contain within it some significant variations of emphasis. The most obvious of these is that represented by the contrast between the work of Parsons and Schutz. The difference between the versions of action theory formulated by these two principal inheritors of the Weberian mantle has been described as that between the 'positivist' or 'instrumental-objective' tradition on the one side and the 'hermeneutic' or 'interpretive-subjective' on the other.[3] The latter, most closely identified with Schutz, sees the primary task of the sociologist to be that of carefully exploring how conduct comes to possess meaning for actors. The positivist tradition, on the other hand, takes its lead from Weber's categorisation of actions and in particular the emphasis which he placed on rational action (*zweckrational*). This has led to a close identification of the meaning of an action with the actor's purposes and the understanding of conduct in terms of a formal means-end schema. Thus although both theoretical traditions trace their origins to Max Weber's work they have drifted so far apart that a meaningful dialogue between them seems to be impossible.[4] Finally, it should be noted that an independent North American tradition, owing nothing to Max Weber but taking its inspiration from the work of George Herbert Mead, should also be identified as an important part of the action theory tradition. Thus Roscoe C. Hinkle traces the antecedents of an action orientation in American sociology prior to publication of Talcott Parsons' *The Structure of Social Action* in 1937, to the work of Florian Znaniecki and Robert M. MacIver, and before them, to the pioneering work of Ward, Giddings, Ross, Small, Cooley, Mead, Thomas, Faris and Park.[5]

Action theory outside sociology

As indicated, however, action theories and interpretive perspectives are not confined to sociology but also exist in other disciplines, and therefore it is necessary to note these together with their possible relationship to developments in sociology itself. Three areas in particular need to be mentioned; these are, the other social sciences, especially economics and political science, individual and social psychology, and finally philosophy; each of which, in different ways, is linked to the fate of action theory within sociology. As far as the other social sciences are concerned the most important recent development has undoubtedly been the increasing popularity of 'rational actor' and 'rational choice' theories. During the 1970s and 1980s, a series of publications appeared advocating the employment of models of human conduct based on such theories. Already widely employed in both economics and political science, there were increasing calls for their use in sociology as well.[6] These theories usually take their cue either directly from classical economics or more indirectly via Weber's discussion of formal rationality. Usually they do not assume that individuals necessarily behave rationally; rather, they are more interested in seeing how much of human behaviour can be explained on the assumption that they do. Such theories generally involve carrying over those premises which characterise economic analysis into the realm of sociology, such as that individuals have consistent preference lists and make decisions which maximise their utility (given their current state of knowledge). In this respect they could be said to represent only the latest wave in the continuing attempt to employ rationalist models to understand action which has marked the social sciences since their emergence in the nineteenth century. Although they can trace their pedigree back to Weber, such perspectives characteristically do not take more than a purely formal interest in the actor's point of view. They do, however, emphasise the element of voluntarism in human conduct and attempt to explain why individuals choose to act as they do. Whilst there are those sociologists who clearly believe that it is 'action theories' like these which represent the best hope of further advance in understanding human conduct and society, to date most British sociologists still appear to regard such a perspective as lying outside the mainstream of their discipline.

As far as psychology is concerned the situation is less clear cut. There has been a growth of interest among individual and developmental psychologists since the late 1960s in an action-theoretical perspective.[7] In part, this development has been a response to the decline in influence of behaviourism whilst also being an off-shoot of the cognitive revolution in that discipline. Action terminology is, however, employed in a variety of different psychological traditions with, as yet, little standard usage[8] although attempts have been made to codify this material and hence stimulate a flourishing action tradition within the discipline.[9] Whilst most sociologists are unlikely to be aware of these developments, many will be acquainted with the recent history of social psychology. Here one of the significant developments over the past twenty years has been the development of the 'ethogenic' perspective associated with Rom Harre and colleagues.[10] This movement was also a reaction against the dominance of behaviourism within psychology, one which insisted that individuals should be treated as self-conscious purposive agents rather than merely the objects of experimentation. Consequently, the emphasis was placed on investigating subjects' accounts of their actions with a view to identifying the rules and conventions used to generate their conduct rather than engaging in direct observation of the behaviour itself. As such it is a perspective which is built upon that distinction between action and behaviour which has long been central to sociological action theories. The ethogenic approach has much in common with another movement which has arisen in psychology in recent years, that which has become known as social constructionism.[11] Like the ethogenic approach, behaviourism is rejected and the focus is turned instead to the knowledge and understanding which people have of the world around them. It is the nature and origin of this body of everyday knowledge and the way in which individuals employ it to make sense of their world (rather than any postulated 'real world') which is the focus of study. These meaning systems are assumed to be transmitted, reproduced and transformed in direct and symbolic social interchanges. Both movements can be regarded as clearly within the 'interpretive' tradition and have many points of similarity with sociological interpretivism. How far their emergence to prominence has influenced events within sociology, rather than themselves being the product of sociological influence, it is hard to say; the truth is probably that both these movements together with parallel developments in sociology are fundamentally the product of events in philosophy.

'Action theory' is a term sometimes used by philosophers in the context of discussions of the problems associated with volition, the freedom–determinism debate and the nature of moral responsibility; the notion of human action being a central concept in issues in philo-sophical psychology, metaphysics, and moral and legal philosophy. Much important work has been published in this field since the 1960s and the influence of the post-Wittgensteinian philosophers of language and action has been particularly significant.[12] More will be said of these developments later since they are the greatest importance in under-standing the recent history of sociological thought. Suffice to say at this juncture that it is events in this discipline which have probably had a bigger impact on the fate of action theory in sociology than any other single intellectual or academic movement in post-war years. Indeed, these developments are the principal reason why some observers do not share the gloomy prognosis expressed above, but believe, on the contrary, that sociological action theory is undergoing a renaissance.

Contemporary action theory in sociology

Ironically, given the comments made at the beginning of this chapter, one reason given for this optimism is the widespread revival of interest in Parsons' work and the renewed impetus which this has given to the study of action;[13] something which, in turn, is related to Jürgen Habermas' impressive theoretical contribution to this field.[14] Habermas not only acknowledges his own intellectual debt to Parsons but claims that 'no social theory can be taken seriously today which does not . . . clarify the relationship to Parsons'.[15] Then, in addition, there is the equally impressive contribution of Anthony Giddens, who has been judged by at least one commentator to be 'the leading theorist of action in contemporary sociology'.[16] In fact, Giddens is one of those who has expressed the view that the prospects for action theory are good, declaring, as long ago as 1976, that 'Recent developments in sociology' have included 'a resurgent interest in action, meaning, and convention in the context of human social life'.[17] Certainly there is little doubt that his own work has been a major factor contributing to this 'resurgent interest'. However, despite Habermas' contention, it is not Parsons' work which has served as the major source of inspiration for contemporary sociologists interested in action theory. This is far more likely to have come from the developments in philosophy noted above. As Anthony Giddens observes, this 'resurgent interest in action' has been one of the features of those 'broad philosophical traditions' which have exerted such an influence on the course of sociological theory since the early 1960s.[18] These he identifies as 'existential phenomenology', 'ordinary language philosophy', and 'the philosophy of the later Wittgenstein', remarking that these have effectively replaced the work of Talcott Parsons as the major source of inspiration for those working in the action tradition.[19] Indeed, although Habermas clearly does draw some of his inspiration from Parsons he actually serves to illustrate Giddens' point since his own theory of 'communicative action' draws heavily on ordinary language philosophy, and especially on the work of Austin. But do these developments really mean that there now exist good grounds for hoping that there will be a revival in the fortunes of the interpretive action theory tradition? Will a current generation of sociologists succeed where earlier ones have failed, and provide the basis for a genuine theory of action? Or will these initiatives also peter out, such that the very stuff of action will once more manage to slip through the fingers of the sociological theorist?

Perhaps it is too early to pass judgement, but a review of what exactly has been missing from earlier theories does not appear to provide grounds for much optimism.

In Parsons' case, as noted, the common judgement has been that 'a theory of orientations' or 'of dispositions to act'[20] is what is offered instead of a theory of action. Or, in Giddens' words, '*There is no action in Parsons' "action frame of reference"*', only behaviour which is propelled by need-dispositions or role expectations. The stage is set, but the actors only perform according to scripts which have already been written out for them.'[21] As the last sentence suggests, Giddens is also critical of Parsons for the lack of voluntarism in his schema, as the 'freedom of the acting subject' has become 'reduced . . . to the need-dispositions of personality'.[22] Indeed there are commonly two different senses in which it is claimed that there is no 'action' in the Parsonian schema. The first is through observing that the loss of voluntarism necessarily means that the individual's conduct is no longer viewed as action but as behaviour. The second is by noting that, like the classical economic theory which served as a point of departure for Parsons' theory, what is actually studied is less action as such, than the individual's preparedness or 'disposition' to perform certain acts. This has been described as embodying a 'contemplative position',[23] the very opposite of 'a theory of action, will and active man'.[24] However, it should be observed that not all sociologists accept that these criticisms are necessarily valid,[25] whilst, as we have seen, Habermas for one believes that, for all its deficiencies, Parsons' theoretical approach still warrants the serious attention of theorists. It remains to be seen, however, whether the recent revival of interest in his work will succeed in redressing the central failure to focus on action itself noted above. Whether, in effect, the commonly-noted deficiencies will be compensated for a 'second-time around' as it were. Giddens makes it clear that he does not think this likely, judging the 'newer versions of Parsonianism' to be 'as flawed as the old'.[26]

A similar absence of a focus can be detected in the phenomenological branch of traditional action theory. It is not that the slippage is in the direction of functionalism and determinism. Rather, the principal subject-matter, instead of being 'action' as such, has now become simply 'meaning'. Giddens has criticised the modern interpretive sociologies for failing to deal with action. As he observes, each of them 'deals with action as meaning rather than with action as *Praxis* – the involvement of actors with the practical realisation of interests, including the material transformation of nature through human activity'.[27] As a consequence of this they ignore the fact that social norms or rules are capable of differential interpretation and fail to recognise 'the centrality of power in social life' or the 'problems of institutional transformation and history'.[28] It is these latter deficiencies in particular which concern Giddens and which his own theory of structuration is specifically designed to address. This preoccupation with meaning at the expense of action results in a marked cognitive bias in the phenomenological image of the individual actor. In Schutz's writings, for example, the individual is someone who reflects, recognises, identifies, plans, comprehends, and interprets, but not really someone who *acts*, who in the last resort actually *does anything*. Schutz has explored, with great subtlety, how individuals employ their consciousness to construct meaning out of the flow of everyday experiences. But this discussion is entirely philosophical and takes no account of the psychological, let alone biological, basis of action. One could say that the picture which is presented is very much a philosopher's image of the human condition in the sense that there is no effort, no whiff of that sweaty straining to achieve results, which attends action in the real world. Heritage – who is generally sympathetic to Schutz' position – also notes the absence of any real treatment of action as such in his work. He comments:

the theoretical situation in Schutzian sociology is not unlike 'Grandmother's Footsteps'. The actor is fully equipped for action, but somehow fails to act within the gaze of the theorist. Within Schutz's theoretical gaze the actors are caught in the frozen postures of actions-in-the-course-of-completion; 'cinema' is never quite achieved.[29]

However, that ethnomethodological perspective which Heritage advocates in place of Schutzian phenomenology (and which, to a considerable extent, is an outgrowth of it) is also open to the criticism that it does not study action. For as Giddens observes, Garfinkel's frequent references, in his reports of interactions and conversations, of individuals 'doing' things, or engaging in 'artful practices' or 'practical accomplishments' is misleading. As he comments, ' "Doing" a social practice is much more than rendering it accountable, and this is precisely what makes it an *accomplishment*'.[30] It is this, Giddens suggests, which explains the 'peculiarly disembodied and empty character' of the reports of 'members practices' provided by ethnomethodologists.[31] Then, in addition, it is important to note that ethnomethodology has little interest in the substantive subjective meanings informing the conduct of individuals and even though much is made of the fact that the sociologist as actor shares a common 'members knowledge' with those he or she observes, there is always a danger that the sociologist's interpretations may come to dominate over those of the actors. Consequently, it is not surprising that, as Paul Atkinson has observed, certain strands of ethnomethodology have developed in such a way that they now have a marked 'structuralist and behaviorist [sic] flavor'.[32] Hence although it long appeared as if there could not possibly be any real danger of the phenomenological-hermeneutic tradition of inquiry suffering the same fate as the 'positivist' or 'instrumental-objective' one and succumbing to a behaviourist indifference to the individual actor's point of view, this is no longer the case.

One might add that a very similar point can be made about the theoretical tradition known as symbolic interactionism, which, as represented by the early work of Mead in particular, has an excellent claim to be one of the most promising of all theories of action. Yet here too one finds that in the version of this tradition which has become popular among sociologists actors are presented as individuals who are predominantly engaged in 'defining' situations or otherwise using their symbolic resources to 'negotiate meanings' with others rather than in actually 'acting'. Indeed, there is a clear tendency, which can also be found in the phenomenological tradition, to substitute communication for physical action as the primary object of study. It could also be argued, as Herbert Blumer does,[33] that there is little action in Goffman's dramaturgical perspective either. This is because he completely ignores what it is that actors are actually 'doing' in their interactions – what Goffman refers to as their 'business at hand' – choosing to focus instead on what he presumes is their endeavour to maintain a viable image in the eyes of others.

It would seem, if we summarise the overall position with regard to theories of human action very crudely, as if at present the practising sociologist has a choice between two broad alternatives, neither of which actually focus on action. On the one hand, there are those theories which ignore action in order to concentrate upon the processes of calculation and judgement underlying the decisions which individuals take which lead them to embark on one course of action rather than another. This alternative, as represented by rational actor and rational choice theories, although enthusiastically endorsed by some, has yet to find favour with the majority of sociologists. It does, however, have the merit of being a perspective which embraces voluntarism and takes seriously the issue of why individuals do one thing rather than another, even though it does not consider the real nature of the actor's point of view nor actually examine action as such. On the other hand, the principal alternative on offer is represented by theories which strangely have a similar preoccupation with intellectual processes. However, in this case the focus is less on decision-making than on meaning or sense-making and hence on those bodies of knowledge, cognitive resources and processes (particularly as manifest in language and talk) through which the actor's experiences of the world are rendered intelligible or 'meaningful'. This is very obviously the case with phenomenologically inspired and ethnomethodologically inspired theories, but it also applies (if in somewhat different ways) to symbolic interactionism, to Goffman's dramaturgical metaphor and to both the ethogenic and constructivist perspectives in social psychology. The merit of these approaches is that they do seem to take the actor's point of view seriously (at least in so far as these are collectively embodied in 'lay' understandings) whilst the study of meaning is not tied to a rationalist framework but actually involves exploring those tacit understandings which themselves make knowledge possible. However, here too there is a similar lack of concern with the actual subjective meaning informing the conduct of individual actors whilst, once again, action as such is not the real focus of study. Indeed, it is noticeable that neither alternative shows much interest in the emotive or conative dimensions of conduct or in the aetiology of action. This leaves us with the promise contained in the work of contemporary theorists of action, of whom Habermas and Giddens would clearly be the most important. Perhaps there are grounds for some optimism here? Clearly it is not easy to evaluate the true promise contained in the complex and sophisticated writings of these two 'grand theorists', whilst in any case it could be judged too early to correctly assess the full impact of their work (which one assumes is not yet complete) on the future direction of the action theory tradition. However, whilst it would appear that there are some grounds for optimism, there are also good reasons for believing that the central problem of the neglect of action has still not been resolved.

In Habermas' monumental and imposing work, *The Theory of Communicative Action* (1984–7), he outlines what he describes as four 'basic, analytically distinguishable' concepts of 'social action' in social philosophy and the social sciences.[34] These are teleological, normatively regulated, dramaturgical, and communicative action. Interestingly, he notes that strategic action, which is a sub-form of the teleological, corresponds with the decision-theoretic and game-theoretic approaches in economics, sociology, and social psychology, and really only 'refers to decisions among alternative courses of action', not to action as such.[35] In addition, he observes that the dramaturgical model is 'parasitic' on goal-directed action; people have to be 'doing something' in order to 'perform' in a particular way, as he puts it,[36] whilst the normatively regulated form of conduct model is open to the accusation of perpetuating the 'cultural dope' view of the actor which has traditionally been levelled against the Parsonian schema. Consequently, it is principally his own distinctive contribution, the 'theory of communicative action', which is the focus for any hope of a revitalised theory of action. Habermas uses this term to refer to the interaction of at least two subjects capable of speech and action who establish interpersonal relations (whether by verbal or extraverbal means) with the aim of reaching an understanding about the action situation and their own plans of action and thus coordinating their conduct. Although he is insistent that such action is not equivalent to communication, it is naturally heavily dependent on it, since this is the means through which agreed definitions of the situation are negotiated and actions interpreted. Consequently, language occupies a prominent place in this model of action. In fact, Habermas draws upon such diverse sources as Mead's symbolic interactionism, Wittgenstein's concept of language games, Austin's theory of speech acts, as well as Gadamer's hermeneutics, in an attempt to develop a workable theory of action by integrating insights from philosophy and empirical social science.

One consequence of this is that although he is clearly conscious of the need for such a theory to deal with actions in the sense of 'events in the world' and thus to embody a view of the agent as someone whose conduct 'changes something in the world',[37] it is not entirely clear that his own theory fully lives up to this aim. For example, although he notes the danger, contained in the ethnomethodological and hermeneutic approaches 'of reducing social *action* to the interpretive accomplishments of participants in communication, of assimilating action to speech, interaction to conversation',[38] the considerable stress which he himself places on the role of language, communication and interpretation suggests that this is a trap which he does not entirely avoid. However, the main problem with the theory which he develops must be that it is a theory of interaction and hence not really a theory of action at all. For although declaring his aim to be the 'development' of the theory of action, and describing his own approach as 'action-theoretic' and an exercise in 'interpretive sociology',[39] he admits to abandoning the paradigm of individual, subjective consciousness as employed by Weber. Indeed, he expresses the view that Weber's mistake was that he 'does not start from the social relationship',[40] arguing that the problem of understanding interaction or co-ordinated action is the central problem which should be addressed. Consequently, he quite deliberately replaces an action paradigm with an interactive one.

Habermas is not alone among contemporary theorists in believing that sociological theory is in need of an effective and viable theory of interaction rather than a theory of action. It is a view which has been forcibly expressed by Jonathan Turner. He puts it very bluntly by asserting that

The basic unit of sociological analysis is not action but interaction; and the presumption that one can begin with elementary conceptualizations of action and then progressively move up to the analysis of *inter*action and structure is highly questionable.

He then adds in a footnote: 'Though it can be argued that a conceptualisation of action must precede one of interaction, I am now convinced that the result is either regression back into psychology or a leap into the macro analysis of social structure – without paying much attention to the dynamics of *inter*action.'[41] Interestingly, a marked feature of Giddens' contribution to the theory of action, as represented by his theory of structuration, is the denial of precisely the contrasts posed by Turner in these remarks; that is, those between micro and macro forms of analysis and between an 'actional' and a 'structural' form of analysis. The popular idea that they are opposed to each other or indeed that one is more 'basic' than another is precisely what his theory of structuration is designed to overcome.[42] Hence, in Giddens' view it is an error to believe that sociologists face any such choice. However, even if Giddens' argument is set aside, it is doubtful if one need accept Turner's conclusions. For it is not clear that there is any logical reason for assuming that sociologists are required to treat either a theory of action or a theory of interaction as being more 'basic' than the other. For whilst it may be true that a convincing theory of interaction cannot be built 'on the back', as it were, of a theory of individual action, it is equally true that a theory of action cannot be 'deduced' from a theory of interaction. As long, therefore, as one assumes that sociologists wish to understand human conduct in general and until such time as some suitably general theory exists which can enable them to do this, it would seem obvious that sociology requires both a theory of action and a theory of interaction. Thus in arguing that sociologists should concentrate upon interaction rather than action Turner is merely stating a personal preference for addressing the problem of how orderly interaction is accomplished rather than that of how orderly action is accomplished. By suggesting that studies of individual action necessarily involve a 'regression back into psychology' (which presumably interaction theories do not), Turner is guilty of the old Durkheimian mistake of equating the individual-social distinction with disciplinary boundaries. In any case, the critical point to make in this context concerning both Turner's remarks and Habermas' theory of communicative action is that no theory of *interaction*, no matter how promising and insightful, is likely to revitalise the moribund theory of *action* in sociology.

The first point to make about Anthony Giddens' work is that although, as we have seen, he has been described as 'the leading action theorist' this label is actually something of a misnomer. In the first place, Giddens' enormous published output is of such a quantity and scope as to suggest that he is really a social, and not merely a sociological, theorist somewhat in the grand, and essentially synthetic, style of Talcott Parsons. In the second place, the essence of Giddens' own distinctive contribution centres on a concept – that of structuration – which seeks to transcend the traditional action/structure distinction. In this respect it is misleading to describe him as an 'action theorist'. Since the term which he appears to prefer is 'social practices' perhaps he should be described as a 'social practices theorist'. However, these qualifications noted, it can be said that action or agency is, as Ian Craib observes, 'at the centre' of Giddens' sociological concerns.[43] Essentially, his is a theory which stresses that social life is the outcome of the skilled performance of social practices on the part of reflexive and creative social agents. Yet despite this stress on the fundamental freedom of the agent and the transformative features of action, Giddens also emphasises the fact that action is a 'given' fact of life and that much of the agent's skilled performance rests on a practical and not merely a discursive consciousness. What is particularly encouraging is that Giddens shows a marked awareness of the deficiencies of present approaches to the study of action. For, as we have already seen, he is very critical both of Parsons' action schema and also of the phenomenologists and ethnomethodologists. As regards the latter, both Schutz and Garfinkel are adjudged guilty of a cognitive bias in their concentration on 'action as meaning rather than with action as *Praxis*'.[44] It is presumably because he wishes to retain – and indeed re-emphasise – this crucial characteristic of action that Giddens' own definition of action refers to '*causal interventions of corporeal beings in the on-going process of events-in-the-world*'[45] thereby stressing the involvement of actors with the practical realisation of their interests and thus the actual material transformation of the world through human effort. This is undoubtedly a refreshing counter-balance to the general neglect of actors' interests and real concerns which tends to mark both the phenomenological and ethnomethodological perspectives, as well as the work of Goffman; so too is Giddens' concern to stress the trans-situational aspects of actors' discursive and non-discursive practices. As we have just seen, Giddens' distinctive contribution to the theory of action lies in the concept of structuration and his insistence on the interdependence of agency and structure. This idea is embodied in the essential 'duality of structure' by which he means not simply that structures are experienced by actors as both enabling and constraining but that the 'rules and resources drawn upon in the production and reproduction of social action are at the same time the means of system reproduction'.[46] In this respect he compensates to some degree for the exclusively 'micro' nature of most action theories as well as for their frequent neglect of the phenomenon of power. Also, unlike Habermas, Giddens is not tempted to substitute a theory of interaction for a theory of action, although he too seems to want to distance himself from what he regards as the excessively individualistic nature of conventional action theories.[47]

However, although the ideas presented by these two major theorists are undoubtedly impressive and promising, there are features of the work of both of them which provide some grounds for concern. In particular, it is hard to reconcile the contention that what is wrong with existing theories of action is that they have concentrated too much on action as meaning – thereby ignoring action as *praxis* – with the increased dependence of both theorists on *philosophy* (especially the Anglo-Saxon form of ordinary language philosophy) for material with which to revitalise a moribund theory of action. For a failure to treat action as little more than a cognitive exercise is precisely what tends to distinguish the work of most of these philosophers, thereby rendering it of dubious value to sociologists. At the same time, it is also hard to see how the unfortunate tendency displayed by many contemporary sociologists to substitute the study of communication for the study of action is likely to be redressed by the construction of theories which draw heavily upon philosophical theories of *language*. How is the very real danger of 'reducing action to an interpretive accomplishment' going to be overcome by developing a theory of *communicative* action? Indeed, the suggestion of Habermas that many of the crucial questions concerning action (free will, causality, mind–body, intentionality, etc.) are ones which 'can equally well be dealt with in the contexts of ontology, epistemology, or the philosophy of language'[48] is surely a recipe which, if anything, is designed to make matters worse in this respect. Now even though Anthony Giddens does not incorporate large sections of ordinary language philosophy into his theory in quite the way that is the case with Habermas, he also appears to share this view. Thus although taking issue with some of the conclusions reached by the philosophers of action he too has, if only by default, largely allowed them to set the agenda when it comes to questions concerning the nature of human action. Consequently one cannot help feeling that both Habermas and Giddens, although correctly identifying what is missing from theories of action, may not be looking in quite the right direction for viable solutions to the problems. There is one point, however, which marks the work of both of them, and indeed almost all contemporary theorists of action, yet which is rarely the subject of comment. This is the fact that they are all presented as theories of *social* action rather than theories of *action* and it is this difference, more than any other, which appears to mark them off most clearly from earlier generations of theorists. Certainly for Weber, social action and action were not identical categories and it is not clear that action theory and social action theory are identical either. If, therefore, one is searching for the immediate cause of the present parlous state of action theory in sociology it could be that this difference provides the vital clue concerning where exactly one should look.

3 Action and social action

Over the past twenty to thirty years, there has been a marked change in terminological usage favoured by British sociologists. Increasingly, the term action has been displaced by the term social action.

In the 1960s and the early 1970s British sociologists tended to regard action rather than social action as the central concept. Thus John Rex in his *Key Problems of Sociological Theory* (published in 1961) refers to action as 'the simplest theoretical term of all in sociology',[1] and does not accord 'social action' a separate entry in the index to the book but relegates it to the status of a sub-heading under 'action'. Similarly, Percy S. Cohen in his *Modern Social Theory* (published in 1968), although discussing social action at length, also sees fit to list it as a sub-heading under 'action' in the index.[2] Again, it is 'Action' and not 'social action' which is the featured entry in David Martin's *50 Key Words in Sociology* (published in 1970) and, what is more, he proceeds to describe it as 'the fundamental concept in the study of social relations and social interaction'.[3] By the end of the 1970s, however, there had emerged a marked tendency to treat the two terms as if they were interchangeable, heralding the beginnings of a reversal of the former order of significance. Thus, both G. Duncan Mitchell (*A New Dictionary of Sociology*, 1979) and Panos D. Bardis (*Dictionary of Quotations in Sociology*, 1985) combine their entries for 'Action' and 'Social Action',[4] whilst Burrell and Morgan refer to 'social action theory *or* the action frame of reference'.[5] In his dictionary, Mitchell asserts that 'social action' is a 'more useful term' than 'action':[6] a view apparently shared by Alan Dawe who, in an intriguing reversal of David Martin's judgement, describes social action as 'the single most central [*sic*]concept in sociology'.[7] By the 1980s the term 'social action' has become predominant and the term 'action' is in danger of disappearing altogether. Thus, David Lee and Howard Newby, in their text *The Problem of Sociology: An introduction to the discipline* (1983) reverse the Rex and Cohen treatment of the two terms by putting '*see* social action' under the entry 'action' in their index.[8] In Stephen

Mennell's book *Sociological Theory: Uses and Unities*, the chapter headed 'Action' in the 1974 edition has been changed to 'Individual' 'Society' and '*Social* Action' (italics added) by the 1980 edition.[9] Similarly, whilst the first (1980) edition of Michael Haralambos' very successful 'A'-level text *Sociology: Themes and Perspectives* contains no reference to either 'action' or 'social action' in the table of contents or the index, by the time the third edition was published in 1990, the heading 'social action theories' is included in the table of contents and in the index, even though there is still no reference to 'action'.[10] Interestingly, a recently published dictionary of sociology appears to indicate a reversal of this trend, for there is an entry for 'action' whilst under 'social action' it simply says, 'see action'.[11] However, closer examination reveals a very different situation, for the entry under action actually reads, 'any unit or sequence of *social* activity or *behaviour*'.[12]

One could argue that the presence or absence of the qualifying adjective 'social' is not really a matter of much significance since whether sociologists refer to 'action' or to 'social action' reflects little more than a stylistic preference. In addition, as has just been noted, some sociologists obviously believe that one can substitute these terms for one another without significantly altering the meaning expressed, whilst a case could even be made for claiming that Weber himself did not always employ the two terms with great care.[13] Of course, even then some explanation would still be required for the changes which have been noted. In particular, one would want to know why it is that social action has become the preferred term. Especially since if it is true that these terms can be substituted for each other one wonders why earlier generations of sociologists considered it important to distinguish between them and why the present generation believe that it is no longer necessary to do so. What is somewhat strange, and indeed a little disturbing in this respect, is the apparent indifference of sociologists towards this issue, for one would have expected such a marked change in usage to be accompanied by some extended debate of the respective merits of the two terms. However, discussions of this issue are virtually non-existent and the change in usage seems to have occurred almost by accident. Indeed, even to this day, it is rare to find any discussion of the relative merits of these two terms either in the introductory textbooks referred to above, in books ostensibly devoted to discussions of the phenomenon covered by the term 'social action',[14] or even in the general theoretical literature.

In fact, this is not a trivial issue because the declining usage of the term 'action' together with the tendency to treat the two terms as equivalents effectively signals the loss of a concept – something which is indicative of a fundamental change in the nature of the discipline. Indeed, it would be one thing to observe that over a period of some twenty to thirty years sociologists have reversed the order of priorities with regard to the two concepts under discussion, now preferring to highlight the term 'social action' whilst treating that of 'action' as secondary (although this would still be important enough to warrant investigation). It is, however, quite another matter to use one concept where formerly there were two. In fact, to be precise, it is rather a matter of three concepts being reduced to two since Weber's original scheme distinguished between behaviour, action and social action, whilst contemporary discussions typically only refer to behaviour and social action.

It is perhaps time to remind ourselves of Weber's original position on this issue and the nature of his distinction between action and social action. Indeed, perhaps it would be best to refer to a classical position rather than to a Weberian one on this matter for this has been echoed by subsequent generations of sociologists. The key features of this position are, first, that a clear contrast is drawn between behaviour (usually envisaged as consisting largely of involuntary reactive responses) and action, defined as voluntary and subjectively meaningful conduct; and second, that a further contrast is drawn between action and social action with the latter envisaged as a sub-type of the former (usually distinguished by the fact that the meaningful orientation is to others). In addition to Weber himself, sociologists as diverse as Schutz, Znaniecki, Mitchell and Cohen[15] have all apparently subscribed (albeit with modifications) to this basic trichotomy. The crucial feature of this classificatory scheme is that social action is a sub-type of the more general and basic category of action upon which it necessarily depends. The trichotomy thus comprises a fundamental contrast (behaviour/ action), in which the second term (action) is then subjected to a further division (action/social action).

The crucial feature of what, by contrast, we might call the modern position is the virtual absence of the concept of 'action' as this classical trichotomy is collapsed into a dichotomy consisting of just behaviour and social action. What follows from this is that the concept of social action is no longer regarded as dependent on a more general concept of action but is rather considered to be a basic concept in its own right. The concept of action, then, if not dispensed with altogether is either treated as a synonym for social action itself, or alternatively regarded as a relatively insignificant (because irrelevant or inaccessible) variant of social action. Indeed, in many instances (especially in introductory textbooks) the term is employed in a solely heuristic capacity in order to enable the author (or authors) to outline the contrast with behaviour prior to its subsequent abandonment in favour of 'social action'.[16]

This contrast between the classic and the modern approach is well illustrated by the manner in which the definition of 'social action' is approached by the different generations of sociologists. Those sociologists writing before the 1980s, and working within an action theory framework, were generally concerned to define the term in such a way as to distinguish it from the associated concept of 'action'. Hence their definition, like Weber's, was an attempt to discriminate social action from a more general category and tend to be structured along such lines as, 'action is social in so far as . . .', 'Social action, as distinct from action in general, begins . . .', or 'action is social when it . . .', etc. Contemporary sociologists, by contrast, in so far as they bother to define the term social action at all, are far more likely to be concerned with discriminating social action from behaviour, thereby collapsing Weber's two distinctions into one or, interestingly, to regard the activity of defining social action as equivalent to specifying the subject-matter of the discipline as a whole.

Change in subject-matter

This latter point shows that what is at issue here is no mere semantic quibble. On the contrary, it is clear that this change in usage is related to a redefinition of the primary subject-matter of sociology. Now one might be tempted to argue that 'social action' has always been regarded as the central subject-matter of the discipline, in the classical approach as much as in the modern, and hence that there has not really been any significant change in this respect. After all, Weber himself wrote that 'sociology . . . is a science which attempts the interpretive understanding of social action'[17] and observed that social action was sociology's 'central subject matter'.[18] Whilst this is true it is important to note that in the sentence from which the second quote is taken Weber also includes the observation that 'Sociology . . . is by no means confined to the study of "social action"'[19] a comment which is hardly in keeping with the modern insistence that sociology is 'the study of social action *alone*',[20] or that the primary purpose of sociology is to understand and '*explain the meaning of social action and interaction*'.[21] The crucial point, however, is less that Weber included action along with social action in the subject-matter of sociology, than the fact that what today's sociologists mean by the latter term is not at all what Weber meant by it. In this respect the continuity of usage is deeply deceptive and merely serves to obscure a fundamental revolution in the meaning given to this term.

For at the same time that the term action has been replaced by that of social action there has been a parallel substitution of the words 'action theory', 'the action approach' and 'the action perspective' with 'social action theory', the 'social action approach' and 'the social action perspective'. What is more, in the course of this 're-phrasing' of the action tradition, Weber's contribution to the discipline has also been 're-located'. Thus, whereas in those books published in the 1960s and 1970s Max Weber's contribution to sociology was typically discussed under the heading of 'action theory' or the 'action perspective' and characteristically linked to the work of Parsons (and sometimes, as noted, to that of Von Mises, or Pareto), today it is to be found under that of *social* action perspectives'[22] or '*social* action theory'.[23] These new headings are then employed to associate Weber's work, not with Parsons, but with symbolic interactionism, phenomenology and even ethnomethodology.[24]

This change can clearly be seen if we compare the two editions of the highly successful A-level textbook *Introductory Sociology* edited by Tony Bilton et al.,[25] the first published in 1981 and the second in 1987. There are two intriguing differences which, since they do not appear to fall under the heading of 'corrections', one can only assume come under the heading of changes which the editors felt it necessary to make in order, as they put it, to 'take account of shifts and developments in certain areas of debate within sociology'.[26] The first change worthy of note can be seen in the table of contents. In the 1981 edition one of the five main subheadings in 'Chapter One: Sociology: Themes and Issues', is given as '1.3 The Individual as a Creative Social Actor' and has, as two of its sub-headings, 'Social Action Theory and Practical Constraints'.[27] Six years later, in the second edition, the same chapter one sub-heading 1.3 has been changed to 'Social Action Theory: The Individual as a Creative Social Actor', whilst 'Practical Constraints' is the only sub-heading.[28] In other words, 'The Individual as a Creative Social Actor' has now become a sub-head to 'Social Action Theory', whilst formerly 'Social Action Theory' was a sub-heading of 'The Individual as a Creative Social Actor'. Secondly, when one turns to examine that section of the text which corresponds to these headings one finds another interesting change. This is the addition in the second edition of a brief paragraph defining 'Social Action Theory'. This reads, ' "Social Action Theory" is a general term within which several different approaches can be identified. These range from *Weber's* micro-sociological work (though Weber was by no means just an action theorist), to *symbolic interactionism*, on to the most recent, and radical, action approaches – *phenomenology* and *ethnomethodology*.'[29]

We can see from all this that something much more than a mere shift in preference for terms has occurred. Indeed, something more than the loss of a concept has taken place. What has happened has been nothing less than a revolution in the discipline, one brought about, at least in part, by the rise to prominence of those very theoretical traditions (or at least the last two) with which Weber's name is now routinely associated.[30] This event has itself been called a 'revolution' and yet its full significance is not usually recognised. For it is not merely that new perspectives have come to prominence, or even that greater emphasis has come to be placed on the 'micro' rather than the 'macro'. Rather, it is, as the above evidence suggests, that the map of the discipline as a whole has been redrawn, with new territories marked out and old names appropriated to new uses. The most significant feature of the new topography is the emergence of a new 'imperialist state', one which has successfully over-run that territory previously known as action theory. For as we have just seen, 'the individual as a creative actor' has been driven out, displaced by something called 'social action', and it is this 'social action theory', or 'social action perspective', which is now the new disciplinary super-power.

4 Action versus social action

The 'social action perspective' is an imperialist power within contemporary sociology. It has not simply displaced traditional 'action theory'. It is fundamentally inimical to it. The recent rise to prominence of the social action perspective is the sole and direct cause of the decline of Weberian action theory. Unless its power and influence are reduced – which depends, in effect, upon broad exposure of its many deficiencies and fundamental weaknesses – there is little chance of revitalising the action tradition. Why is there so little awareness of the dramatic nature of this change? How is it possible for so many sociologists to believe that the modern position of social action, if not exactly identical with Weber's original action theory programme, is at least compatible with it? Indeed, the radical difference between the 'modern' and 'classical' positions gives rise to a further question. How is it that sociologists can employ a concept of social action which is independent of a more general concept of action?

One simple answer to this question is that contemporary sociologists are able to employ the concept of social action without reference to the more general concept of action because the adjective 'social' tends to qualify the noun 'meaning' rather than the noun 'action'; that is to say, social action is the term typically used to refer to action which is regarded as possessing a social meaning rather than to action which is itself social. This is illustrated by David P. and Lynn S. Levine's definition: 'Action . . . becomes social action in so far as the orientation of the act is to a socially shared meaning.'[1] Whereas in the classical position 'social' is the adjective which qualifies the noun 'action', with the 'meaning' of all action necessarily subjective in nature (with action deemed social only if it 'involves others', or is affected by, or affects others in some way), the modern position does not depend on any prior notion of non-social action, but rather (as it would seem) on that of non-social meaning. Not that it is quite as simple as that, however, for the modern approach to defining social action is somewhat ambiguous on this question, as we shall see later.[2]

It is this shift which explains why the modern interpretation of social action differs so radically from the classical Weberian one. For Weber was first and foremost an action theorist, not a social action theorist, and his primary emphasis was placed, not on social, communal or inter-subjective meaning, but on subjective meaning. His perspective thus differs markedly from the social action perspective currently prevalent, and it is not easy to justify his identification with it. In place of Weber's definition of action as 'all human behaviour when and in so far as the acting individual attaches a subjective meaning to it' and the social variant of this which includes the 'orientation to others',[3] the modern position not only involves substituting 'all human behaviour when and in so far as there is a social meaning attached to it', but even goes on to claim that *all* action is of this kind. Naturally, this has the consequence of cutting off the phenomenon of social action from any connection with a theory of non-social action; moreover, it divorces the study of meaningful conduct from any inquiry into the actor's subjective states or intra-personal processes.

It is therefore important to state that the key feature of classical action theory was the attempt to explain the conduct of individuals via an understanding of the meanings which their actions have for them. Its most crucial concept, therefore, is that of subjective meaning, and it is consequently this which serves to define the phenomenon of action itself.[4] Consequently, it is the move away from an interest in subjective meaning which explains the loss of the concept of action. The new 'social action perspective' apparently shares with traditional interpretivism a common concern with 'action'. But the original Weberian emphasis on 'subjective meaning' has been displaced by one on 'inter-subjective' and 'communal' meaning, thus breaking the intimate connection between action and the actor's viewpoint. Despite this, contemporary sociologists still struggle to identify Weber with the modern position, collapsing his two distinctions into one, sometimes with bizarre results. Lee and Newby, for example, in their introductory text, begin by quoting Weber's definitions of both action and social action correctly, only immediately to over-ride his distinction in order to conform with the modern position. Their quotations from Weber are followed by what is presented as an inevitable conclusion: to wit, 'Mere behaviour becomes action, then, (a) when it derives from dealings with others and (b) when it is meaningful.'[5]

Why is it that so many sociologists seem genuinely to believe that such an approach to the definition of social action and the subject-matter of sociology is consistent with Weber's? In part, this would seem to be the result of carelessness in the employment of terms, coupled as often as not with a failure to establish what Weber's position really was. It is not unusual to encounter observations such as Tony Watson's 'Sociology . . . is not just about social *behaviour* but about socially meaningful behaviour, or, in Weber's terms *social action*'.[6] As noted above, one reason why this revolutionary change has not received the attention it warrants is the general indifference which sociologists have shown towards the issue of carefully distinguishing action from social action. But there is undoubtedly a deeper reason why this revolutionary change has not been the subject of more comment and discussion in the discipline. There is a popular belief that the 'social action perspective' represents a development of classical action theory; that it is not actually in direct contrast to it, but is rather a working out of themes inherent within that tradition; and thus that it represents in effect a 'building on' the work of Weber, or a 'teasing out' of ideas implicit in his work, rather than, as argued here, a radical departure from the position which he held. It is this belief which helps to explain the apparently unproblematic inclusion of Weber under the general heading of the 'social action perspective'. Consequently, it is not so much the writers of modern textbooks who are really to blame for this confusion as those sociologists who have represented their own work as consistent with Weber's when this is not in fact the case. One can single out two important culprits in this respect: C. Wright Mills and Alfred Schutz.

Although Schutz' writings have probably had a more profound effect on the development of that distinctive 'social action' approach which now dominates contemporary sociology, it would be a mistake to under-estimate C. Wright Mills' influence. As a major representative of the symbolic interactionist tradition, he is also responsible for the wide-spread view that treating social action as conduct with a social meaning is consistent with Weber's position. This is due largely to his highly influential 1940 article 'Situated Actions and Vocabularies of Motive'.[7] In this he first cites Weber (correctly) to the effect that a motive 'is a complex of subjective meaning which seem, to the actor himself or to the observer an adequate ground for the conduct in question' but then follows this with the strange comment: 'The aspect of motive which this conception grasps is its intrinsically social character'.[8] It is strange because whatever 'intrinsically social' quality Mills is able to detect would seem to apply only to his own reconstruction of Weber's concept. For his own definition of a 'satisfactory or adequate', motive is a '*word . . . which is to the actor and to the other members of a situation an unquestioned answer to questions concerning social and lingual conduct.*'[9] However, even if we ignore Mills's substitution of 'word' for 'a complex of meaning', his definition still involves changing Weber's 'actor . . . *or . . . observer*' to 'actor *and* . . . *other members of a situation*' (italics added). Thus, whilst Weber's formulation of the concept of motive allowed for the possibility of its operation in a non-interactional and purely private or personal context, Mills excludes it. At the same time, Mills eliminates the reference to an 'observer' (which could, in the context of Weber's discussion, have referred to the sociologist rather than another actor), and by substituting 'the other members of a situation' *necessarily* attributes a social function to the concept of motive. What is more, Mills treats 'satisfactory or adequate' as if they were adjectives which necessarily contained an ethical or moral referent, such that a motive is seen as functioning to 'justify' conduct, when Weber's original usage clearly embraced a purely technical sense of 'adequate'. In fact, there is nothing 'intrinsically social' about Weber's insistence that a motive is 'a complex of *subjective* meaning' (italics added) despite Mills' claim to the contrary. As we shall see later, this article by Mills initiated an important tradition of work in sociology – one which has become known as the 'vocabulary of motives' – which is still influential today within the discipline. Consequently, the fact that his misuse of Weber's name has gone unchallenged has meant that his name has been employed, unjustifiably, to provide an authoritative seal of approval for this tradition of work.

However, the work of Alfred Schutz is probably the major reason for the difference between the new orthodoxy and Weber's original position, as well as, paradoxically, the reason why it is widely assumed that they are compatible. The second assumption stems in large measure from the fact that Schutz does take Weber's work as his starting point and, what is more, echoes Weber's concern with subjective meaning. Indeed, Schutz is very explicit in his claim to be building on Weber's pioneering work on the study of social action. However, what he does in practice is radically to *redefine* what is covered by that term. He begins by noting that whilst Weber's concept of action has 'no necessary social reference' the concept of social action obviously implies a reference to another human being.[10] Now Schutz takes this to mean that an actor's actions are focused on another person regarded as an experiencing human being, or 'Thou'.[11] Thus he suggests that social action is a term which implies more than a mere awareness of the existence of an other person; it implies recognition of the other as a 'conscious living being' or 'self'. To act towards another person as if he or she were merely a physical thing should not really count as social action.[12] An act does not warrant the adjective 'social', he says, merely because 'its activating stimulus was someone else's behavior as opposed to a natural event'. What makes conduct social is 'the fact that its intentional object is the expected behavior [*sic*] of another person'.[13]

Hence, the term should be taken to imply that the actor is oriented towards the Other in the sense of the 'consciousness and the subjective experiences being constituted therein'.[14]

Schutz' interpretation specifically excludes from the concept of social action any conduct 'directed to the other person's body as a physical object rather than as a field of expression for his subjective experiences'.[15] He justifies this position as follows:

Suppose, for instance, that I act toward the other person as if he were merely a physical thing, paying no attention to his subjective experiences as another self. My own conscious experiences accompanying my action are here not, following the above definition, intentionally directed toward the other self. My action, therefore, is in this case no social action. Weber would apparently agree with this point. Remember that he said the collision of two bicycles does not have the status of social action but that the conversation that follows is indeed social action. The doctor who performs an operation on an anaesthetized patient truly acts 'upon the body' of that patient, but this is not social action in Weber's sense.[16]

From this Schutz draws the conclusion that 'Weber thus requires that the person who is engaged in social action be aware of much more than the mere existence of the other. He must be aware of and interpret the meaning of the other's behavior.'[17] Such a position is clearly in accord with the dominant theme which comes to pervade Schutz' writings, which is 'the understanding of the other person within the social world'.[18] Yet despite the claim made above, this was not Weber's position. Schutz has not recalled Weber's words correctly. What Weber actually said was not that 'the conversation' following the cyclists' collision was social action, but that 'their attempts to avoid hitting each other, or whatever insults, blows, or friendly discussion might follow the collision, would constitute social 'action'.[19] Now it is perfectly clear that 'attempts to avoid hitting each other', as well (in all probability) as 'blows', *do not* imply that the action is oriented towards another human being in their capacity as a 'Thou' or experiencing self but, on the contrary, can be considered to constitute conduct directed to the other person's body as a physical object or thing. It is not at all clear, for example, that 'attempts to avoid hitting' a non-human animate obstruction encountered blocking the road, such as a cow, would differ in any way from the conduct under consideration here. An exceptionally irate cyclist might well swear at, if not actually threaten, such an unfortunate animal. There seems little to support Schutz' suggestion that Weber would agree with the interpretation which he gives to the term 'social action'.

In fact, it becomes very clear that he would *not* have done as soon as one turns to consider some of the other examples which Weber mentions. Weber writes that an action is social 'if in relation to the actor's own consumption the future wants of others are taken into account'.[20] Does such an activity necessarily involve the subjective meaning contained in the conduct of the others, or treating of the other as a Thou or experiencing self rather than as a thing? After all, if, in the course of allocating economic resources, an individual takes the wants of his or her dog into account and sets aside a sum for dog food, this activity would seem to be an exact parallel to that mentioned, even though the dog is not treated as a self-conscious actor. Equally, an individual can engage in a deliberate act of imitation (as a mimic might do, for example) without the conduct of the person imitated being treated as the manifestation of subjective experience; yet Weber identifies such acts as instances of social action (so long as they are intentional and not merely reactive in form).[21] Thus, although some of Weber's comments might appear to lend support to Schutz' claim, most of his examples do not.

What this suggests is that Weber was operating with a broader conception. Indeed, what his examples seem to imply is that the crucial criterion relates to the *decision* underlying the action in question. Indeed, he specifically states that an act of consumption is social if 'the future wants of others *are taken into account* and this becomes one *consideration* affecting the actor's own saving'.[22] In other words, it is the content of the actor's deliberation which is the key, and the crucial question here is whether this process includes any explicit consideration of an other or others or of their actions, wants or characteristics. Hence, the act which follows a decision to imitate another person (or even non-action following the decision not to imitate another person) would be a social act, whilst unconscious imitation would not be. For a cyclist to alter course on sighting another cyclist coming towards him or her (or indeed to decide not to, despite the risk of collision) are thus also social acts. If, however, an individual decides to alter his or her pattern of consumption, or of saving, and does not consider others in any way in arriving at this decision, then that would not be social action. Similarly, if the cyclist took a decision to alter course but without any consideration being given to the presence of another cyclist (say, to avoid a pothole) then that too would not be social action. It is clear from such examples that the actor does not have to regard the other person as a 'Thou' rather than an object; let alone have to engage in an 'interpretion' of the subjective meaning of the actions of others. The critical feature is merely that of 'taking others into account', which in effect means that some recognition of their existence figures in the decision-making process.

All of this is actually clear from Weber's initial definition of social action, where he writes that action is social 'in so far as . . . *it takes account of the behaviour of others* and is therefore oriented in its course'.[23] In effect, Schutz changes Weber's notion of social action as conduct which is subjectively meaningful *and* oriented to others to conduct which involves '*a meaningful orientation* to others'. What is more, he goes on to insist that a 'meaningful orientation to others' must involve treating them as experiencing subjects. Now, there are undoubtedly difficulties with Weber's definition of social action and it could well be that, as Schutz claims, it is 'too broad and imprecise to determine the object of social science'.[24] And, of course, Schutz is free to define social action in any way he wishes.[25] However, what he is not at liberty to do is to invoke Weber's name in support of an interpretation which is clearly at odds with Weber's own usage. The long-term consequences of this largely unnoticed redefinition have been profound. For Weber, social action simply meant 'taking others into account'. For Schutz, it is an activity which *by definition* involves an exercise in the interpretive understanding of another's conscious experiences together with the subjective meanings which, it is assumed, inform their actions. In other words, Schutz has turned social action into a phenomenon which *necessarily* involves interpreting the experiences of others, and excludes from the scope of the concept any conduct not so oriented. Under this view, conduct which simply involves 'recognising', or 'noting' the existence of others is not social action: moreover, neither is that which involves simply perceiving their conduct to be intelligible. For conduct to count as 'social action' it must involve ascertaining the subjective meaning informing the actions of others.

There are two critical consequences of this major redefinition of what contemporary sociologists insist on regarding as the exclusive subject-matter of the discipline. First, it enables Schutz to draw a direct parallel between an actor who engages in social action and the sociologist who engages in the analysis of social action; consequently Schutz is able to argue that Weber's method of *verstehen* is common to both ordinary actors and sociologists. However, whilst one could argue that sociologists, because of the very nature of their discipline, are required to penetrate to the real subjective meanings informing the actions of others if they are to be at all successful in gaining a true understanding of human actions, it remains necessary to prove that ordinary people must do this if they are to interact successfully with others. Schutz, however, does not prove this (as we shall see below) but instead builds the assumption into his definition of social action. Secondly, by defining social action as necessarily involving processes central to an 'understanding of the Other', Schutz effectively makes the 'problem of intersubjectivity' – or how it is that actors can share common experiences of the world and communicate successfully about them – the central problem in the study of (social) action, thereby displacing Weber's primary concern with the 'problem of action'. Consequently how individuals manage to 'know other minds', or come to possess knowledge of the other person's subjective meaning (that is to say, how they interpret the acts of others), has come to displace the question of how they themselves manage to act.

And it is this preoccupation with the problem of intersubjectivity which largely explains why there is no action theory in contemporary sociology. This shift of focus accounts for the fact that contemporary 'social action theories' do not, in general, concern themselves with the contents of the agent's consciousness. In so far as they do, however, the focus is less on the meanings informing the actions of individuals than on their capacity to understand and interpret what others mean by their actions. Emphasis on the individual as observer or 'interpreter' leads in turn to a preoccupation with language and with verbal and non-verbal forms of communication in general. This takes the place of any real interest in action at all – except, of course, for that form of action which *is* communication. Where action theory stresses the importance of discovering the actor's definition of the situation, social action theory stresses the importance of understanding how the actor understands the conduct of others. It is this which makes social action theory virtually indistinguishable from interaction theory. As Bilton et al. admit, 'The general social action approach thus emphasises fluidity and change in social *interaction*.'[26] The reinterpretations of Weberian action theory presented by both C. Wright Mills and Schutz are actually social action theory reconstructions of Weber's original 'subjectivist' formulations. For Weber, neither social action itself nor the concept of motive necessarily implied that conduct was taking place in a context which either the actor or the sociologist had any good reason to define as a 'social situation'. 'Taking others into consideration' does not imply that the actor is interacting with others in a face-to-face manner or indeed necessarily anticipates doing so. Nor does being 'oriented to others' imply any effort to ascertain the subjective meaning of their actions. Nor indeed does identifying a complex of meaning as adequate grounds for one's conduct necessarily have anything at all to do with others. Weber's name has been hi-jacked to endorse positions which he did not hold.

With such reinterpretations of Weber's position as those of Schutz and Mills going largely unchallenged it is hardly surprising that sociologists are able not merely to represent Weber's position as compatible with a 'social action perspective', but actually to believe that it is. Indeed, Heap even goes so far as to assert that although Schutz has criticised and significantly altered Weber's definition of social action, 'he has retained the core of Weber's notion of social.'[27] As we have seen, this is quite untrue. Hence, it is all the more important to state, categorically, that Weber's action theory perspective and the modern social action perspective are not compatible. They are incommensurate. Primarily, this is because for Weber social action was a sub-category of action. Consequently it was a category which *necessarily* consisted of acts which were subjectively meaningful to those who performed them. By contrast, the modern position treats social acts as primary, not as a sub-category of any more general concept. The meaning which social acts embody is thus not necessarily 'subjective' at all, but instead is treated as embodying an 'intersubjective', communal or conventional meaning. Usually this is taken to mean that within a particular culture, social group or interactional context, such acts are recognised by members as possessing a given meaning. From this perspective 'subjective meaning', if indeed it is recognised at all, is presumed to be a sub-category or 'variety' of inter-subjective meaning. The difference between these two perspectives is profound. There have been those theorists (Schutz is the most obvious case) who have endeavoured to demonstrate the necessity of a high degree of overlap between the subjective and the inter-subjective. But it is not at all clear that there are good arguments for believing that this will be the case.

5   The rise of social situationalism

As we have seen, the 'social action perspective' is distinguished by two assumptions. The first is that the subject-matter of sociology comprises social action and/or social interaction (the way that social action is defined effectively obscures the difference between these terms). The second is that the term 'social action' means conduct which possesses a 'social meaning'. Naively, one might have thought that shifting the criterion of definition from action to meaning would involve some attempt to indicate how 'social' meaning differed from 'non-social' meaning. But contemporary sociologists have generally opted for a more radical solution which serves to justify the treatment of social action as the exclusive subject-matter of the discipline. This involves defining non-social action out of existence altogether – something which is achieved by presuming that *all* meaning is necessarily social. Consequently, not only can there be no such thing as non-social action, but defining action and defining social action inevitably become one and the same. This position is reached by accepting a basic syllogism, one which it is not unreasonable to suggest underpins the central dogma of contemporary sociology. This syllogism is as follows: (a) all actions possess meaning (this is their defining characteristic); (b) all meaning is essentially social; therefore (c) all actions must be social actions. As can be seen, this syllogism builds on the presumption that social actions are actions which possess a social meaning. Whilst acceptance of this syllogism leads on to the claim that the meaningful features of an individual's conduct, those which justify describing it as action, are themselves to be viewed as socially derived, socially constructed, socially situated or in some other way essentially 'social' or 'intersubjective' in nature: a position which is therefore seen as implying that action itself must necessarily be conceived of in the same way. Thus one finds that the first premise and the conclusion are frequently run together in an unproblematic fashion as if it unquestionably followed that all action was necessarily social. It has become something of a commonplace for sociologists to represent the contrast between behaviour and action in such a way as to imply that both meaning and action are social in nature. This is illustrated by J. E. Goldthorpe's simple, if startling, statement that 'action is a unit of behaviour that has a social meaning'.[1] The social psychologists Rom Harre and P. F. Secord also claim that 'Action' (again, it is important to note that it is not social action which is being defined) 'has significance and *meaning*, and it occurs in a *social* and not a physiological context'.[2]

Such an approach to the definition of social action is not without its ambiguities, although these are rarely commented on. An obvious problem arises from the natural desire to want to employ the term 'social action' in what appears to be an essentially 'common-sense' manner to refer to conduct which occurs in a 'social context' or a 'social situation', terms which are usually taken to refer to the 'co-presence of two or more actors'.[3] On the other hand, commitment to the central syllogism means that there is an even more powerful tendency to employ the term to refer to any conduct which has a 'social meaning' whether or not it occurs in a social setting. These two approaches do not appear to be reconcilable. There is no good reason why all conduct which has a social meaning should be confined to that which occurs in a 'social situation'. Nor is there any good reason why all conduct performed in a 'social situation' (as defined above) should have a social meaning. It is indicative, however, of the taken-for-granted status of the belief that social action is the exclusive subject-matter of modern sociology that this difficulty is regularly brushed aside. Consequently, what one might call the Goffmanesque fallacy of assuming that all action performed in a 'social situation' *must* have a social meaning (which, in the case of the dramaturgical analogy, would be a 'message' for the other 'occupants' of the 'social situation') is widespread and generally unchallenged within the discipline. Understandably, therefore, sociologists who assert that social action is conduct which possesses a social meaning are usually also keen to claim, as Goldthorpe does, that 'Most of the things we do in the company of human beings . . . are *obviously* social actions'.[4] This 'social imperialism' with its consequent refusal to recognise forms of meaningful human conduct which are not social, is a recognisable trademark of all the social action perspectives. Yet there is more to these perspectives than this, for they also all tend to share other assumptions about the nature of the sociological endeavour – assumptions which concern, in particular, the location of meaning and how it should be studied. Since these stress the importance of the 'social context' or 'social situation', that social action perspective which dominates contemporary micro-sociology can also justifiably be described as 'social situationalism'.

Social situationalism: the paradigm

Social situationalism, so described, cannot be equated directly with any one theoretical tradition or school of thought within sociology or the social sciences. It is not a distinct 'ism' of the kind generally outlined in sociology textbooks. Rather, it should be seen as a set of closely related assumptions which are contained in the theoretical premises of several recognisable traditions but which also pervade and underpin the work of many sociologists (and indeed some philosophers and social psychologists) who ostensibly owe allegiance to none. This new orthodoxy thus resembles a paradigm rather than simply a movement or perspective.[5] Its central tenet is the belief that actions can be identified only by reference to the social context in which they occur. Indeed, situationalists frequently go so far as to equate all meaningful human conduct with socially situated action. As we have seen, such contexts or situations are usually assumed to be 'social' in the sense that the conduct in question is either part of an on-going interaction, publicly witnessed, or if neither of these, embodies meanings which can be considered 'social'. Naturally, this implies that action is always treated as an overt phenomenon. Furthermore, it is claimed that actions can be understood only by means of a study of the contexts of their occurrence and that no extra-contextual factors should be invoked. Great stress is also placed on the 'intersubjective' character of meaning and on the nature and function of language, which phenomenon is itself regarded as wholly 'social' and 'situated' in character. Closely linked to the centrality accorded language is the tendency to treat communicative actions as paradigmatic of all actions and consequently to presume that to inquire into the 'meaning' of an act is to ask a question concerning what the act denotes rather than what it might indicate. Following on from this, meaning is treated as predominantly a matter of cognition and closely equated with 'knowledge'; it is taken for granted that such knowledge, like 'meaning', both 'arises' and is transmitted from individual to individual through 'public', interactional processes.

This disciplinary paradigm has come to prominence largely as a result of an apparently coincidental convergence of several quite distinct sociological (and extra-sociological) traditions and areas of work. In particular, one can single out American symbolic interactionism (as represented, for example, by C. Wright Mills and Herbert Blumer), Goffman-style dramaturgical analysis, and Continental phenomenologically inspired sociology (as represented especially by Schutz). Within sociology itself, those areas of study where it is most apparent would be the 'vocabulary of motives' tradition of analysis inspired by Mills, the sociology of knowledge stemming from the work of Berger and Luckmann,[6] together with some aspects of the sociology of science.[7] However, social situationalism is also marked in the 'ethogenic' and 'social constructionist' movements within social psychology,[8] whilst in the form of discourse analysis[9] and conversation analysis,[10] it straddles the disciplines of sociology, psychology and linguistics. The prominent emergence of Garfinkelian ethnomethodology in recent decades has been crucial, not only as a means of bringing such diverse traditions into contact with one another but also because it is itself (at least in some forms) a crucial part of this movement. Indeed, its importance for the long-term development of sociology may well prove to be less its own distinctive contribution than the fact that it has fulfilled the critical function of acting as the catalyst for a meaningful encounter between what had, until then, been very different philosophical traditions. The origins of contemporary social situationalism undoubtedly lie in the (somewhat fortuitous) coming together of Continental phenomenology and existentialism (especially as represented by Schutz), and British 'ordinary language' and post-Wittgensteinian philosophy of language and action (especially as represented, for example, by Winch).

Whilst ethnomethodology's debt to phenomenology is obvious, its relationship to a post-Wittgenstein philosophy of language and action is rather less apparent and indeed the points of similarity seem to have been largely discovered by ethnomethodologists once their movement was under way. Thus, although there is evidence that Garfinkel was aware of Wittgenstein's work,[11] he appears to have made little use of it, preferring to draw extensively upon the work of Schutz. Indeed, it was not really until the 1970s that references to British 'ordinary language philosophy' became common in the work of ethnomethodologists and those influenced by their work. An interesting example of this changing awareness and associated increasing use of post-Wittgensteinian philosophy can be seen by comparing two well-known articles on motives and accounts: that by Scott and Lyman published in 1968 and that by Blum and McHugh published three years later. In the course of developing their own 'sociology of talk', Scott and Lyman observe in a footnote that 'Contemporary British philosophy, following the lead of Ludwig Wittgenstein, has (apparently) independently advanced the idea of a "vocabulary of motives"', and they go on to cite R. S. Peters (1958) as 'an exemplary case'.[12] However they actually make little use of this alternative tradition in their own work. Significantly, however, only three years later, Blum and McHugh, writing from a perspective more markedly informed by ethnomethodology (if also critical of it), are not only aware of, but actually draw upon, post-Wittgensteinian philosophy.

Thus, they adopt arguments taken from Melden's *Free Action*, judging his discussion to be 'The best criticism of the causal account of motive'.[13] Interestingly, Scott and Lyman drew their inspiration from the work of C. Wright Mills, and it is clear that his position accords very well with that of the post-Wittgensteinians. This is because not only was an interest in language a central feature of the Millsian version of symbolic interactionism but, in addition, he had a special interest in the 'functional conception of language' as opposed to the idea of language as an 'expression of antecedent ideas'.[14] Mills appears to have adopted this position as a result of reading the work of developmental psychologists on the functions of speech, together with that of anthropologists and ethnologists, independently of any input from a British philosophy of language.[15] However, whatever the sources used, Mills' version of symbolic interactionism was clearly compatible with the new approach to language adopted by Wittgenstein's disciples, and can be seen, in retrospect, to have been an important context in which anti-behaviourist and anti-mentalist tendencies could meet. One further important tradition of thought contributed, albeit indirectly, to the rise of social situationalism. This is structuralism and post-structuralism. The popularity, during the 1970s and 1980s, of the work of Saussure, Lévi-Strauss, Foucault, Lacan, Barthes, Derrida, together with that of their many followers, meant that a generation of sociologists came to maturity already inclined to be critical of Cartesianism and the traditional treatment of consciousness as the 'datum' or starting point for the analysis of meaning. On the contrary, these sociologists were temperamentally inclined to be critical of 'intentionalist' forms of analysis whilst sympathetic to theories which attempted to 'de-centre the subject'.

However, whilst no doubt both Millsian symbolic interactionism and structuralist and post-structuralist tendencies have contributed in some measure to the emergence of the new orthodoxy within sociology, it is clearly the confluence of the two previously independent philosophical traditions which has played the key role, a confluence facilitated, as Heritage notes, by the perception of a 'striking convergence' between the work of Schutz and Wittgenstein,[16] or, in Giddens' view, between Schutz and Winch. For, as Giddens observes, although there are 'striking, and not very widely acknowledged, points of connection between . . . Heidegger and the later Wittgenstein', the critical point, so far as the social sciences are concerned, is that between the 'lesser figures of Schutz and Winch'.[17] These very different figures have a common interest in 'the study of the everyday world, the world of the layman as opposed to that of the scientist'.[18] An everyday world is mediated via the communicative categories of language and the 'definite forms of life' which they presuppose. More specifically, Schutz and Winch have a common perception that 'self-understanding is connected integrally to the understanding of others'. Which is to say, 'self-understanding is held to be possible only through the appropriation by the subject of publicly available linguistic forms.'[19]

Following Giddens' remarks, social situationalism champions 'lay' knowledge and understanding over any formal rational, 'scientific', or behaviouristic perspectives, and rejects foundationalism and causal explanation in favour of an espousal (if sometimes qualified) of relativism and an essentially descriptive methodology. More substantive features include a predominant focus on communication and especially upon the nature and function of language, and a stress upon the generally 'situated' nature of all knowledge and meaning. It is this last point which justifies employing the label 'situationalism'. It is 'the social context', or 'situation' which is regarded as both the source and the location of meaning and order; systems of meaning are presumed to be transmitted, reproduced and transformed in specific, interactional social contexts. Indeed, as Jonathan H. Turner has observed, what all the micro-sociologies have in common, despite their apparent diversity, is the belief that 'Social reality involves (1) individual action in (2) concrete social settings and contexts'.[20]

What is most characteristic of the situationalist approach to action is that the concern with 'meaning' or 'the meaningful' is sharply divorced from any study of its subjective location in the consciousness of the individual actor and hence from its role in the initiation and accomplishment of action. Indeed, because of the widespread incorporation of Wittgensteinian anti-mentalism into situationalism, the assumption that given mental states and intra-subjective processes generally constitute a necessary prerequisite for action to occur is often overtly denied. Thus, whilst Weber stressed the need to discover the individual actor's view of the world, the contemporary, situationalist approach requires that sociology should approach its subject-matter, as Mills puts it, 'socially and from the outside',[21] which is effectively the same as arguing that it should be approached 'horizontally in terms of the objective features of the actor's situation rather than vertically in terms of his subjective processes',[22] or indeed that one's analysis should be confined to 'events that are "scenic" to the person'.[23] Mental states or intra-personal processes or, in fact, anything 'internal' or 'under the skull' of the individual is deemed to be of no interest or relevance to sociology. Accordingly situationalists deny that meaning resides in the minds of actors, insisting instead that it is located in social situations and it is shared, 'intersubjective' and contextually determined and manifest. The prime (if not the exclusive) subject-matter of sociology thus consists of 'situated' conduct together with such features of social situations as those rules, conventions, assumptions and practices which are considered to constitute or generate meaning. Talk, especially conversation and discourse, is seen as paradigmatic of socially situated action in general being symbolically 'meaningful' in character and communicative in function. Consequently, situationalism tends to be reliant on certain theories of language both for much of its theoretical inspiration and for its legitimation. It is this 'horizontal', 'external' or 'scenic' approach which characterises all the prominent 'social action' movements within contemporary sociology and reveals the extent to which a concern with 'situations' actually takes precedence over any interest in 'action' itself. It is revealing, for example, that Goffman, who does not find it necessary to define either 'action' or 'social action' (at least as far as this author can discover), does take the trouble to define 'social situation'. He defines it as 'any physical area anywhere within which two or more persons find themselves in visual and aural range of one another'.[24] Equally significant in its way is the fact that C. Wright Mills, in one of the most seminal of situationalist texts, his 1940 article on motives, uses the word 'situation' (or situations, situated and situational) no less than fifty-five times in the course of a brief ten page article.[25]

In practice, this means that there is actually a marked absence of any real concern with 'action' in these perspectives. Either actors' accounts of their actions are studied in place of the physical actions themselves, as in the vocabulary of motives tradition, or talk (including writing) is itself the only form of action examined, as in discourse analysis and conversation analysis. Alternatively, the physical actions of individuals are examined but assimilated to a communications paradigm rather than an action one, and viewed as 'messages' of some sort, as in the case of Goffman's dramaturgical analogy, or that branch of semiotics which studies gestures. Finally there is such an emphasis placed on those processes through which 'knowledge' in general is generated or acquired, or specific actions or action sequences 'take on meaning' or are perceived as 'meaningful' or 'intelligible' by others, as in the case of most branches of phenomenology or ethnomethodology, that little interest is shown in how such understandings might give rise to actions. In the main, attention is focused on the understanding *of* actions, or on the processes through which events and actions are, in general, perceived as *understandable*, together with the bodies of explicit and implicit knowledge drawn on in the process of rendering them so. Talk, discourse, actions *as* talk not as actions, understanding the actions of others, bodies of knowledge, how events and actions are rendered 'intelligible': the list includes everything except how actions themselves are actually accomplished. Hence whatever social situationalism studies and whatever value it might have, it would not appear to offer much in the way of a theory of action.

The principal reason for this failure lies in the strange coupling of a stress on meaningful conduct and a rejection of the subjective viewpoint. Since in practice meaning cannot really be 'located' in social situations, such formulations can only be taken as shorthand for statements which specify the precise circumstances under which given meanings are registered in the minds of particular individuals. For to talk of meaning is necessarily to talk of conscious aware subjects. Objects, symbols, actions or events must always 'mean something' *to someone* (even if the someone is merely the sociologist); strictly speaking, 'meaning' cannot be 'located' anywhere except in 'minds'. Since there is such stress placed on rejecting the mind of the actor as the appropriate site in which to search for the meaning of an act what actually happens in practice is that meaning is re-located in the minds of observers. A common characteristic of social situationalism is thus the privileging of the observer's viewpoint. Indeed, one could claim that situationalism typically replaces the viewpoint of the individual as actor with that of the individual as an observer of action. This is why social situationalist studies of forms of action generally focus on action as a *post hoc* phenomenon, something which has already been accomplished. The observer bias also explains why action is also always assumed to be something overt, necessarily witnessable by others. The question of how and why action occurs is always bracketed out, set aside in order to focus on the question of how that which has been performed is perceived by others as meaningful and hence as action. Thus, in ethogenics the stress is on the way that 'movements and behaviour only *take on meaning* in the context of specific, and often very local, social conventions'.[26] Similarly, the emphasis in ethnomethodology is upon how conduct is 'perceived' as normal, or 'rendered accountable' or 'intelligible', or in Goffman's dramaturgical perspective action is *perceived by others* as carrying a particular message. Hence, although the explicit programme of several situationalist movements has been to 'subjectivise the objective', as far as action theory is concerned the actual result has been to 'desubjectivise' the actor. It might seem paradoxical, if not actually perverse, to include phenomenological sociology in a movement which effectively stands accused of 'desubjectivising' the actor, but there is little doubt that Schutz's writings have been used to this end. In part this is because his own stress on the 'intersubjective' nature of all knowledge and understanding is easily assimilated into straightforwardly situational claims.

But it is also due to the importance which he places on the 'problem of intersubjectivity' and the need which he presumes individuals possess to 'understand other minds'. This means that he necessarily turns the spotlight away from the subject as actor and on to the subject as observer. Although he is ostensibly still preoccupied with the consciousness of the actor, it is actually the subject as interpreter of the actions of others which is really the focus of attention.

Situationalism: the new orthodoxy

The influence of social situationalism upon the discipline of sociology is enormous, as can be seen by consulting any textbook. This is because situationalism has become powerful enough to constitute the orthodoxy on a variety of crucial issues. As we have seen, these include the definition of the subject-matter of the discipline (at the micro level, at least), but it also covers such matters as the treatment of actors' accounts, the general view of the nature and function of language and the conceptualisation of motives. In all these fields the majority of sociologists, no matter what their explicit theoretical affiliation, now seem to subscribe to situationalist doctrines. One illustration of this is the way in which contemporary sociologists tend to view the concept of motive, generally considering it a 'fallacy' to see motive as an 'internal state'.[27] It is hardly necessary to ask to what, in that case, the term is presumed to refer. For, unsurprisingly, the answer is Mills' 'anticipated *situational* consequences of questioned conduct'.[28] Another excellent example of the extent to which situationalist views have now attained the status of sociological orthodoxy is provided by the treatment accorded to actors' accounts of their conduct in contemporary sociology. For the term 'account' is actually *defined* in *The Penguin Dictionary of Sociology* as 'the language by which people justify their behaviour when challenged by another social actor or group'.[29] This extraordinary statement presents two highly contentious situationalist assumptions – that actors only present accounts of their conduct when 'challenged' by others to do so, and that any accounts given are necessarily intended to function (or do in any case fulfil the function of) 'justifying' their conduct – as if they constituted unquestionable sociological premises. What, in effect, has happened to sociology over the past twenty years or so is that social situationalism has attained a position of almost complete domination over the interpretive tradition, such that Jack Douglas' statement (made, in fact, as early as 1971) that 'there is no doubt that almost all of them (sociologists today) agree that social actions are *meaningful* actions, that is, that they must be studied and explained in terms of their *situations* and their meanings to the actors themselves',[30] has today become the accepted dogma of the discipline.

However, despite Douglas' attempt to run together explaining actions in terms of 'their situations' with explaining them in terms of 'their meanings to the actors concerned', these are distinct and incompatible perspectives. Or, at least, this is true if we insist that the term 'actors' really does mean people who perform actions and is not simply a loose term for those individuals who occupy 'social situations'. For the assumption which pervades so much of social situationalism, which is that any action must, for all practical purposes, possess approximately the same meaning for those performing it as those observing it, is ultimately unconvincing. Subjective meanings cannot be assimilated to intersubjective meanings in this simple fashion, either on empirical or on theoretical grounds. If we ignore for the moment the alternative situationalist strategy of asserting that the identification of actions has nothing whatever to do with the meanings present in the mind of the actor (an argument to be considered later), then there are good grounds for believing that these two will not coincide. For to account for action in terms of its meaning to the actor is to arrive at a different conclusion from that reached by trying to understand it in terms of its meaning to an observer.

The full grounds for making this assertion cannot be outlined here but will become apparent in the course of the arguments advanced in the following chapters. Let it be sufficient at this stage to observe that there are two good reasons for believing that the 'subjective' and 'inter-subjective' meanings of any action will differ, the one based on empirical observation, the other on conceptual grounds. The first concerns the well-known phenomenon of inadequate or inappropriate socialisation and the consequent contrasting 'readings' of an action which can occur when individuals do not share a common definition of their situation. Thus, a tourist or traveller, ignorant of the ways of the people among whom he or she temporarily resides, may unwittingly perform an act which is deeply meaningful to them but not to him or her. In such cases, conduct which is judged by observers to possess a given meaning may well be regarded by the actor as mere behaviour. Thus, an English person, on first joining a group of Greeks, may not be aware of the fact that her failure to greet each person individually is perceived as evidence of indifference and hence as an insult to those present.[31] Consequently what is an 'insult' from the perspective of an observer is not even an 'act' from the perspective of the actor. It may be thought that such instances of cultural 'dissonance' are uncommon and that the vast majority of everyday interactions proceed smoothly enough because the interactants have indeed undergone common socialisation experiences. This, however, is an empirical issue and the degree of common understanding (if it exists) has to be established. It should not be an axiom of sociological thought that individuals *must* share common interpretations of their actions. Even if the majority of everyday interactions appear to be successful, this only *suggests* that a degree of common understanding exists, it does not prove this to be the case. After all, there are other possible explanations for the fact that interactions do not break down. The second and more important point, is that the subjective and intersubjective approaches necessarily imply contrasting approaches to the issue of identifying what is an action, ones which are logically independent of one another. While in the one case actions are identified by *what* is performed, in the other they are identified by the *manner* in which they are performed. This can be seen, and the full extent of the contrast between a situationalist 'social action' approach and a Weberian action approach illustrated, by considering the range of phenomena which according to contemporary orthodoxy is included under the rubric of 'action'.

The first point to make is that situationally influenced sociologists seem to have few qualms about using the term 'action' to refer to what are clearly conditioned behaviours; that is to say, to aspects of an individual's conduct which although perhaps of significance to observers, are from the point of view of the actor, habits or mannerisms which possess little 'meaning'. The classic instance of this is the famous 'bidding at an auction by inadvertently scratching one's nose' example, imported into sociological discussions along with the similar 'signalling a turn when approaching an intersection in a car' example, from philosophy. Now it is clear that in the first case (and possibly in the second, although this is unclear, see p. 59 below), the conduct of the actor, although probably intentional, is very close to, if not actually on the other side of, that line which Weber drew between meaningful action and 'merely reactive' or habitual behaviour.[32] Thus here the term action is employed to refer to movements which, although the individual may be aware of undertaking them, have so little subjective meaning that it is doubtful if they deserve the appellation 'action'. Because situationalists are concerned merely with what is done and whether it possesses a social meaning or not, this item of conduct is defined from that perspective as 'an act'. Subjectively, however, as Weber's quote suggests, it is not an 'act', because what was done was not performed consciously and deliberately. This contrast is even more obvious when situationalists use the term 'action' to encompass events which are of special interest or significance to members of society yet which are in fact no more than respondent behaviours. That is to say, to refer to movements which from the actor's point of view are not only involuntary but of which he or she may actually be unaware. An example of this kind is provided by J. E. Goldthorpe who justifies identifying the beating of the heart of a dying man as a 'social action' on the grounds that it possesses a 'social meaning' for the relatives gathered round the bedside.[33] Indeed, the contrast between the two perspectives may even lead, under some circumstances, to the term 'social action' being applied to items of conduct which are not even meaningful to the other members of the situation, let alone the actor, but are merely judged to be so by the sociologist. That is to say, either sociologists presume that they are meaningful to others present (without the evidence necessary to corroborate such a judgement; something which could be said to characterise Veblen's theory of conspicuous consumption, for example, and also much of Goffman's work), or sociologists use the term to refer to conduct which they judge to be of social significance, even though they recognise that it has no meaning for either the actor or other lay observers (something which could be said to characterise much of semiotics). This interpretation not only allows the incorporation of conditioned and respondent behaviours but also events which are not even recognised by members of the society under investigation as constituting a part of human conduct. This may seem a rather odd position for any self-declared 'interpretivist' to adopt, but it is important to remember that, having defined the subject-matter of sociology as 'social action', this is the only interpretation which would allow such phenomena as unconsciously motivated acts or Mertonian latent functions to be the object of sociological inquiry. It is thus perhaps not so surprising that Goldthorpe's formulation of 'social action' also allows for the inclusion of whatever is regarded as 'of sociological interest'.[34]

It is important to stress that the grounds for doubting whether subjective and 'social' (or 'intersubjective') meaning are likely to correspond has nothing whatever to do with the fact that the former might possess some unique or idiosyncratic quality. It may well be the case, as Schutz seems to believe, that there is an 'ineffable' and hence incommunicable dimension to subjective meaning, but to treat this as the critical issue is to make the mistake of assuming that all meaning is essentially a cognitive matter and hence only varies on one dimension. In fact, action is likely to have a completely different character for the person performing it to the person who merely observes its performance. This is because 'accomplishing an action' is a complex process which frequently involves the actor in a good deal of largely covert, intra-subjective activity of a cathectic and conative as well as cognitive nature;

whereas 'recognising' or 'identifying' an action, is by comparison, a relatively straightforward and largely cognitive activity. Hence, it is extremely doubtful if observer and actor ever regard 'what is going on' in a similar manner. Indeed, once the unjustifiable situationalist restriction of the term 'action' to overt conduct has been discarded, in addition to its illegitimate extension to merely habitual performances, it becomes possible to see that there must be considerable doubt over whether actor and observer are in a position even to share a common definition of what is 'going on'. The real problem which needs to be addressed is not so much whether actor and observer attach similar or different meanings to a given action; it is whether there are any grounds for believing that observers can ever know what constitutes the actions of individuals unless they take the trouble to ask them.

These issues will be developed below. The key point here is that the representation of social action as conduct which has a social meaning (in the sense that meaning is 'situationally' given or determined) is an approach which necessarily leads to the label of 'action' being attached to conduct which may have little or no meaning to the actor undertaking it, whilst at the same time neglecting conduct which does have subjective meaning for the person undertaking it. Consequently, the 'social action' or situationalist perspective is quite clearly and unambiguously incompatible with Weber's notion of action. At root, this incompatibility is quite simply the consequence of the fact that whilst the one position accords priority to that view of the world which is held by the individual as actor, the other accords it to the individual as observer of the actions of others. This category of 'observer' is not assumed to be the scientific observer of classical behaviourism but the 'lay' observer or 'ordinary member' of society. However, as we have seen, Schutz's conception of social action provides the justification for equating the techniques of the sociologist with those of the 'ordinary member'. The critical point about situationalism, however, is the highly doubtful central assumption that there will be a close overlap between the views of the individual as actor and the individual as observer, together with the equally doubtful assumption that actors themselves will assume that they overlap. These assumptions, so convenient for resolving the problem of intersubjectivity, none the less remain assumptions.

We have reached the point of concluding that since social situationalism and Weberian action theory are exclusive of each other the rise of the modern position does not simply indicate a changed preference by sociologists – a shift, as it were, of interest from one area of sociological inquiry to another (let alone simply a new fashion in terminological usage). What it indicates is a clear *rejection* of action theory. Sociologists are effectively being forced to choose between the two paradigms. It is simply not possible to endorse the central tenet of social situationalism and, at the same time, still claim that action should be understood in terms of the meaning which it has for the person performing it. In the words used above 'outside' precludes 'inside', and 'horizontal' precludes 'vertical'. Now, what is not clear is precisely how many sociologists realise that by committing themselves to the modern position they are necessarily drawn into a rejection of Weber's, and that by accepting the view that action is conduct which has a social meaning they are being pushed into rejecting the view that action is conduct which has a subjective meaning – or, at least, into rejecting the idea that it is the meaning located in the mind of the actor which actually gives action its character of meaningfulness. For as long as some sociologists continue to believe that Weber's name can legitimately be attached to the 'social action perspective' then the stark opposition between the two positions is unlikely to be fully recognised.

The very viability and continued success of social situationalism is intimately bound up with the need to invalidate or somehow discredit the classic action theory tradition and its assumptions. The two perspectives are in direct competition with each other over the question of how action should be defined and identified as well as how 'meaning' should be 'understood' and action 'explained'. The case for the one is thus at one and the same time the case against the other, such that it is hard to see how they can co-exist. The new orthodoxy of social situationalism is accompanied by a set of arguments which have been deployed to show either that action is not accompanied by subjective meaning or that if it is it can safely be ignored by sociologists. These arguments must be identified and countered if there is to be any hope of reviving the action perspective.

6   The argument by denial

By subscribing to the new situationalist orthodoxy sociologists have presented themselves with a difficult problem. Common sense (as well as their own personal experience) strongly suggests that the subjective meanings located in the minds of individuals are critically implicated in the construction and accomplishment of human actions. To focus instead upon 'social', situationally defined actions and their meanings, sociologists need powerful arguments which can undermine such 'common sense' notions. This was indeed what happened in the 1970s and early 1980s when material from philosophy was drawn upon both to justify the increasingly popular micro-perspectives, but also and more importantly, to undermine and discredit traditional action theory assumptions. At that time, there was some debate between representatives of the old and new orthodoxies, with arguments assessed and exchanged, even if, to a considerable extent, this was a dialogue of the deaf.[1] Today, however, such debate has largely died away, allowing the beliefs which underpin social situationalism to solidify into dogma. It is therefore vitally important to identify and challenge those arguments which situationalists employ in their efforts to marginalise or otherwise exclude the study of subjective meaning from the subject-matter of the discipline. There are, in essence, three main strategies which situationalists have adopted. They amount to arguing: (1) that it doesn't exist; (2) that its study is not part of sociology; and (3) that it is really subsumed under the heading of 'social' or 'intersubjective' meaning.

The first of these, the 'argument by denial', involves the simple assertion that there are no subjective states relevant to the performance of actions. This is the most radical argument and the one which has been imported directly from philosophy. The other two arguments do at least involve accepting the reality (and up to a point, the relevance) of such states. However, they either delegate – or perhaps one should say, more properly, *relegate* – their study to another discipline or paradigm, thereby effectively excluding their study from sociology, or alternatively try to represent them as necessarily dependent on, or effectively incorporated into, the central concept of social action. This latter tactic is then accompanied by arguments which aim to belittle their significance by stressing either their inaccessibility or their irrelevance to an understanding of human conduct. In addition, a critical part of all three strategies, and indeed of the situationalist position as a whole, involves dismissing any possibility of using actors' accounts of their conduct as an interpretive resource, that is, as a principal means of understanding and explaining their actions. This is obviously a crucial part of the situationalists' creed since such accounts are the principal vehicles through which subjective meaning is embodied and conveyed to others. If sociologists were to take these accounts at face value then they would have little choice but to recognise the central role which subjective meaning plays in the initiation and accomplishment of all action. In order to maintain the viability of situationalism, a whole battery of arguments has been marshalled for the sole purpose of demonstrating that, whilst actors' accounts of their conduct may well be of interest to the sociologist, they cannot (and indeed should not) be used as a means of shedding light on the actions which they purport to describe. Each of these three crucial strategies, together with their supporting arguments, will be dealt with in turn, beginning in this chapter with the argument through denial. Successive chapters will deal with the treatment of actors' accounts (including especially the treatment of motive accounts); the argument through exclusion; followed finally by the argument through incorporation.

The simplest tactic of all for reducing the classical trichotomy to the modern dichotomy and hence eliminating subjective meaning from the arena of sociological inquiry is naturally to deny that such a phenomenon exists, or at least, since it is inherently implausible to suggest that human beings are not conscious subjects, to deny that the content of their consciousness has any direct connection with the actions they perform. In essence this claim centres around an empirical assertion concerning the impossibility of both defining actions and ascertaining their meaning according to the traditional criterion, that there is no 'subjective event' or 'mental state' present in the actor which either immediately precedes or accompanies action. Or rather, the actor is not conscious of any distinctive subjective experience which could be called an 'intention', 'purpose', 'plan', 'project', 'motive', or whatever and which, if it existed, would serve both to define the parameters of the act and constitute its 'meaning'. Hence the central denial thesis amounts to the claim that it is wrong to see action as 'behaviour plus a mental component which gives it meaning'.[2] This means not only that action cannot be distinguished from behaviour by the presence of such an ingredient, but some other method of identifying action and establishing its meaning is required. Not surprisingly perhaps, the other method advocated turns out to involve recourse to the social situation in which the conduct in question occurs.[3] Now, although this argument essentially centres on an empirical claim, it has gained considerable plausibility because of its association with certain imported, logical arguments which have their origins in British linguistic philosophy. Particularly important is the anti-mentalism which has been attributed to Wittgenstein: notably his attack on what he called the 'myth of mental process' or 'the belief that meaning, understanding and so on require, or consist in, something that exists or existed in the mind of the person concerned'.[4] Wittgenstein's position has influenced most sociologists not directly but through its subsequent espousal by such writers as Anscombe, Peters, Winch and Melden.[5]

It is important to note that Wittgenstein was not, as some interpreters have suggested, trying to deny the reality of mental processes. Nor, indeed, did he argue that they were unconnected with the actions which people perform. As Hanfling observes, 'it was far from Wittgenstein's intentions to deny or cast doubt on the existence of mental processes';[6] on the contrary 'he was fascinated by these phenomena'.[7] His aim, in fact, was 'to clarify the role of these phenomena, and not to question their existence'.[8] In attacking the 'myth of mental processes', Wittgenstein was attacking the belief that meaning, understanding, remembering and the like 'require or consist in, something that exists or existed in the mind of the person concerned'.[9] He was interested in the vocabulary of mentalistic terms – such words as 'memory', 'belief' and 'motive' – and he was sceptical of the prevailing assumption that each of these had an 'inner' mental referent: something like a 'picture' or 'image' for example to which such mentalistic terms could be said to refer. He came to the conclusion that they could not be regarded as just describing distinct mental states or processes but rather gained some of their meaning from the contexts in which they were used in everyday speech.

It is not clear, however, that concluding that the meaning of such a term as 'understanding' or 'motive' cannot be found by a simple process of identifying the appropriate 'inner' mental referent, but also requires establishing something about its actual use in discourse, has any very obvious connection with empirical claims concerning the nature of action. Wittgenstein himself considered that it was very important to distinguish between causal and logical explanations because if this was not done pseudo-explanations would be produced. Yet there is little doubt that his is a logical rather than an empirical argument. What is more, attempting to establish how words gain their 'meaning' (which was Wittgenstein's principal concern) is not the same exercise as searching for the 'meaning' of an event like an action. Indeed, the very presumption which marks the study of meaning and language, which is that words have *a* meaning which is *the* referent, does not apply to the study of actions, which being events and not mere symbols, can be said to be 'meaningful' in more than one respect. Indeed, establishing the 'meaning' of an event necessarily involves more than identifying a referent; it involves explaining its occurrence. In assuming that an action is preceded by mental processes such as deliberation or reasoning, one is not necessarily committed to the assumption that some non-linguistic mental 'entity' constitutes the 'meaning' of such processes. The point is not that such language may or may not relate to entities but that self-reports refer to covert, intra-personal activities in which the individual engages. These activities include thinking, imagining and feeling. An understanding of the nature and function of these activities is critical for an understanding of overt actions. In making this claim, one is not committed to logical claims of a 'mentalist' variety in the sense of implying that linguistic terms such as understanding or memory necessarily 'refer to', 'express' or 'stand for' prior thoughts or mental images in the mind of the actor. All one is asserting is that knowledge of certain internal states and processes is critical to an understanding of the act and its occurrence. Indeed, this need not imply that the 'meaning' of such events is located anywhere other than in language since such intra-personal processes may themselves be mediated by inner or internal speech. In other words one is not committed to the belief that 'something' existed such as a 'thought' or 'image' prior to the expression of a thought in words and which supplies the word with its 'meaning'.

However, despite the doubtful applicability of Wittgenstein's theory of meaning and language to the study of human action, many sociologists have eagerly seized upon this philosophical tradition. One suspects that this is mainly because it appears to strengthen greatly that suspicion of the tendency to invoke factors 'internal' to actors when accounting for action which already existed in other traditions of thought in the discipline, notably, that present in the 'social behaviourism' of symbolic interactionism (see Mills above). At the same time, this Wittgenstein-inspired scepticism is easily linked with the argument, present in forms of Continental philosophy, that the subjective is intrinsically incommunicable. This particular claim now exists in a variety of forms.[10]

This position centres upon the claim that whilst there are mental processes occurring in individuals these are unconnected with the occurrence of actions and consequently fundamentally unrelated to their meaning. However, there are at least four variants of this argument. The first and most radical is simply the assertion that there are no subjective events or mental states associated with the initiation or accomplishment of action. The second is that there are such states but that the actor is not conscious of them and hence is not in a position to report them. The third is that such phenomena do exist and that the actor is aware of them, but that they are irrelevant to the performance of action. The final variant is the view that there are mental and emotional states associated with actions and pertinent to their performance, and what is more, that actors are actually aware of these, but that such subjective phenomena are 'ineffable', incommunicable to others, and hence beyond the reach of sociological investigation. Now, although all four of these arguments have been advanced, the first three are commonly rolled together and hence will be the focus of the following discussion whilst the fourth will be discussed later in connection with the exclusionist and incorporationist theses.

Since all four of the above assertions are claims about the nature of reality one might have assumed that their acceptance by sociologists was due to the convincing nature of the evidence which supports them. However, those research findings which are most pertinent to such issues – that derived from the work of cognitive and action psychologists – are rarely consulted. This is because these issues have largely been imported into sociology from philosophy where, as we have seen, they have arisen in the course of discussions focusing on logical and conceptual questions (mainly concerned with meaning and language). The 'evidence' cited by sociologists in support of these claims has consisted primarily of arguments taken from philosophers, backed-up in the main by the kind of imaginary and anecdotal-style examples which they tend to favour. Hence, in practice, it is logic and (somewhat paradoxically) the world of 'common sense' which is typically invoked to support the contention that when individuals 'act' there is no relevant accompanying or distinguishing mental event for either the actor to report or an observer to discover.

Interestingly, though, that 'common sense' which does tell us that our actions are related to some inner state or mental processes is actually acknowledged (if only in passing) by some situationalists. They are usually prepared to accept that *some* actions do indeed accord with the traditional view; these being the ones which patently require elaborate intellectual effort, such as playing a game of chess, for example.[11] In such cases, it is clear that distinct mental processes do accompany overt actions and can quite properly be said to constitute their 'meaning'. What is more, the actor is conscious of these processes and can report them to others. This would seem an important, if not a damaging, admission yet it is played down by situationalists on the grounds that such forms of conduct are exceptional and hence that the majority of human actions still cannot be said to conform to the traditional model. The reason for making this claim is the fact that much conduct is habitual in character and hence, even though it is clearly voluntary and intentional in nature, is carried out 'automatically' whilst the actor is busy thinking about something quite different, or else possibly about nothing at all. The very prevalence of this form of behaviour together with the fact that we recognise this as a description of much of our own conduct, helps render the situationalists' appeal to common sense plausible.

There is a problem with this argument, however, since it does not demonstrate that there is no subjective meaning accompanying action. Whilst it appears reasonable to claim that habit constitutes the larger part of the overt forms of human conduct it is not at all clear that it can be assumed that this is equivalent to saying that habit forms the majority of human *action*. After all, as we have already had occasion to note, Weber clearly identifies habitual conduct as a marginal phenomenon, situated on the borderline between action and behaviour. As he puts it, 'Strictly traditional behaviour . . . lies very close to the borderline of what can justifiably be called meaningfully oriented action'.[12] Hence one can hardly cite the prevalence of habit as evidence for the invalidity of Weber's theory of action, although one could suggest that this fact greatly limits its applicability.[13] The difficulty here clearly surrounds the question of what should count as 'action' and whereas situationalists appear to presume that Weber's position involved including any intentional item of conduct under that heading, this is not what the above quote suggests. On the contrary, since Weber talks of habitual conduct 'shading over' into other forms,[14] it strongly suggests that he considered that there were *degrees* of action and that his famous categories are less 'types' than limiting or 'ideal' forms – something which is especially true of the terms 'action' and 'behaviour'. This implies that all real items of conduct are likely to comprise a mixture of behaviour and action and should not simply be placed in one category or the other. It follows that the presence of intentionality or voluntarism is insufficient in itself to establish that the conduct in question should properly be dubbed 'action'. In fact habitual conduct is not really a problem within Weberian action theory. This is because all habitual acts (assuming that they are indeed intentionally performed) are merely 'decayed' versions of earlier 'true' actions and obviously have to be understood as such. If, therefore, conduct as presently performed appears to lack any accompanying subjective meaning, it is still the case that it must have been so accompanied at the point in the past when the actor learnt how to do it. The action characteristics of habitual conduct necessarily stem from the same source as those for 'true' actions – that of the mind of the actor.

However, it is not just over the question of what constitutes action that situationalists have misrepresented the action theory position. They also fail to understand how the unit of action, or act, is identified. For in order to claim that action is not accompanied by any subjectively observable event or mental state it is absolutely crucial to know precisely what constitutes an act and in particular exactly where it begins and ends. What situationalists characteristically do (and in this they have merely followed the example of the philosophers whose arguments they have adopted) is to identify a given slice of conduct as an act on the basis of a situationalist definition (that is to say conduct which is presumed to possess a social meaning) and then go on to claim that there is no evidence of an accompanying mental event. Yet as we saw earlier, such a definition is incompatible with a subjectivist definition of action; hence, such a conclusion is hardly surprising. Melden cites the driver of a car who performs 'the act' of signalling a turn on approaching a cross-roads, noting that although this is a 'full-blooded . . . intentional act'[15] its performance does not depend on the presence of any particular subjective state within the driver. But it is not clear why he should assume that what he has singled out from the individual's flow of conduct should count as 'an act' rather than a larger unit which should rightly deserve that name, such as 'driving a car', 'driving home', or 'trying to pass a driving test'. Nor, indeed, is it clear why it should be distinguished from a series of even smaller ones, such as 'identifying the correct turning', 'looking in the mirror' or 'moving to the crown of the road'.

This issue is critical because one would normally expect a distinct subjective event to be discernible only at the beginning of an act. If there is uncertainty over where an act commences, then there is little basis for declaring that no accompanying 'mental state' or process has been discerned. After all, the very fact that for many people much of their conduct does consist of automatically performed routines means that all that they have to attend to is the process of initiation. Once under way, the series of 'behaviours' unfolds in an 'automatic' manner as the execution of each movement serves as a sufficient stimulus to prompt the next in the sequence. This is the way that most of us get undressed, for example, or brush our teeth, walk, cycle, type or, as in the example above, drive a car.[16] Only if the usual sequence is interrupted or frustrated in some way does it normally happen that we need to attend to what we are doing and so turn our conduct into the proper form of meaningful or true action reminiscent of the chess player. This means that the only place where we would expect to find a 'mental event' accompanying conduct of this kind is at the very beginning, when we make the initial decision to engage in it. Thus, for most accomplished drivers signalling a turn would simply not constitute an act, it would merely be a constituent movement in a sequence of movements routinely and inattentively performed once the driver had made the initial decision to 'drive home' or 'take a short cut' or whatever it was that he or she considered themselves to be 'doing' at that time. On the other hand, a learner driver, or someone concentrating on passing a driving test, might well define signalling as an 'act' and consequently be conscious of this portion of their conduct as a separate and willed item. In such a case, it would indeed be accompanied by subjectively observable mental processes. We can see from this discussion that when situationalists claim that actions are not accompanied by subjective meaning they arrive at this conclusion as a consequence of their prior commitment to a general conception of action and to a definition of what represents an individual act which are both at odds with the meaningful experiences of actors. In other words, actions are perceived as unaccompanied by subjective meaning largely because action itself has already been defined in a manner which is inconsistent with the actor's subjective world.

Finally we need to recognise that the question of whether action can be said to be accompanied by identifiable subjective, mental events has been regarded by both philosophers and social scientists as important for two different, if closely related, reasons. The first is because the central activity of the interpretive endeavour is to seek to elucidate the nature of human activity by discovering the meaning which it has for the individuals engaged in performing it. At one level, this can be regarded as no more than an exercise in the re-descriptive 'understanding' of conduct. However, the second reason is that there is the additional question of whether or not it is possible to discover an event, located in the mind of the actor, which can be invoked as the initiating factor or 'cause' which serves to 'explain' the occurrence of the act in question. Now, although situationalists are usually keen to deny both these possibilities they are especially hostile to the second of them and indeed to the very suggestion that human conduct is in any way amenable to causal-style explanations. This second possibility, with the related complex of matters surrounding such issues as free-will, determinism and the status of causal explanations in the social sciences, has served to unite the concerns of both philosophers and sociologists. Situationalists have been quick to adopt the arguments of those philosophers (like Wittgenstein himself, but more especially Winch) who have expressed scepticism about the possibility of identifying the 'cause' of an action. We have already seen that the claim, as advanced by some philosophers, and subsequently adopted by many sociologists, to the effect that there is no observable subjective mental event accompanying action, is suspect because of the manner in which the definition of action is handled. But there is an additional point which needs to be made.

As indicated earlier, the traditional concept of action is one which suggests that what distinguishes it from behaviour is the presence of some additional factor, usually described as 'subjective meaning' or more specifically as an intention, purpose, goal, project or motive. Since behaviour is conventionally regarded as that form of conduct which 'happens to us' whilst action is that which we 'do', it has naturally been assumed that it is the presence of an additional factor of this kind which explains the voluntary nature of action and hence 'explains' its occurrence.[17] The only problem with this formulation is that it does not recognise the real nature of the developmental process through which individuals actually acquire voluntary control over their behaviour and consequently causes philosophers and sociologists to look in the wrong place when seeking to explain voluntarism. Traditionally, philosophers discussing the problem of human volition have not been inhibited by their lack of an acquaintance with the findings of psychology. One might have hoped that sociologists would have a greater regard for research findings. Had they consulted psychologists instead of philosophers, they would have realised that what distinguishes voluntary from involuntary conduct (at least in the first place) is that which is absent rather than that which is present.

There are psychological theories of volition which make it clear that no special mental fiat or act of will is required for behaviour of the voluntary type to occur.[18] Since a true act is behaviour which the individual has chosen to perform it necessarily implies the rejection of one or more contemplated alternatives. In order to understand the faculty of volition, it is crucial to understand how agents are able to contemplate engaging in an act without actually performing it. This is achieved through the power of inhibition which ensures that the thought does not 'naturally' give rise to the deed. Once an actor has learnt how to inhibit those responses which he or she does not wish to exhibit, voluntarism is achieved by the simple expedient of suspending inhibition with respect to the chosen course of action. In such a case, the natural expression of the thought as action is allowed to occur.[19] The initiation of voluntary acts is thus not in practice distinguished from 'mere behaviour' by the addition of some 'extra' component. This is simply not necessary as essentially willed conduct consists of 'natural acts'. Rather it is the refraining from engaging in acts which the actor contemplates but does not wish to perform that involves the 'added' component of inhibition. Consider the process through which people come to gain voluntary control over their natural functions. It does not usually require the presence of a specific 'mental event' for an actor to commence urinating but it may well require precisely just such a 'mental effort' to prevent this from happening when, despite having a full bladder, an actor needs to delay this natural response. Or consider those instances where individuals do things which they did not wish to do, even though (theoretically at least) they possessed the power to refrain. An individual 'blurts out' something which they had not intended to say; subsequently, they admit that they 'acted without thinking'. In other words, what they omitted to do was to prevent the thought from manifesting itself as the deed. Of course, voluntary willed action will be preceded by the thought processes related to decision-making. However, this can take place at any time prior to the action in question and does not need to precede it immediately. It does not function as any kind of 'trigger' for the action to commence.

We are now in a position to summarise the 'denial position' and the objections to it. The situationalist argument is that the traditional conception of action is invalid because there is no observable subjective mental event immediately preceding or accompanying action which could serve either to explain its occurrence or to supply its meaning. They do not invoke any body of research to support this contention but point instead to arguments advanced by British linguistic philosophers and philosophers of action. These either rely on 'common sense' claims concerning the nature of human conduct as individuals have experience of it, supported by *ad hoc* examples intended to illustrate the primary contention, or they derive from Wittgenstein-inspired scepticism of the possibility of there being 'inner' referents for mentalistic terms. However, as argued above, it is not at all clear that Wittgenstein's theory has any particular implications for an understanding of action; identifying the 'meaning' of an action is a rather different exercise from establishing the referent for a word. In addition, it is not necessary to contend that the 'meaning' of 'mentalist' terms is to be found in thoughts and images in order to claim that the occurrence of action is dependent on intra-personal processes.

The other problems with this position are as follows. First, even on the situationalists' own admission a not insignificant category of actions does indeed appear to be accompanied by just such relevant mental events, ones of which the actor is conscious and hence able to report. Secondly, the principal evidence advanced in favour of the claim does not relate to action at all but to the hybrid category of 'habit'. Even so, the 'meaningful' features of this form of behaviour are only explicable in terms of its prior status as action in the traditional sense. Thirdly, items of conduct are cited as examples of acts which lack accompanying subjective meaning when there is no good reason for believing that they qualify as whole actions (rather than ingredients of actions) in the first place (unless of course one is already committed to the situationalist definition of action). Fourthly, and finally, the failure to discover a distinct 'mental event' which immediately precedes voluntary acts and hence which could be invoked as their 'cause' involves a confusion over where precisely one should look for the source of the power of voluntarism. On the one hand, as far as habitual actions are concerned the initiation of one item of behaviour is prompted by its immediate predecessor in the chain of learnt responses. On the other hand, the source of the power to will genuine actions into being stems from the ability to inhibit unwanted responses and not from the presence of any special ideational 'prompt' to produce those which are desired.

7   Accounts and actions

If the situationalists are correct in claiming that actions are not accompanied by any 'mental event' or intra-subjective process that could be said to constitute its 'meaning' (let alone function as its cause), then it would indeed follow that actors' accounts of their actions would not be of much value as a resource for understanding their conduct. But how then should such accounts be regarded? It is obviously consistent with the overall situationalist position to treat the giving of accounts as itself a socially situated act and thus also a form of conduct which requires understanding in situationalist terms. Hence the self-same social rules and conventions which it is believed give ordinary actions their meaning would similarly act as the source of meaningfulness for the accounts of those actions. Thus all accounts are to be treated as acts in their own right, and analysed as such: the focus being on how they are constructed and what social functions they can be said to fulfil. It is in this context that one encounters such statements as 'words are actions too'[1] or Mills' insistence that the verbalisation of an act 'is a new act'.[2]

However, regarding an account of an action as a new act understandable primarily in terms of the social context in which it is produced rather than in terms of the action to which it refers, does leave two questions unanswered. First, some explanation is needed for the tendency of actors to refer to internal processes and states when reporting on their actions. In particular, there is a need to explain the common tendency of individuals to invoke such supposedly internal factors as 'reasons', 'motives', 'intentions', 'goals', 'purposes,' etc., when providing explanations of their own conduct as well as that of others. Why should they do this if, as the situationalists claim, such accounts do not relate to any real experience connected with the act in question? Secondly, there remains the intriguing question of how one should regard the relationship between acts and actors' accounts of them. Are they considered to possess no determinate relationship of any kind? Surely this is somewhat implausible. If they do possess some relationship how is it that the latter is regarded as incapable of shedding any light on the former?

63

In fact, there would appear to be something of a tension within situationalism between these alternative positions. On the one hand there are those who are keen to emphasise the lack of congruence between what people do and what they say they do,[3] and indeed between what they say about what they do in one context and what they say about what they do in another.[4] With this emphasis comes an eagerness to embrace a wholeheartedly situationalist position and a readiness to deny the connection so crucial to traditional action theory. This has led some sociologists into such complete scepticism concerning the possibility of any trans-situational components of behaviour as to give rise to doubts about the possibility of there being any such unit as an 'individual' in the conventional sense at all. Such an extreme situationalism effectively constitutes a collapse into relativism. On the other hand, some situationalists are keen to argue that there is a determinate relationship between actions and actors' accounts of them, especially those working in the so-called 'vocabulary of motives' tradition, who espouse a broadly functional theory concerning the way that actors' accounts serve as 'justifications', 'excuses', 'apologies', 'disclaimers' and the like.[5] Since these perspectives serve to undermine the traditional view, situationalists often appear to endorse them both, even though the perspectives would appear to be contradictory.

As far as the second 'determinate relationship' theory is concerned, there are two influential arguments about the nature of their linkage, a philosophical one stressing logic and a sociological one stressing functionality.[6] The philosophical theory addresses the question of what the point of reference could be for such terms as 'reason', 'motive' and the like if it is not to states or processes located within the actor. The primary answer given is that they simply serve to amplify the description of the act. Hence, eliciting the 'reasons' why an individual performed a particular act or discovering the 'motive' lying behind it is not to refer to some other entity or process but simply to achieve a fuller description of the original act. This fact makes it impossible to invoke such concepts as the causes of action since analytically they are inseparable from it. They are, effectively, correlative concepts, ones which form a logical (or hermeneutic) circle with the actions to which they refer. This has been referred to as the 'logical-connection argument'.[7]

This argument has come to prominence largely because of its significance in what has become known as the 'reasons as causes debate'. The issues involved here are complex. They are closely related to the larger naturalist versus anti-naturalist debate over the possibility of explanation in sociology. However, the central question at issue is whether 'acting for a reason' can or cannot be reconciled with 'behaving from a cause',[8] and it is a distinctive feature of the situationalist position to argue that it cannot because, as noted, a 'reason' is logically linked to the action to which it refers. Now, what has to be noted at this point is the highly restricted usage of the terms 'reason' or 'reasons' which is such a marked feature of the situationalist position on these matters. For in order to render this argument convincing, it is necessary to represent 'the reason' or 'the reasons' for acting as synonymous with the intention, goal or purpose subsumed within it. In so doing, the critical difference between actions and decisions, as well as that between intentions and motives, are necessarily glossed over.

One widely recognised weakness of the situationalist argument is this. Even if it is accepted that the reasons cited by the actor are perceived as having a logical connection with the particular action which is performed, this would probably also have been true of any of the alternative courses of action and their associated reasons which the actor contemplated yet decided against undertaking. Thus, as Porpora among others has pointed out,[9] although the concepts of action and purpose are conceptually linked, particular actions and purposes are not and may vary independently of each other. A person may intend to perform one action and fail or perform another by mistake. In learning, therefore, about the reasons given for performing *this* action the investigator could be said to obtain more than an extended description of the act. He or she could be learning something about the decision-making process which preceded it. In fact, when an individual is asked to give 'the reasons' why he or she did what they did, more often than not they volunteer the reasons associated with the contemplated alternatives in addition to those linked to the act performed. The very question, 'why did you do X?' often carries with it the implied 'as opposed to Y or Z?' and people acknowledge this in the form of their answers. Thus, in eliciting the reasons for performing an action one is gaining much more than an account of logically linked or correlative concepts; one is learning about a decision-making process. Winch, Melden and the other anti-naturalists all seem to presume that when an actor is invited to 'give the reasons' for their conduct they will merely respond with a statement of intentions, goals or purposes. They conclude that this information merely helps to make clear what the action in question *is*. But individuals also 'give the reasons' why they *decided to do* what they did and this information extends beyond a mere description of that action to include a description of the considered alternatives together with the manner in which a decision was reached. None of this information is logically linked to the action in question. If you ask actors to 'give the reasons' for their actions, you may well get far more than a further description of the action in question. You may get descriptions of other (unperformed) actions, together with a description of a decision-making process – information which is crucial to a proper understanding (if not an 'explanation') of the action performed.[10]

Recognition of the fact that there are two classes of 'reasons' leads on to the important point. Where 'reason' is used as a synonym for goal or intention (e.g. the 'reason' why I am running is because I want to catch the bus) then there is force to the argument that 'reasons' and the actions to which they relate are logically inseparable (e.g. the action is more properly described in the first place as 'running to catch the bus'). However, where 'reason' is used in its proper sense as a short-hand term for the outcome of a process of mental reasoning which typically precedes the initiation of an action, then this argument does not apply. (E.g., the 'reason' why I decided to run and not let the bus go without me was because I didn't want to wait an hour for the next one.) Unlike the first category of 'reasons', this second type does not amplify the action in any way (in a description of the kind 'running to catch the bus so that I won't have to wait an hour', the last part does not amplify the action in any way) but sheds light instead upon how the decision to perform it was reached. These reasons are logically linked to decisions but not to actions. There is no logical relationship between the reasons which an actor may advance for performing an action and the action itself (assuming that is, that the term 'reason' is used properly). The logical relationship exists only between the reasons advanced and the *decision* to perform that act. This can be seen by the fact that typically individuals say that they 'decided to do X because Y'; a full description of a decision involves stating the reasons for making it. To suggest, therefore, that discovering the reasons why an individual performed an act is to do no more than obtain a full or proper 'description' of the act is incorrect; it is, in fact, to gain a full understanding of the decision which preceded it.

But what implications does this conclusion have for the debate over whether it is correct to regard 'reasons' as the 'causes' of action? It follows from the above argument that if reasons are not logically related to actions then the principal objection to their being presented as causes has been removed. However, it has also been argued that they are logically connected to decisions. What, then, is the relationship between a decision to perform an action and the action itself? Is the relationship to be regarded as logical or causal in character? One could say, on the one hand, that the description of a decision does seem logically to include a description of the action to which it refers. That is to say, one never simply decides, one always decides to *do* something (even if it is, in fact, to *do* nothing). On the other hand one can quite easily describe an action independently of the decision which preceded it. In fact, there would seem to be good grounds for declaring the two to be independent of each other since one can decide to engage in actions which in the event one never actually performs, just as one can perform actions which one has no recollection of ever having decided to undertake. In that respect, actions and their decisions do not possess the intimate logical inter-dependence which marks the connection between an action and an intention or a decision and a reason. Hence, it would seem that the way is open to propose that decisions (if not in the first instance reasons themselves) can be invoked as the 'causes' of actions.[11] However, for the purposes here, the pertinent conclusion is that the situationalists' contention that internal states are logically linked to actions is uncon-vincing. Indeed, it is made to appear plausible only by a glossing of certain crucial distinctions, notably that between reasons and intentions and that between actions and decisions.

Actions and motives

The sociological version of the argument concerning how accounts are related to the actions to which they refer lays the stress on functionality rather than logic. That is to say, actions and the accounts which actors give of them are generally regarded as having a determinate relationship in which the second facilitates the performance of the first. This approach is best exemplified by the work of C. Wright Mills and the so-called 'vocabulary of motives' tradition which has developed out of his work.[12] It assumes that accounts serve to meet the specific needs experienced by actors in social situations. These needs are generally taken to involve defending or justifying the action in question to others. For example, one should not regard the giving of accounts as involving merely the neutral 're-telling' of events; rather, it constitutes the active creation of a version which is understandable only in terms of the circumstances of its 'production'.

In fact, this sociological tradition, as it has developed over the past forty to fifty years, probably provides the clearest example of the way in which an imperialistic social situationalism has resulted in the exclusion of the study of subjective meaning from the discipline. Probably more than any other single factor, the loss of the traditional concept of motive has impoverished and undermined the action theory tradition in sociology. Most of the blame for this loss must lie with the unfortunate observations made by C. Wright Mills in his 1940s paper, together with the extraordinarily uncritical and rather selective reading of this article by subsequent generations of sociologists. Mills can be credited with founding that sociological tradition of treating human conduct as if it were unmotivated, focusing instead on the topic of 'motive talk'. In fact, the study of motive talk is one thing: understanding the part played by motives in human conduct is quite another.

This development has occurred through a quite extraordinary series of substitutions and conceptual slippages. First, Weber's concept of motive was redefined in order to make it equivalent to that of the goal of action or the reasons for pursuing that goal. Secondly, by suggesting that the only part which 'motive-reasons' of this kind play in human life (or which is amenable to study) is through that form of public talk which constitutes the 'giving of reasons' to others (also that motives only become an issue when an actor's conduct is 'frustrated' in some way). Only, thirdly, to go on to represent this process as equivalent to that of providing 'justifications' for prior actions which are now queried by others. In this way a concern with the issue of motives in human action has been eroded, its place taken by the study of 'motive talk', or how it is that an individual's conduct is perceived as acceptable or meaningful by others. More specifically this slippage involved two vital stages. The first was a move from viewing the concept of motive as embracing a range of phenomena including both current states and future ends to using it to refer just to future ends (or intentions) and then to refer just to the reasons for choosing those ends. The second was a move from using it to refer to the reasons given for actions to referring simply to the words used to articulate these reasons to others, and finally to using it to refer to just the words used to articulate reasons in the course of defending one's action to those who have queried it. So one passes through goals and intentions to reasons, to words and then accounts, and finally to justifications and excuses. A quite remarkable evolution of usage.

The first, and in many ways most critical, development is the impoverishment of the term 'motive'. Instead of embracing what 'motivates', 'moves' or 'causes' an action, as indeed it does in ordinary speech, its use is now confined merely to the actor's 'reasons' for acting. Sociologists have abandoned the long-standing recognition that the term is commonly used in two senses and not one. Bentham, for example, distinguished between what he called motive 'in prospect' and motive 'in esse'.[13] That is to say, between the use of the term to refer to an event in the future and that usage which refers to an event prior to the action in question. Thus as he says, whilst 'Motive . . . in one sense of the word, must be previous to such [an] event, to speak of a man being governed by a motive is also to suggest that the man looks beyond the event itself to its consequences, to some event posterior to the act in contemplation; an event which as yet exists not, but stands only in prospect.'[14] This distinction is familiar to psychologists. J. A. Hadfield, writing in the 1920s, noted the 'confusion in which we find ourselves . . . due to the fact that we use "motive" in two senses – the *primary or initial motive* and the *end motive*.'[15] He continues,

When, for instance, we say that the 'motive for the crime was theft', we mean that this was the 'end in view' which moved the prisoner to commit the crime. But it would be equally true to say that the motive of the crime was avarice, or the instinct of acquisition, in which case we use 'motive' to mean the instinctive motive or *force* which impelled him to perform the theft. The money was the end motive, the greed the *primary* motive or motive force, which urged him to the crime.[16]

Now there has been a natural tendency for those sociologists who identify with the interpretive tradition to emphasise the 'end motive', or Bentham's motive 'in prospect', rather than the 'primary motive', or Bentham's motive 'in esse', when discussing action. This is largely because to do so appears consistent with the stress on voluntarism and the central role of meaning in determining conduct. Emphasizing the dynamic interpretation of motive, however, or viewing it as a 'force' of some sort, has been seen as tantamount to embracing behaviourism and thus turning one's back on the interpretive tradition. Whether sociologists are indeed faced with such a stark choice is highly debatable. However, the clear consequence of adopting this view and abandoning the 'moving' connotations of the concept of motive is that interpretivists have also largely abandoned any possibility of 'explaining' action. Although there are still some who insist that 'reasons' can indeed act as 'causes', for the majority of sociologists the choice appears to be between either viewing conduct as meaningful and voluntarily undertaken – in which case explanation is ruled out; or conduct is explained in terms of energy and force – in which case meaningfulness and voluntarism are ruled out. The position adopted here is the same as Weber's, which is that this is an unreal choice since these positions do not, in fact, exclude each other.

It is clear that for Weber the concept of motive was absolutely central to the sociological enterprise for it lies at the very heart of his programme for the interpretive-cum-explanatory account of human life. Under-standing conduct was a process which had two stages, firstly that of 'direct observation' (essentially an identification or naming of the actions to be accounted for), and secondly that of 'explanatory' or 'motivational' understanding and it is the concept of motive which is crucial in this second and more important stage.[17] Weber defined motive as 'a complex of subjective meaning which seems to the actor himself or to the observer an adequate ground for the conduct in question'.[18] To which must be added his observation that 'we understand in terms of *motive* the meaning an actor attaches [to his action] . . . in that we understand what makes him do this at precisely this moment and in these circumstances'.[19] Hence, this process of understanding essentially consists of placing the act in question in 'an intelligible and more inclusive context of meaning', that is to say within 'an understandable sequence of motivation'; a process which can be treated as equivalent to 'an explanation of the actual course of behaviour'.[20] Finally he adds that 'Thus for a science which is concerned with the subjective meaning of action, explanation requires a grasp of the complex of meaning in which an actual course of understandable action thus interpreted belongs'.[21] Weber then illustrates these points with a series of examples. Thus we understand the actions of a man multiplying 2 × 2 when we know that he is balancing a ledger or engaged in a scientific demonstration. We understand the action of a man in chopping wood when we know that he is working for a wage, making firewood for his own use, or 'working off' a fit of rage. Similarly we 'understand' the action of the man in pointing a gun when we learn that he is a member of a firing squad, or that he is acting out of revenge, etc. Now the 'complexes of meaning' referred to in these examples differ considerably. In some, discovering the motive means understanding the place which the act in question occupies in a means–end chain (earning a wage, creating firewood). In others, the actor's goal is unclear as the act is merely located in a broader institutional context (an execution by firing squad; a scientific demonstration). Two relate the act to states within the actor which indicate in what way the act was 'motivated' in the dynamic, energising sense of that term (a fit of rage, a feeling of revenge). It is very clear from these examples that for Weber gaining a 'motivational understanding' of an individual's action was certainly not merely a matter of discovering the actor's 'reasons' for acting. This becomes all the more obvious when one turns away from this very attenuated theoretical discussion to examine the treatment of motive in what one might call Weber's more 'applied' works. This is especially true of *The Protestant Ethic and the Spirit of Capitalism*, an essay which is devoted, as Weber makes clear, to exploring 'the *motives* of moral action'.[22] In this work he explores all dimensions of the 'meaningful context' of action, including the institutional, cultural and psychological, tracing in detail the manner in which the concept of 'motive' is implicated in all three. What is very obvious is that he does not restrict this concept to the actor's goals or ends in view, or even to the actor's reasons for choosing one course of action rather than another. On the contrary, he uses the term to refer to the psychological pressures which impelled both Protestants and capitalists to embark on specific courses of action; pressures such as the desire to serve God in a calling, the need for reassurance concerning one's state of grace, and other similar 'psychological motive force[s]'.[23]

An attempt, only partially successful, to retain this meaning of motive is made by Schutz. His distinction between what he calls 'in-order-to' motives and 'because' motives is clearly reminiscent of the two forms of motive outlined by Bentham and Hadfield, with his 'in-order-to' motive being equivalent to the goal or end of action and his 'because' corresponding to the 'primary' or energising sense of motive. As he notes, the nature of language is such that statements can sometimes be 'fudged' so as to make in-order-to statements appear as if they are 'because statements' when they are in reality only 'pseudo because-statements'.[24] Genuine 'because statements' cannot be translated into 'in-order-to' statements but explain the project in terms of the actor's past experiences. He supplies the somewhat doubtful example of 'a man [who] became a murderer because of the influence of bad companions'. This, he suggests, is the 'explanation of the deed', one which occurred because past experiences created a 'disposition . . . to achieve goals by violence'.[25] He also provides the example of an individual opening an umbrella 'because it is raining', observing that the individual 'remembers' that he could get wet and that this would be unpleasant. This appears to be as far as he goes in elucidating the 'because motive', simply noting that it is located in the 'lived experience temporally prior to the project'.[26] Schutz's discussion of motives is far from clear containing, as Bernstein notes, more than one 'crucial ambiguity'.[27] Schutz is less than clear, for example, over whether actors need to be aware of their because motive before it can indeed be described as a 'motive'. Also he appears to confuse intentions with in-order-to-motives; as Bernstein notes, 'I may have the explicit intention to kill X, but this does not reveal my motive, even my in-order-to motive'.[28] But the more serious error is his suggestion that a 'because' motive relates to an actor's past experience. In fact, as he hints, it is the operation of the murderer's disposition in the present which makes it an effective motive force, whilst similarly it is the individual's current desire to remain dry or current anxiety about ruining his (sic) clothes which prompts him to act. Whilst these states may well have their origins in past experience it is their operation in the present which turns them into motives. 'Because' motives necessarily refer to factors at work in the present, not to features of the past.

However, whilst it is clear that some aspects of Schutz' work have been heavily influential, his observations on the topic of motive have been largely ignored. His acknowledgement of the second 'dynamic' sense of motive (flawed though it is) has had little effect on contemporary sociologists. On the treatment of motives they are much more likely to have been influenced, directly or indirectly, by C. Wright Mills, and yet as we have seen, it was Mills who, whilst overtly maintaining that he was employing Weber's usage, radically departed from it. In particular, Mills fiercely rejected any suggestion that the concept of motive might refer to a 'force' of any kind. Indeed, in the chapter which he wrote with Hans Gerth, Mills states categorically that the problem of motive is the problem of 'understanding and explaining . . . why and how human conduct takes a specific direction. It is a problem of *steered conduct* rather than a problem of *motive power*.'[29] Mills' influence in spreading this view has been greatly enhanced by the work of a group of British post-Wittgensteinian philosophers who also worked hard to eliminate this dimension from the concept of motive, thus contributing to the present consensus of opinion to the effect that 'motive' is equivalent to 'the reasons' for acting.

R. S. Peters, Peter Winch, and I. Melden have all been significant influences in persuading sociologists that, as Peters puts it, 'motives are a special class of reasons'.[30] Now Peters does note the 'moving' connotation of the word 'motive' and hence its common connection with emotional states and desires. Indeed, at one point, he even tries to accommodate this by describing a motive as an 'emotively charged reason'.[31] However, he goes on to attribute this view to psychologists and tries to dismiss it by suggesting that it is 'odd' when assessing someone's conduct in a court of law to 'ferret around for answers to questions about emotions'.[32] Why he should assume this to be 'odd' he does not say, any more than he explains why a court of law should be taken as the natural setting for inquiries into the nature and causes of human conduct. Even if we accept that he is right in this latter point, however, he is surely wrong to assume that questions concerning the influence of emotion on action are excluded in such a setting; for they are certainly not. Indeed, there is even a specific offence – the *crime passionel* – in which the nature and extent of the emotion influencing the offender is the central issue to be decided. Peters assumes, in addition, that treating a motive as a force means that one is committed to viewing it as equivalent to a 'drive' and hence is related to the question, not of why individuals perform the acts they do, but rather why they act at all. This may well be true, but not only are these two questions not as easy to separate as he appears to assume, but it is hard to see why both issues should not be equally of interest to sociologists (or indeed philosophers).

Peter Winch is also at pains to equate motives with reasons in the sense of cognitions, and hence to claim that 'motives can have nothing to do with . . . physiological states'.[33] In fact, he proceeds to try and distinguish between motives and reasons in a rather strange way. He says that the two terms are not synonymous on the grounds that motives may be 'unreasonable'.

To say, for example, that N murdered his wife from jealousy is certainly not to say that he acted reasonably. But it is to say that his act was *intelligible* in terms of the modes of behaviour which are familiar in our society, and that it was governed by considerations appropriate to its context.[34]

This would seem to be a very inadequate way of distinguishing between reasons and motives. Because a person 'had a reason' for acting as they did it does not therefore follow that they could be said to have 'acted reasonably'. These are two entirely different matters. Therefore it is hard to see how motives could be distinguished from reasons on the grounds that they constitute a special class of 'unreasonable' reasons. Viewed in its proper sense, as a concept which implies movement, a motive is not a reason at all. Rather it is a complex of meaning and affect which serves to energise action, and as such cannot be judged to be either reasonable or unreasonable, merely either more or less effective.

Finally I. Melden, although claiming to be seeking to clarify some of 'those obscurities and confusions that mark and surround the term "motive"',[35] is also at great pains to restrict its meaning to the 'reasons for acting' in a purely cognitive sense. For, after attempting to demonstrate that a motive is neither a necessary nor a sufficient condition for an action to be performed (an argument somewhat vitiated by the lack of a clear definition of action) he then develops the extremely influential argument concerning the necessarily logical connection between motives and actions which we encountered earlier. He presents the typical situationalist argument in the following words: 'Since a motive, in explaining an action, makes it clear *what* the action in question is, any description or account of the motive must of necessity involve a reference to an action being performed.'[36] However, this discussion is preceded by the following significant qualification: 'Now the term "motive" applies not only to emotions (e.g. of rage, jealousy, etc.) but also to intentions. In order to simplify the discussion, I shall restrict the application of the term "motive", in this chapter, to the case of intentions'.[37] It is this unwarrantable restriction, consistently overlooked by those who cite him with approval, which would appear to negate the whole force of his argument.

It is natural to wonder why these philosophers (as well as C. Wright Mills) have been quite so concerned to eliminate the dynamic connotations of motive and restrict its meaning instead to 'reasons' in a purely cognitive or ratiocinative sense. Why have they been so eager to accept the equation of 'motive' with 'reason' when neither common usage nor Weber's own example support such a limited view? As suggested it would seem at least in part to be due to the feeling that interpretivist sociologists must assume that *the* reason for an individual's action must equal *his* or *her* reason for acting for if any other stance were adopted it would not be possible to describe the conduct in question as 'action' in the sense of willed conduct. That is to say, if the actor's reason for acting was not treated as the motive which initiated it then it would not be possible to sustain the image of the conduct as voluntaristic or freely determined. Yet, as we have seen, this was not Weber's view. Hence, it is hard to escape the feeling that the eagerness to dispense with the dynamic connotation of motive is, at root, linked to the fundamental inability of a situationalist perspective to account for the origins of actions or offer any 'explanations' for human conduct generally. Because of this there has been an effort to argue that explanation is itself impossible, a position which requires that human conduct should be presented as purposeful yet, in essence, 'unmotivated'. What is clear, however, is that the consequences of this orchestrated chorus of cries for motive to be equated with reasons is, firstly, to strengthen that marked cognitive bias which is such a feature of situationalism in sociology but also, and more specifically, to prepare the way for the subsequent equation of motive with words, public talk and hence justifications and accounts.

The starting point for this move is Mills' observation that questions of motive only arise when conduct is 'frustrated' in some way, and that the 'question' is a lingual index of such conditions;[38] together with his subsequent equation of this condition with situations in which an actor's conduct is challenged by others. As we noted, Weber did not make these assumptions, but, on the contrary, treated motive as a complex of meaning which was regarded as 'adequate' enough to account for the action in question. Hence, he did not assume, as Mills does, that questions of motive only arise when an individual's conduct is thwarted in some way. Equally, he did not make the gratuitous equation between being frustrated and having one's conduct challenged by others. Unfortunately, having equated motives with reasons, Peters also imitates Mills in assuming that the question of motive is only likely to crop up 'when there is a breach of conventional expectations', for it is 'in just these sorts of contexts that men have to justify their actions'.[39] He continues, 'Motives are reasons for action which are asked for when there is an issue of justification as well as of explanation',[40] asserting that the term 'is used in contexts where conduct is being assessed and not simply explained, where there is a breakdown in conventional expectations'.[41] This position is echoed by Lyman and Scott (1964) who declare that an account is 'a linguistic device employed whenever an action is subjected to valuative inquiry'[42] and is thus used to explain unanticipated or untoward behaviour; with the consequence that accounts are not called for when people engage in routine common-sense behaviour.[43] In addition, Blum and McHugh, although emphasising a somewhat different aspect of 'motive talk' – its role as a class of devices for 'making a social environment orderly and sensible' – also presume that the ascription or avowal of motives occurs when the action being talked of is presupposed to be 'fishy', 'odd' or 'deviant' in some way and that it must be, at least potentially, a 'public' phenomenon.[44] Harre and Secord also make the assumption that accounts or, as they say, 'commentaries', are usually produced 'in justificatory contexts, and it is in these that rules and conventions are usually adverted to in explanations of social behaviour'.[45] Finally Semin and Manstead suggest that motive talk only occurs when action is viewed as 'questionable' in some way and that something 'more desirable or appropriate' should be enacted, whilst in their subsequent discussion they refer to such action as constituting an 'interactional offence'.[46]

Now there are several debatable assumptions contained in these claims. First, let us take the suggestion that questions of motive arise when conduct is 'frustrated' in some way and that 'the question' is 'the lingual index' of such a condition. What Mills says is that

Men live in immediate acts of experience and their attentions are directed outside themselves until acts are in some way frustrated. It is then that awareness of self and motive occur. The 'question' is a lingual index of such conditions. The avowal and imputation of motives are features of such conversations as arise in 'question' situations.[47]

Now we can certainly assume that if an individual experiences some frustration in the course of his or her attempts to attain a given goal this may well cause them to become self-aware and reflect on the nature of their own conduct, as Mills suggests. It is also possible that actors may, when finding themselves in such a position, question the adequacy of their own motivation and consequently interrogate themselves with such questions as, 'Am I trying hard enough?', or 'Is the goal really worth all this effort?', or 'How can I motivate myself to work harder to overcome this obstacle?' But it is hard to see why being frustrated in this way should have any connection with being questioned by others. After all, the actor's frustration need not be apparent to others, either because the action concerned is private or covert, or because the individual is able to conceal any overt manifestation of the experience. But then, even if it is apparent to others there is no particular reason why they should be interested in the fact that someone else is experiencing difficulty in attaining their desired aims. On the other hand, viewed from the reverse perspective, there is equally little reason for believing that those occasions when individuals find their conduct queried by others correspond to situations where they experience 'frustration' in accomplishing their aims. Unless, of course, we assume that the frustration which Mills has in mind is limited to that which arises from being questioned by others. We can conclude from this that questions of motive may well arise for the actor when there are no such issues for observers and correspondingly that when such questions are posed by others there may well not be any awareness of motive issues present in the mind of the actor. Of course, if an actor's conduct is queried by others then this might well cause the individual to query his or her own conduct; on the other hand the reverse does not follow. What is more, it is also hard to see why the questions which arise in the mind of the actor as a result of frustration should have anything to do with the avowal and imputation of motives. One would have thought that experiencing difficulty in accomplishing one's goals would be more likely to raise questions concerning the appropriateness and adequacy of motives.

It follows from this lack of correspondence between the actor's experience of frustration and the observers' experience of puzzlement or indignation that there is also no reason to assume that motive issues are less likely to arise when the conduct in question consists of 'routine common-sense behaviour', as Lyman and Scott suggest. It may well be the case that such conduct is less likely to be queried by others, but on the other hand it may actually pose just as many motive issues for the actor as any instance of unusual or exceptional behaviour. This is because the routine is often experienced as tedious and boring and hence difficult to sustain without effort. Consequently everyday activities like housework, or the repetitive tasks of the kind that unskilled operatives in factories are often called on to perform, may well occasion an individual to experience one form of 'frustration' and thus prompt an awareness that they have a 'problem of motives'. The simple fact is that there is no particular connection between an actor's experience of frustration in accomplishing programmes of action and conversations with others in which the avowal and imputation of motives occurs. Once again, the attempt to 'retranslate' an essentially subjective experience so that it can be represented as if it were an interpersonal and situational phenomenon is shown to be unjustified.

Indeed, one can go further and state that even when public inter-personal discussion about motives does occur it does not necessarily resemble the 'vocabulary of motives' pattern which assumes that avowals and imputations are associated with condemnations and indictments. This is because questions of motive often enter the public arena as a result of an actor confiding to one or more others concerning the 'motivational difficulties' which he or she is currently experiencing; or indeed which they have recently experienced, or anticipate experiencing. Thus one worker may confide to another concerning the fact that they 'just can't get motivated this morning', or one student may admit to another that they 'lack the motivation', 'can't be bothered', or 'can't see any good reason for bothering', to revise for the forthcoming examinations. Such a confession may then prompt similar confessions from others, or alternatively a general discussion over what is and is not successful in motivating different people to undertake unappealing tasks, without there being any suggestion that a particular person's conduct is being evaluated, let alone condemned. Indeed, it is not unusual for individuals to reveal specific motives for their acts to selected others, secure in the knowledge that their actions will not be evaluated or condemned.

All of which clearly suggests that Mills' attempt (in which he has been followed by all those working in the 'vocabulary of motives' tradition) to claim that motives do not denote any elements 'in' actors is contrary to existing usage. For this is precisely how individuals do use the term 'motive' and they may initiate a conversation on the topic with their companions as a direct result, not of being challenged by others, but of introspection or self-observation. His attempt to suggest that because the reasons which people give to 'justify' their conduct may vary from one situation to another, the term motive cannot refer to something 'in' individuals is invalid. When an individual claims that his or her conduct was motivated by 'fear', or 'anger', or 'jealousy', they are likely to arrive at these judgements as a result of reflection on personal experience. That is, by observing the processes through which their own conduct comes to take the form it does. Consequently they are indeed referring directly to elements or states which are 'within' themselves (at least in part), and quite reasonably they assume that similar forces operate within others. To suggest that individuals engage in such discussions without knowledge of any first-hand experiential referent, but do so merely on the basis of convention or as a result of observing others is bizarre. What is more, Mills' suggestion that such a conception of motive is purely 'inferential' and hence, unlike motive avowals and attributions, is not open to direct investigation is also untrue. All individuals are in a position to 'observe' their own motives as they experience them and it is of course this direct first-hand experience of the nature and role which motives play in conduct which underlies any subsequent motive attributions which individuals may make with respect to others. The basic truth is that our understanding of the actions of others is grounded in our own experiences of agency. The fact that talk occurs in which motives are avowed or imputed does not mean that there cannot be such forces as 'motives' operating within individuals. Indeed, on the contrary, the fact that there are is precisely why they are talked about. The study of the functions which motive talk may fulfil with regard to the controlling and integrating of social interaction has no special implications for the study of motivated conduct. It is certainly no substitute for it.

Of course, the empirical claim that accounts are only formulated by actors when they find themselves in the position of needing to defend their actions in the face of a challenge from others cannot itself be allowed to pass unchallenged. It is this strange assumption which has resulted in the 'vocabulary of motives' tradition focusing largely on the accounts provided by criminals and deviants. But the fact that actors may be called upon by others to present accounts of their actions does not necessarily mean that their conduct is considered questionable or unworthy. It may simply be regarded as puzzling.[48] Indeed it may even be regarded as highly praiseworthy but sufficiently extraordinary as to warrant an explanation, as is often the case with people who perform exceptionally noble or heroic deeds. But then the 'vocabulary of motives' perspective holds to a strange view of the relationship between actions and actors' reports of them in the first place. It tends to presume that individuals will normally have no need of such accounts themselves and will only bother to construct them when called upon to do so by others. This necessarily presents accounting as an activity which always occurs in a public context and is subsequent to the conduct to which it relates. But Mills was probably closer to the truth in a remark which, in general, has been largely ignored by those who have developed his ideas. He observed that individuals often anticipated the possible need to defend their actions prior to engaging in them, and consequently might sometimes actually refrain from acting if they were unable to think of an acceptable 'justification' in advance.[49] Now this remark is important because it involves recognising both that the actor's need for an account is not simply related to the actions of others and that accounts may actually precede the conduct to which they relate. Indeed, as one might expect, situationalists are generally reluctant to acknowledge the real role played by accounts in the complex processes through which action is accomplished. For accounts are not just functionally related to actions in a simple *post hoc* manner; they play an equally critical role before and during the performance of the action; whilst accounts are as likely to be self-directed as produced to satisfy others.[50]

Accounts and actions: some contradictions

It has been necessary to consider the orthodox treatment of actors' accounts of their actions at some length because this issue is so central to the key situationalist strategy of denying the relevance of subjective states to an understanding of human action. The conclusion we have reached, both in relation to that logical argument imported from philosophy as well as the functional, 'vocabulary of motives' argument initiated by Mills, is that the situationalist position is riddled with unwarranted assumptions and conceptual confusions; rather too many, in fact, to summarize here. There are, however, at least six more contradictions contained in the general situationalist position which should be noted. Firstly, the fact there might be a discrepancy between saying and doing does not in itself lend support to a situationalist approach to the study of accounts. Thus although Heritage observes that 'there is a variety of evidence to suggest that the attempt to correlate accounts with actions, words with deeds, may not be a very fruitful one', and deduces from this, not only that actors' accounts stand 'in a bafflingly complex relationship' to the actions they depict,[51] but that a situationalist approach to account production is justified, it is doubtful if this is the case. For the evidence which he cites hardly supports this conclusion, as it mainly concerns the difference between expressed attitudes and behaviour rather than that between actions and self-reports of those actions. An 'attitude' is a construct, something inferred from motor and verbal behaviour and as such can hardly be equated with an 'account', whilst behaviour, by definition, is bound to differ from actors' reports of 'what they were doing'. In any case, a discrepancy between words and deeds is a different thing from a discrepancy between deeds and words. People often say that they are going to do one thing only to find that, in the event, they are unable to do it. There is no need to invoke a sociological theory of account production to explain such discrepancies as these. Equally, the fact that there may be, on occasions, discrepancies between deeds and actors' subsequent accounts of them can be explained by means other than resort to Millsian 'vocabulary of motives' theories. It may be due to memory loss or inaccurate recall, or simply to the fact that people are 'telling more than they know'.[52] What is more, any discrepancies between what people do and what they say they do would seem to have little significance for 'vocabulary of motive' theorists; for, by definition, they are only really interested in discrepancies between why people did things and why they said that they did them.

Secondly, there is a serious logical difficulty with the whole situationalist argument. For if accounts cannot be used as a 'resource' by sociologists in order to discover what actions their informants engaged in, then equally they cannot be used as a resource in order to discover what actions they *did not* engage in. Either inferences can be drawn from actors' accounts concerning the actions to which they refer or they cannot. If they cannot, as situationalists aver, then they should remain silent on the issue of their validity. For the only alternative is to assume that situationalists believe that actions can be identified independently of the accounts of them supplied by actors. But, as noted above, it is doubtful if we can be certain what constitutes an action except by reference to the subjective meanings present in the mind of the actor. From this perspective actions can only be identified in the first place by means of the agent's account. To rely on observation in order to establish 'what someone was doing' would be an unacceptable and unreliable way of identifying actions, one which is actually guaranteed to result in the creation of a discrepancy between actions and the actor's account of them. In fact, all one could possibly conclude on the basis of such an approach would be that there was a difference between the actor's report of his or her 'actions' and their 'behaviour'.

But then, thirdly, the whole situationalist position with regard to accounts is plagued by exactly the same difficulty over deciding what counts as *an* action that we noted earlier. Only here we also have additional problems (for exactly similar reasons) over what should count as *an* account. Once again it is the analyst and not the actor who is engaged in the process of breaking the overall flow of conduct up into these units and then declaring, first, that accounts contradict the nature of the action, and, second, that different accounts contradict each other.[53] This issue is crucial because unless these units have been correctly identified it becomes impossible to conclude that the differences in verbal reports which have been noted actually constitute different accounts of the same act rather than different accounts of different acts or partial accounts of the same act, let alone that they amount to contradictory statements rather than mere differences in selection and emphasis. Yet why should the sociologist rather than the actor be the person to decide what constitutes '*an* account'? For if this decision is left to the situationalist-inclined sociologist then the claims will be fundamentally self-validating. For that 'evidence' which, it is claimed, shows that actors' reports of their actions are too variable and self-contradictory to be employed as reliable sources of information about the actions to which they ostensibly refer is derived from studies which already embody the assumption that what counts as 'an act' or as 'an account' is situationally determined.[54]

Fourthly, even setting this issue aside, it remains difficult to see why the fact that accounts vary from one social context to another should mean that there is no possibility of using them as a source of reliable data about the acts to which they refer. For presumably this variation is not random, but relates directly to differences in the accounting context; whilst a central feature of this variation is presumably the 'truth' or 'accuracy' of the account with regard to the action it portrays. Now, although some situationalists have flirted with relativism, declaring in effect that all accounts (or none) should be regarded as equally true, such a position is inconsistent with the claim that accounts do not tally with the actions to which they refer; a position which necessarily implies some basis for judging truth. Given that situationalists also claim that their evidence indicates discrepancies between accounts and the actions to which they refer, they obviously have some way of knowing what a 'true' account would look like. (If they deny this possibility and embrace relativism then they cannot also claim that accounts are unreliable.) It should therefore be possible to rank different social contexts in terms of the accuracy of the accounts which they generate. Armed with this knowledge, sociologists should be in a position to ensure that they always interview their informants in just such contexts. If it is indeed the case, as some of those who work in the vocabulary of motives tradition appear to believe, that it is possible to identify a determinate relationship between different forms of accounts (such as justifications, excuses, apologies, etc.) and different aspects of the accounting situation (such as severity of transgression, the status of the 'offender', etc.),[55] then there should be no special difficulty about doing the same for such forms of account as 'telling the truth' and 'lying'. Then, armed with this knowledge, all the sociologist has to do is ensure that informants are interviewed under those conditions which facilitate 'telling the truth'. For to imply that sociologists cannot know if actors are telling the truth about their actions would be to suggest either that this is a form of conduct which never occurs, or to admit that as yet they have failed to identify those social situations in which such accounts are actually produced.[56]

Fifthly, one point which seems particularly odd is how the essentially functionalist 'vocabulary of motive' approach to accounts can be married to the denial of subjective meaning thesis. For it is difficult to understand how if accounts are to be treated like any other action actors could succeed in producing them 'whilst anything or nothing' is going on in their minds. Perhaps this is true; perhaps some people do produce excuses and apologies when challenged in an 'automatic' or 'habitual' fashion whilst busy thinking about (or even doing) something else. Perhaps individuals even succeed in justifying or excusing their actions inadvertently, having set out to 'engage in idle conversation' or 'inquire about their neighbour's health'. But it must be said that this seems extraordinarily unlikely. On the other hand, if individuals are consciously and deliberately constructing accounts with the intention of defending their conduct why is it then that most forms of action cannot also be regarded as consciously and deliberately constructed in the same way? Or is it proposed that the only time that mental events accompany and inform actions is when individuals are busy defending their conduct to others?

Sixthly, there would also seem to be a problem concerning the relationship between the philosophical thesis concerning the linkage between actions and mentalist terms such as reason and motive and the vocabulary of motive perspective. On the one hand, philosophical situationalists argue that when either the actor or the sociologist attempts to 'explain' an action by providing information about the actor's reasons or motives for undertaking it this 'account' is no more than an elaborated description of the original act. The terms, such as 'reason' and 'motive' which are embodied in such accounts are described as being 'analytically inseparable' from the act itself, or the act and such terms are identified as 'correlative concepts'. In Melden's words, cited earlier, 'any description or account of the motive must of necessity involve a reference to an action being performed'. Now since the reverse is not the case; that is to say, the action can be described without any reference to the motive for undertaking it, it necessarily follows that an actor's motive account adds to the general understanding of the original action. On the other hand, sociological situationists are very keen to stress the fact that the accounts which actors give of their actions do not possess any close connection with the original acts, but must be viewed as new and 'independent' acts, incapable of shedding light on that which they purport to describe. The only relationship which they are prepared to contemplate existing between the two is a functional one. But in that case how are these two different positions to be reconciled? According to the one theory if an actor is asked to supply the motive for a particular action what will be obtained will be an amplified description of the former act; in other words one will learn something more about the action in question, even if that something cannot be deemed to qualify as an explanation of it. On the other hand the vocabulary of motives theorists insist that an actor's motive account will not add anything to one's knowledge or understanding of the original act, but that, as a new and independent act, it possesses only a 'functional' relationship to the original. It is hard to see how both positions can be valid.

All the above problems stem directly from the situationalist insistence that actions are not accompanied or initiated by any mental states or intra-personal processes, but that, on the contrary, actions can be studied without any reference to anything 'internal' or 'under the skull' of the actor. It should be clear by now that this is not plausible and that the attempt to study accounts without reference to the phenomenon to which they ostensibly refer simply leads to logical contradictions and conceptual confusion. Not surprisingly, therefore, some advocates of situationalism have sought for a simpler solution, one which recognises both the reality and relevance of subjective states and subjective meaning, yet still seeks to protect the orthodox status of situationalism by presenting the study of such phenomena as lying outside the discipline of sociology.

8   The argument by exclusion

In advancing this argument, the advocates of situationalism hope to resolve the problem of justifying restricting the subject-matter of sociology to social action and hence disregarding action by allocating the two phenomena to separate paradigms or disciplines. The rationale for reducing three concepts to two is thus provided by claiming that 'action' actually belongs to a different interpretive or explanatory schema to that which applies to 'social action'. This tactic of representing the theory of action as entirely separate from, and indeed in large measure opposed to, the theory of social action is a very effective means of reducing the classical conceptual trichotomy to the modern dichotomy. What can be said in its favour is that, unlike the argument by denial, it does at least have the merit of recognising the existence of individual action and subjective meaning and hence the necessity of studying them under one rubric or another. However, it still represents an attempt to marginalise their investigation, either by restricting it to some form of theoretical ghetto within sociology, or by displacing it into another discipline. Whilst, at the same time, the aim remains that of claiming a monopoly over the study of 'meaning' and the interpretive tradition for the social action paradigm.

Julian Freund is one sociologist who employs this tactic. He declares that action and social action relate to contrasting paradigms and that interpretive sociology is only interested in the latter.[1] Non-social or individual action, by contrast, he deems to be only suitable for study by 'causal sociology'.[2] Understandably perhaps, given situationalism's close links with the sub-discipline, this is also an argument which appeals to social psychologists. Thus Rom Harre claims that action and social action relate to different conceptual schemes for the ordering of data.[3] Action, he suggests, (or what he calls 'act theory') concerns a 'means–ends' schema, whilst social action (which he refers to as 'action') relates to a 'socially defined unit (something which divides the stream of action into meaningful sections').[4] He provides an example of what he has in mind; hand-clapping, he suggests, can be treated as an 'act' when individuals use it as a means of attracting someone's attention (as a customer in a restaurant might do in order to summon a waiter), whilst clapping at the end of a public performance such as a concert is regarded as a social action since in this context it has a purely expressive function. Others have also argued in favour of a similar paradigmatic contrast in conceptual schemes for the two forms of action, as indeed Habermas appears to do in distinguishing between 'teleological action' on the one hand and the normatively regulated, dramaturgical, and communicative forms on the other.[5]

In Julian Freund's comments mentioned above, the contrast between the study of social action and the study of action is presented as that between 'interpretive' and 'causal' sociology. This is a surprising way of expressing the difference and in particular, it seems especially odd to find a Weberian, 'action theory' perspective described as 'causal sociology'. One would have thought that the study of action and the study of social action could both be described as 'interpretive' in character, since each claim to be concerned with 'meaning'. Why then should it be the study of action which is regarded as the one which has a natural affinity with a positivist or 'causal-style' analysis? It is easy enough to see why situationalists might want to present the study of action in this light as in so doing the task of defending social situationalism and attacking the action perspective is made a great deal easier. For by associating the two perspectives in this way with the contrast between interpretive and causal forms of analysis their ideological purpose is linked to the fierce and long-standing naturalist versus anti-naturalist debate over the place of causality and natural-science forms of explanation in the social sciences.[6] In addition, we can observe that it is very much to the advantage of situationalism to seek to relegate causal-styles of analysis to another discipline or paradigm. For social situationalism is a theoretical perspective which is inherently unable to account for the aetiology of actions (whether individual or social). This is inevitably the case with any perspective which eschews a diachronic approach to conduct in favour of a *post hoc* and situationalist perspective. So it is perhaps unsurprising that situationalists should not only attempt to make a virtue out of a necessity by declaring that no causal explanations of human conduct are possible but, in addition, seek to insist that any such misguided attempt be contained within another paradigm. What is more, such a strategy also enables that deep-seated suspicion of positivism, which is such a feature of British sociology, to be exploited in favour of situationalism and to the disadvantage of its 'rival'.

Yet none of this explains how the designation of the study of individual action as 'causal', or 'positivistic' has come to be accepted by sociologists when its origins so clearly lie in the Weberian 'interpretive' tradition. It is easy to see that one purely logical consequence of reducing the classical trichotomy to the modern dichotomy is the natural tendency to 'push' the concept of 'action' into the more general category of 'behaviour' and thus into a positivist and behaviourist theoretical framework. But why should such a practice be tolerated unless it was accompanied by some very persuasive arguments? One possibility that comes to mind is that action theory is perceived in this way as a direct consequence of Parsons' influence. For, as we have already had occasion to observe, his herculean theoretical endeavour to develop an 'action schema' tended to result in practice in changing Weber's interpretive programme for the study of human conduct into one with a distinctive non-voluntaristic and functional, if not wholly positivistic, flavour. The irony here, of course, is that Parsons' whole aim was to extricate a fledgling 'voluntaristic theory of action' from what he took to be an unduly utilitarian and (in some respects at least) overly positivistic framework of assumptions.

So the question which this suggests is whether there is perhaps something intrinsic to the study of individual, non-social action which means that it is *bound* to develop in this manner, something which causes the analyst, no matter how interpretive his or her leanings might be, to move towards an observer-based, positivistic form of inquiry. For only if this can be shown to be the case would the division of sociology into a causal study of individual action and an interpretive study of social action be justified. The obvious candidate here is the tendency of action theorists to adopt a 'means–end' form of instrumental analysis in which *rationality* plays a key role.[7] This is certainly the case with Weber's own theory of action as it is too with Parsons' schema, so it might be argued that it is this which is ultimately bound to lead, not merely to a utilitarian, but eventually to a positivist if not a behaviourist, form of analysis. The reason that this might be the case is the importance which is attached to the actor's knowledge and beliefs and the fact that the criterion of 'rationality' is routinely used as a standard against which to judge them. For although a means–end analysis ostensibly adopts 'the actor's point of view' what this tends to mean in practice is that whatever calculations and assessments the individual may make are examined in relation to a 'rational', or 'scientific' criterion. Hence the importance which in Weber's typology is accorded to *zweckrational* action. Now the problem here, as Garfinkel has noted, is that such an approach tends to lead to a position in which the actor's view is only accepted as valid where it coincides with scientific knowledge; otherwise there is a tendency for it to be 'explained away' as error. Consequently either actors are portrayed as individuals who make rational decisions based on verifiable knowledge (as in neo-classical economics, decision-theoretic and game-theoretic perspectives), or they are portrayed as effectively acting irrationally, in which case their subjective meanings are considered largely irrelevant to any explanation of their conduct (as in the classic behaviourist position). However, it is not clear that these alternatives really differ very much from each other. For in each case action is accounted for in terms of logically constructed models which are not derived from the study of real subjective meanings and thus not dependent on the interpretive method. Hence, it seems justifiable to claim, as indeed Homans does, that utilitarianism and rational-choice theories in general are really only ' "stripped-down" versions of behaviorism [sic]'.[8] Hence, although the former do embody at least a formal concern with both subjective meaning and voluntarism, in practice no recourse to the actual subjective meanings which inform the actions of individuals is involved; instead, what are invoked are general principles – such as the maximisation of satisfaction – which could apply to animals just as readily as humans. Consequently it could be that it is this pre-occupation with rationality which is the principal reason why this perspective is seen as inherently leading away from a truly subjective viewpoint and towards an inevitable behaviourism. In which case the crucial question to be answered is whether such an emphasis upon rationality is an inescapable feature of theories of individual conduct.

The reason one can confidently declare that this need not be the case is because, as already noted, the decision-theoretic and game-theoretic approaches whether in economics, sociology, political theory or social psychology, do not constitute fully-fledged theories of action at all but are merely theories of *decision-making*. An individualistic interpretive schema which takes the form of a rationalistic and instrumental means–ends form of analysis does not address the fundamental question of how ordered action is accomplished, merely the question of why an actor decided to act one way rather than another. Consequently, a proper theory of action encompasses more than merely matters of knowledge and belief; it also addresses the role played by emotion, imagination and effort, aspects of conduct for which there is no applicable 'rational' or 'scientific' standard and consequently little possibility of a dispute between the actor's and the observer's perspective. For there is no 'right' or 'wrong' way of achieving or maintaining agency; no 'scientifically correct' means of preventing the deterioration of action into behaviour; only ways which 'work' for the individuals concerned.[9]

In fact, the study of individual action is no more intimately tied to a 'causal', positivistic or behaviouristic paradigm than the social action perspective is necessarily divorced from one. For, as already noted, situationalism in general tends to involve the privileging of the observers' viewpoint, whilst ethnomethodology in particular has distinct behaviourist tendencies. But then the separation of interpretive and causal analysis and their confinement to unrelated paradigms as advocated by Freund and by Harre and Secord should not go unchallenged. For it is not clear that these paradigms need be counterposed against each other in such a fashion. Weber for one did not think that this was necessary. For although he is often represented as the founder of interpretive sociological analysis, his own position quite clearly emphasised the importance of combining the two. His words are not open to dispute. He wrote, 'Sociology . . . is a *science* which attempts the interpretive understanding of social action in order thereby to arrive at a *causal explanation* of its course and effects'.[10] It is important to remember that it was principally Schutz who was responsible for deviating from this commitment, largely as a result of his preoccupation with purely cognitive questions, together with his determination to redefine the concept of social action so as to make its study an exclusively *verstehen*-style exercise.

A more extreme version of the suggestion that the study of action and of social action should be allotted to separate paradigms is the claim that they should be allotted to different disciplines. To some extent the second suggestion is implied in the first, since an instrumental 'means–end' and decision-theoretic form of analysis is basic to both economics and certain branches of political science. However, when sociologists think along these lines it is more likely to be the discipline of psychology which they have in mind as that most suited to the study of 'action' in a causal or positivistic fashion. Consequently this form of the exclusion argument tends to draw upon and indeed merge into the long-established yet still on-going debate over psychological reductionism. Indeed we have already seen how Jonathan H. Turner has tried to argue that sociologists should focus on theories of interaction rather than action not simply on the grounds that 'The basic unit of sociological analysis is not action but *inter*action' but also that to focus on the conceptualization of action is to risk 'regression back into psychology'.[11]

Once again, Mills has played a major part in suggesting that analyses in terms of factors 'internal' to the actor are necessarily 'psychological' and 'behaviourist', if not actually 'biological' and 'determinist' in character. Mills repeatedly represents any analysis of action which makes reference to internal factors as necessarily committed to the view that such elements 'lie deeper' than verbalizations, and are 'fixed', 'springs of action'; a view which presupposes that such elements have ontological supremacy over social factors. It is this portrayal which enables him to consistently dismiss such a position as 'unsociological.'[12] What in effect Mills does when representing intra-personal states and processes as 'psychological' is to imply that this places them if not outside of consciousness, at least outside of conscious control; therefore necessarily casting any such analysis in a quasi-biological and deterministic mould. But it is quite gratuitous of Mills to suggest that an analysis of motives which makes reference to internal states or intra-personal process is necessarily committed, as he puts it, to the 'metaphysical view' that these are more 'real' or 'deep' than overt verbalizations; let alone that such an analysis necessarily assumes that such entities are 'fixed' or 'in some way biological'.[13] What Mills does is to associate two dubiously dichotomous theories of language and psychology to produce a markedly Manichean sociology. On the one hand he invokes the authority of 'the modern study of language' to claim that linguistic behaviour should be studied by observing 'its social function in coordinating diverse actions' and not by referring it to private states within individuals; whilst on the other he cites Dewey to the effect that 'All psychology is either biological or social psychology'[14] By thus reducing the study of human conduct to these stark alternatives he is able to advocate his situationalist programme for the study of motive vocabularies by the simple device of representing any alternative as necessarily biological and reductionist. The irony here, of course, is that Mills himself owed a considerable intellectual debt to the work of George Herbert Mead, a philosopher and psychologist who managed to analyse intra-personal processes and their relationship to inter-personal ones in a remarkably insightful fashion without being either reductionist or relying on biological explanations. But then, as we shall see, it is typical of situationalists to be extraordinarily selective in the conclusions which they choose to draw from Mead's work. However, it seems both unhelpful and unrealistic to separate intra-personal from inter-personal processes in the stark Millsian fashion. For as Michael Chapman has observed 'the intersubjective perspective does not preclude the study of intrapsychic conflicts, functions or processes (even if) it does present their *origins* in a different light'.[15]

The reality would seem to be that if sociologists attempt to treat intra-personal processes as 'off limits' and consequently concentrate solely on interpersonal ones, then they will never be able to provide any comprehensive explanation of human conduct, whether social or non-social in form. The fact that a theorist may invoke psychological concepts, such as motive, for example, or personality, does not in itself imply that the theory propounded is 'psychological' rather than 'socio-logical' in form. That depends much more on how these concepts are handled and in particular which factors are treated as constants (and hence not subject to detailed investigation) and which are treated as variables (and hence do, in fact, represent the principal objects of study). Finally, one can observe that there is no particularly good reason why action which is performed in public or is 'oriented to others' or even which 'contains a social meaning', should be any less amenable to psychological analysis than actions which are performed in private, or performed covertly, or which embody 'personal' meanings. There is, after all, a perfectly respectable and well-established discipline entitled *social* psychology and there are psychological theories of interaction just as there are psychological theories of individual action. The division between the disciplines of sociology and psychology does not neatly parallel that between the social and the individual.

There is, however, also another long-debated issue closely associated with the argument through exclusion. This is the suggestion that the study of action, since it takes individuals as its principal unit of study, represents an illegitimate attempt to explain social phenomenon by 'reducing' them to nothing more than facts about individuals. In other words, that traditional action theory is guilty of the error of methodological individualism, if not psychological reductionism, an error which is quite sufficient to warrant excluding such an approach from the discipline. This is a large topic with a pedigree reaching back at least as far as Durkheim's attempt to exclude all 'psychological' facts from the purview of the discipline.[16] However, it would seem important, as Runciman suggests, to separate out the three questions; (a) does sociology necessarily involve reference to 'facts about individuals', (b) can (or indeed should) sociology be reduced to a matter of nothing more than statements about facts about individuals, and (c) should such 'facts about individuals' necessarily be regarded as 'psychological' or not.[17] In brief and in accordance with the points made above, the position adopted here will be, firstly, that adequate explanations of social phenomenon usually require reference to more than one level of analysis, and so (b) is unlikely to be supportable. However, the need to provide an explanation will almost certainly mean that one of these levels will have to pertain to the conduct of individuals. In that sense reference to facts about individuals is likely to be an essential, if not a sufficient, condition of any explanation of social phenomenon.[18] Finally, there is nothing wrong with describing these facts about individuals as 'psychological' in form, provided that this term is interpreted broadly to encompass the actions, beliefs, values, and attitudes of individuals and not considered to refer merely to their 'behaviour'.

Exclusive paradigms or exclusive phenomena?

So far, that aspect of the argument through exclusion which has been the focus of discussion is the suggestion that action and social action should be regarded as appropriately studied within the parameters of contrasting 'causal' and 'interpretive' paradigms. Yet even if the controversial nature of the paradigm to which action is assigned is set aside, there still remains the issue of whether action and social action do indeed constitute such different phenomena as to warrant the application of different paradigms. Since, for Weber, social action was merely a sub-type of action, it is clear that he did not consider that different paradigms were required. Now what is not always clear when such assertions are made is whether it is believed that separate paradigms are required because action and social action constitute distinct phenomena, or whether these paradigms are merely viewed as alternative ways of examining the same phenomena. When Harre and Secord refer to 'different conceptual schemes for the ordering of data'[19] it is not entirely clear whether they mean schemes for the ordering of *different and exclusive* data or contrasting schemes for the ordering of the *same* data. Although one may indeed clap one's hands as a means to the end of attracting the waiter's attention, there are other actions which, in principle, could have served the same end (whistling, stamping one's feet or yodelling, for example). Few of these, however, are recognised as conventionally acceptable ways of attracting attention in a British restaurant. At the same time, the suggestion that clapping at the end of a performance has a 'purely expressive and communicative function' and is not in any way a 'means' to an end, is less than convincing; since presumably some members of the audience may indeed see this activity as a means to the end of conveying their pleasure and appreciation to those on stage (especially perhaps those who have friends or relatives among the performers). Indeed, Harre and Secord do somewhat muddy the water here by stating, in this latter case, that the clapping serves a 'purely expressive and *communicative* function',[20] for communicative acts do, of course, serve as a means to an end, that of successfully communicating a 'message' of some kind to one or more other people. The problem here is that whilst the instrumental-expressive contrast is the basis of several important theoretical and conceptual distinctions and typologies in sociology (Weber's types of action, Tonnies' *Gemeinschaft/ Gesellschaft* distinction and Parsons' pattern variables come to mind), it is one which refers to *qualities* of actions and hence does not correspond directly to real, concrete acts. In other words actions usually fulfil both instrumental and expressive functions, albeit in differing degrees.

Because an action can be analysed in terms of one of these paradigms, it does not follow that the other is not also applicable. Indeed, it is not only perfectly possible, but very probable, that most actors perform actions which, in Harre and Secord's terms, turn out to be both action and social action at the same time. This can be illustrated by reference to a Goffmanesque treatment of Weber's famous woodcutter example.

If we assume that he is alone in a clearing in the forest and engaged in chopping wood for firewood for his own use (such that his decision to engage in this activity did not involve reference to any 'others'), this can then be regarded as non-social action in both Harre and Secord and Weber's terms; for it is an instrumental task in which the actor's conduct is oriented to the inanimate logs. Now let us imagine that the situation is complicated by the arrival of someone else on the scene; perhaps a neighbour has called by and now stands watching the woodcutter who, as a result of having acquired an audience now wishes to impress his onlooker. Consequently he now concentrates on trying to demonstrate a certain easy skill and nonchalance in the manner in which he executes his blows. His conduct can now definitely be said to be meaningfully oriented to an other, as well as having a clear 'expressive and communicative' dimension. It thus becomes 'social action'. What is interesting, however, is that the original 'action' of wood-cutting has not been displaced by the 'social action' of seeking to impress another person, but has rather been added to it such that the action in question is now that of 'seeking to impress through the way in which the activity of chopping is performed'. The original meaning (in Weber's sense) has certainly not disappeared; the woodcutter has not ceased to orient his action to the inanimate logs. It is merely that another meaning or orientation has been added to it. So it would seem that, in Harre and Secord's formulation (and, interestingly, in Weber's) the phenomena of 'action' and 'social action' do not exclude each other. Indeed, in this example, the phenomenon of social action is *dependent* on that of action, without which it could not exist. On the other hand, the reverse is not the case. But then if social action can be dependent on action in this way is it sensible to assume that the first can profitably be examined without reference to the second?

The conclusions to be drawn from this discussion would seem to be first, that there is no necessary connection between the study of individual action and a causal-style analysis, or between the study of social action and an interpretive analysis, and second, that it is not obvious that, in reality, social action and action refer either to exclusive sets of data or to phenomena which can sensibly be examined independently of each other. In which case, it is unjustifiable to counter-pose the study of social and non-social action and the argument by exclusion falls. Indeed dividing human conduct into the two categories of action and social action and assigning each to contrasting paradigms does not seem like a sensible way to proceed. On the contrary, it seems rather like a recipe for ensuring that human conduct will never be understood. Certainly, it is hard to see how the discipline could possible benefit in the long run from a strategy which creates such a fundamental division. Having to accept that the study of human conduct should be divided into two distinct fields of inquiry, each operating independently of each other and accepting contrasting premises, seems a very heavy price to pay merely in order to protect the privileged position of social action as the principal subject-matter of sociology. It is however a price which not just sociology but the social sciences in general could already be paying. The rise to dominance of social situationalism has meant that its monopolistic claim over the interpretative tradition has increasingly forced those sociologists who wish to study individual conduct into considering adopting rational action and rational choice theories. It would appear to be more than a coincidence that what Goran Therborn has called 'The forceful advances of rational choice models in a number of fields of social study'[21] has coincided with the rise of situationalism. For this now seems to be the stark alternative facing those sociologists who do not wish to work at the macro-level (and indeed, even for some of those who do). This is a tragic breach which can only really be healed by the revival of a genuine interpretive action tradition.

9 The argument through incorporation

The third and most common argument employed by situationalists to justify reducing the classical trichotomy to the modern dichotomy is the argument through incorporation and reverse dependency. The advocates of this argument resolve the problem of the relationship between action and social action by collapsing the two concepts into one: more specifically, by absorbing the first into the second. Something which is achieved by claiming that the critical defining feature of action, that is its 'meaningfulness', is necessarily a social quality. Consequently, it is claimed that there cannot be such a thing as 'action' which is not, in reality, 'social action' (or at the very least, dependent on it) and hence that the former term is redundant. In effect, therefore, this position involves denying the possibility of an interpretive action theory tradition, claiming that there can only be an interpretive social action theory tradition. As we have seen, this position rests on a critical syllogism concerning action, social action and meaning and especially upon its major premise, the assertion that all meaning is necessarily social. This empirical claim will thus be the focus of the following discussion. But first there are two general observations to be made about the logical status of the incorporationist justification for collapsing the classical trichotomy to the modern dichotomy.

The first thing to note is how strangely illogical is the conclusion reached in relation to the use of terms. For even if one were to accept the case for reducing the three terms to two it is hard to understand why it is the concept of action which should be abandoned when both logic and the principle of parsimony clearly indicate that the more general term should be retained. It would seem obvious enough that if meaning were necessarily social in character then the single term 'action' could presumably suffice to cover all such phenomena whilst the term 'social action' would constitute a tautology, as too would any reference to 'social meaning'. The retention therefore by incorporation theorists of the adjective would seem to indicate that there is some conceptual confusion underlying this position. Indeed as noted earlier, this would seem to relate to a desire to use 'social action' in both a 'common-sense' and a more general and all-embracing manner. Thus while there is clearly a general eagerness among situationalists to accept the contention that all action is social there also exists a widespread, if somewhat reluctant, recognition that two discrete forms of action exist. Consider, for example, the following quote from Mary F. Rogers' summary review of Schutz' phenomenology of social life. She declares, in the full spirit of the modern position, that 'The Schutzian theory of action insists that human action is necessarily social. Action is always implicitly social inasmuch as it rests on the natural attitude and language. With profound frequency, action is explicitly social. Schutz' theory subsumes both sense of "social action".'[1] Setting aside the question of whether this is an accurate presentation of Schutz' position, what we have here is an interesting example of someone who is clearly keen to deny that there is any meaningful distinction between the two categories yet never the less finds it necessary to employ one in the course of that very denial. This tendency to elide the meaning of the term 'social action' such that it always serves to include all forms of action is a characteristic of the argument through incorporation. An even more fascinating example of this practice is exhibited by O'Donnell in his textbook, where in place of Mary Rogers' 'implicit social action' he employs the extraordinary term 'individual social action' to refer to what, in previous decades, would simply have been called action.[2]

What both writers appear to be trying to do is to acknowledge the reality of two different phenomena whilst at the same time preserving the pre-eminent position of social action, a tactic which results in an inversion of Weber's original conceptualisation of the relationship, with action transformed into a sub-variety of social action. However, what constitutes the difference between 'individual' or 'implicit' social action and 'explicit' or 'non-individual' social action is far from clear in the discussions of these reverse dependency theorists. The impression given is that it relates to the presence of other social actors. The problem here, however, is that one then ends up using two different definitions of 'social' at the same time; social in the 'common sense' interpretation of 'with others' or 'in the presence of others', and social as in the sense of containing social meaning, thereby raising intriguing problems about the precise relationship between these two forms of the social. It is obviously far more satisfactory if the difference between 'explicit' and 'implicit' social action can be treated as simply a matter of variation along a single axis and the obvious candidate here is that of 'meaning'. Hence there is a prevailing tendency to treat 'implicit' social action as differing from the primary form in so far as the meaning contained in it is 'individual' in some way, with 'subjective meaning' represented as a particular variant of social meaning. Indeed, the ambiguities surrounding the word individual provide the apologists for situationalism with a perfect opportunity in this respect for presenting 'implicit' social action as unworthy of serious sociological attention. This is because they facilitate the claim that 'individual' social action differs from the purely social form by constituting an 'individual' – in the sense of individuated or unique – variation of intersubjective or social meaning. An argument which, in turn, paves the way for such a phenomenon to be disregarded on the grounds either that, being unique, it is of no interest to a social scientist, or that its very uniqueness actually renders it inexpressible and hence inaccessible. It is important to state, therefore, that by referring to action as 'individual' one is not necessarily implying that its meaning is in any way 'individuated' or unique. For the term, like the associated 'subjective', refers to the *location* of meaning and not to its character. This meaning may or may not be shared with other actors (either present at the time the action is performed or not), just as it may or may not possess some 'unique' or idiosyncratic features. Indeed a major situationalist error lies in the assumption that there is only one dimension of meaning and consequently that the only possible variation is along the unique-general axis. However, there are in practice several dimensions to the meaning of actions with the consequence that subjective meaning and social meaning may differ radically without this implying that the former is in any way unique or inexpressible.

This point relates closely to a second logical problem surrounding the situationalist treatment of the 'meaning' of action which is the presence of a certain confusion between the use of the adjective 'social' as a description of the content of an action's meaning or as a description of the character of meaning in general. One would assume that to argue that an action has a social meaning is to make a claim about the substantive content of action; it is to say something about what actions actually 'mean' in the sense of the exact nature of their denotative or indicative referents or of the intentions, purposes, motives, or 'projects' which can be considered as informing them. By contrast, to claim that all meaning has a social character is to say something about the intrinsic nature of meaning as a phenomenon; to comment, for example, on its logical, epistemological or even developmental characteristics. Hence, it is to identify a quality which all formulations of meaning possess and consequently does not involve any claim about the substantive nature of individual items of conduct and their meaning. It naturally follows from this that the second claim can be conceded without this having any necessary implications for the first. Indeed, one can say that the first is fairly obviously false (on most if not all definitions of the term 'meaning'), whilst the second is equally self-evidently true. To claim that the meaning contained in any given action depends for its 'meaningfulness' on larger, socially shared systems of concepts or typifications, or even that it depends on the general concepts of a 'rule' and 'rule-following', or indeed upon the fact that the individual concerned has undergone a lengthy experience of socialisation, may well be true up to a point. However, it amounts in effect to little more than the observation that the possession of meaning is a function of being human and hence a member of society. One suspects that Weber would have had little difficulty in accepting it. But then Weber used the adjective 'social' to refer to the content of the subjective meaning accompanying an action whilst the social imperialists typically employ it to refer to the character or source of meaning in general. Consequently such claims do not provide any reason for denying that there is a distinction between action and social action or that all action necessarily possesses a 'social' content.

This tendency to carry over claims concerning the character of meaning to embrace those concerning its content is a common feature of situationalist arguments, especially those which arise from the work of Schutz and the suggestion that meaning is an 'intersubjective phenomenon', resting on 'the natural attitude and language' to quote Mary Rogers. In fact it turns out that what Schutz meant by the latter observation is merely that all rational beings take up the same basic attitude towards the world, a 'natural attitude', which involves treating it as a taken-for-granted reality. Indeed Schutz makes it clear that his usage signifies 'no more than' this.[3] Within the common context of this attitude there still exists, therefore, plenty of scope for differences in the actual meanings which individuals may ascribe to objects and events. Berger and Luckmann, in echoing Schutz' view, also begin by making it clear that the crucial feature which unites actors is a shared sense of the reality of the world rather than an identity of actual meanings or perspectives.[4] However, they go on to talk about an 'ongoing correspondence' between '*my* meanings and *their* meanings in this world' whilst referring to a 'common-sense knowledge' which is shared between the individual and others.[5] Finally, they appear to have no qualms in concluding their discussion by asserting that 'The reality of everyday life is shared with others', when the arguments advanced would only appear to justify concluding that the *sense* of reality is so shared.[6]

It is worth re-iterating the point that the claim that all meaning is social in character is *not* the same as the claim that all action has a social meaning. All languages could be said to be social in character, in the sense that speakers share a common competence in the application of its rules of grammar or a common knowledge of its vocabulary. This does not mean that all utterances made by proficient speakers of that language must have a social content. One can, for example, use language without intending to communicate with an other or others (let alone attempting to influence them), or indeed with the intention of 'orienting' one's conduct to them in any way. Equally, the ideas and sentiments articulated through language may relate to events (like dreams, for example) which individuals cannot experience in the company of others or simply to events to which they are the only witnesses. Of course, meaning, like language, can reasonably be described as a social phenomenon. But this does not mean that actors cannot use their general capacity to construct meaning to express personal or private ideas, any more than in making use of language the statements people make must, by definition, have a 'social' content. To suggest this is to be guilty of a logical confusion between the general characteristics of a phenomenon and its particular substantive forms. It may well be the case that individuals cannot have a purely private language;[7] but then they do not need one in order to express meanings which are personal to them. This can be accomplished using a vocabulary and grammar common to all. Similarly, the fact that meaning is in general dependent on shared typifications or common rules does not imply that these cannot be employed to express experiences which are known only to the individual concerned.

The 'all meaning is social' thesis

This confusion between the substantive content of an action's meaning and the general characteristics of meaning-systems is closely related to the situationalist tendency to employ the adjective 'social' in place of 'human'. Time and again one encounters discussions by sociologists in which those features characteristic of human life in general are referred to as if they were distinctly social in nature; something which is achieved by either failing to distinguish adequately between the social and the cultural or between the social as shared and the social as that which is experienced in common. The psychologist Richard Totman has drawn attention to the logical fallacy contained in this line of argument in the context of his attempt to define the subject-matter of social psychology. He takes as his example the activity of gardening:

A gardener often works alone, yet he or she follows rules and strives towards ends that are collectively defined and upheld. The way a good garden is established is not arbitrary. One must have an idea of what such a garden should look like, what constitutes a weed, when to water plants and so on, and these things are the result of consensus and are passed through the community. The concept of a desirable garden, methods of gardening, and the role of gardener are categories expressive of one fragment of social order within our culture. The products of people's labours, gardens themselves, are shown off, judged, admired, and scorned. They are the source of pride, hope, frustration, and despair. Although gardening is something that is often done alone, it is by no means free of social associations.[8]

As Totman goes on to note, such an approach to defining the social is so all-encompassing as to be virtually 'void of meaning on the grounds that there are no other forms of behaviour against which to contrast what we are calling social'. Hence, to speak of gardening as possessing 'social meaning' on these grounds is, as he suggests, effectively to 'class all learned human performance as social'.[9] One might have thought that this conclusion was obvious enough to prevent sociologists from making the same mistake. But then, as observed above, social situationalists are keen to find arguments which they can use to justify their neglect of the phenomenon of action; hence it is perhaps not so surprising to find that arguments of this kind are commonly encountered.[10]

As Totman rightly points out, if the term 'social' is to mean anything then there must be something non-social with which to contrast it and although the 'individual' is what most readily springs to mind a more pertinent contrast in this instance is with the 'cultural'. For what the above passage serves to illustrate is the mistake of employing the word 'social' when 'cultural' would be more accurate. After all, if an individual's action implies that he or she knows the difference between a weed and a plant, as well as when to prune a rose bush, or is prone to place a high value on a neatly-mown lawn, then these facts justify concluding that the conduct in question reveals an obvious cultural, rather than a purely social, dimension. That is to say, it reveals that at some time or other the individual concerned has been socialised into a given 'gardening culture' one from which he or she has acquired these beliefs, values and attitudes. By itself, it implies nothing at all about on-going patterns of social interaction or current membership of social groups. Any explanation of such forms of conduct requires reference in the first place to cultural rather than social processes.

But then those theorists whose work has served to inspire the situationalist dogma have themselves typically treated the boundary between the social and the cultural with a certain cavalier disregard. Schutz' use of the term 'intersubjective' is a good case in point. The term itself would seem to have obvious social rather than cultural connotations, suggesting as it does a relationship between experiencing human subjects. However, although Schutz repeatedly uses it to refer to features of actual face-to-face interactions he also uses it to refer to an individual's relationship to bodies of knowledge and systems of meaning, writing in this context of the 'intersubjective world of culture'.[11] As a consequence, his oft-repeated assertion that meaning is 'constituted as an intersubjective phenomenon'[12] is an essential ambiguous observation. On the one hand, it could mean no more than that meaning is 'intersubjective' in the sense of being dependent on the existence of a culture which is common to a group of 'subjects', or alternatively it could imply that meaning is the outcome of processes which occur in interactions 'between subjects'. In other words, does inter-subjective describe that necessarily impersonal and extremely indirect form of 'contact' between experiencing subjects which is implied by their common resort to similar cultural material, or does it imply that form of direct interaction which would actually warrant the label 'social'? When Schutz suggests that 'every act of mine through which I endow the world with meaning refers back to some meaning-endowing act . . . of yours with respect to the same world',[13] is one meant to interpret this literally, as implying a direct, even a personal relationship, or as merely indicating that both parties make reference to the same interpretive schemes and systems of meaning? For whilst the former would seem quite implausible, the latter would only justify the conclusion that inter-subjectivity is a cultural and not a social phenomenon. In fact, most of the time Schutz appears to represent the cultural dimension of human experience as if it was necessarily 'intersubjective' in the sense of involving reference to other 'experiencing subjects'. For example, when he suggests that 'A tool . . . is experienced . . . in terms of the purpose for which it was designed by more or less anonymous fellow-men and its possible use by others.'[14] However, not only does he not supply any evidence to show that individuals actually do experience tools or other cultural objects in this way, his reference to 'more or less *anonymous* fellow-men' shows that no social inter-subjectivity is really involved here at all. For Totman's gardener who has learnt to weed with a hoe or prune with secateurs from consulting a gardening manual is clearly 'experiencing' these tools via a cultural and not a social process.

This failure to distinguish adequately between the social and the cultural is closely related to a similar confusion between that which individuals have in common and that which they experience collectively. Consider another passage from Schutz: 'the phenomena of the external world have meaning not only for you and me . . . but for everyone living in it. There is only one external world, *the public world*, and it is given equally to all of us.'[15] In equating the 'external world' with 'the public world' Schutz is apparently treating individuals' experiences of this 'external world' as if they were in effect communal experiences, open to observation and scrutiny by others. Yet in practice that world which we experience in common is most definitely not the same world as that which we experience collectively. Obviously for this to be the case not only would all actions have to be overt but they would also all have to be performed in public. The fact that individuals may have experiences of the external world 'in common' does not warrant identifying those experiences as part of a 'public world'. This is to play games with the meaning of words. If two individuals both undergo similar experiences of delight at the sight of a beautiful sunset, or of fear when coming face-to-face with a wild animal, this does not warrant describing these as 'public' experiences. Nor are there any grounds for suggesting that the experiences of the one 'relate to' those of the other, except in the most indirect 'cultural' sense mentioned above. Even then, it is important to remember that two individuals may draw on identical cultural sources in relation to identical subjective experiences only to arrive at differing interpretations of their meaning.

Again it must be stressed that this does not of course imply that the meaning which an individual attaches to his or her actions or experiences will be unique to them. Others may well have acted in the same way and for similar reasons at other times and in other places. It does not follow, however, that because the meaning of an act is the same for two individuals that they can therefore be said to 'share' its meaning, let alone that their experiences 'relate' to each other. After all, they are probably quite unaware of each other's existence, let alone of their actions or the meanings they attach to them. The fact that they may all have employed similar cultural material in the course of constructing their actions does not mean that the *actions* can be considered to 'relate' to each other in a social or intersubjective fashion. For this is to confuse the sharing of beliefs, values and attitudes among social groups or collectivities with the identity of any specific actions (and their associated meanings) which may stem from these.[16]

What is more, the 'external world' to which all individuals have to adapt consists of more than an external environment (whether defined as physical or social). It also comprises that internal psycho-biological environment comprised of our bodies.[17] This too is a world 'given equally to all of us' and yet it could never be a 'public' world. Rather it is one which each of us necessarily experiences and interprets 'privately' (even when in the company of others) since the sensations, feelings and thoughts which constitute it are not ones which are open for others to directly experience. In what sense can an individual's experience of claustrophobia, indigestion or incestuous urges be said to 'relate' to those of others? After all, whether others know of such experiences at all depends on whether the individual chooses to report them. Thus here too it seems bizarre to suggest that an individual's meaning-endowing acts with respect to this covert world 'relate' to those of others with respect to their covert world. This can only be true in the most indirect, culturally-mediated, sense, mentioned above. In addition, as an assertion it probably has much less truth than the claim that such experiences 'relate' to others which the individual has experienced previously. Indeed the claim that meaning is an inter-subjective phenomenon is less convincing in this connection than the claim that it is an intra-subjective one. The point here is less that 'the world' which we have to interpret is different for each individual (it may not be), but rather that each individual confronts their private world independently and unwitnessed by others.

It is noticeable that one factor which is common to each of these confused treatments of the term 'social' is the significance which is attached to language. For it is largely because of the considerable importance which is attached to this phenomenon that the content and character of meaning are easily conflated, as too is the difference between the social and the cultural and that between what people have in common and that which they share. Now one might naively have thought that observations on the crucial part played by language in the construction of meaning (and hence action) would have led to a stress being placed on the importance of culture. However, the influence of situationalism is such that it is a very different conclusion which is drawn. Thus, one encounters Mary Rogers' claim that action is social because it 'rests on language',[18] or Harre and Secord's assertion that action is social because it is 'inextricably bound up with the nature and limits of language'.[19] How strange that commentators do not reach the conclusion that action is cultural because it rests on language.[20] Surely the truth is that the characteristics of language, like those of action itself, are such as to suggest that it is a fundamentally *human* phenomenon, and consequently can justifiably be described as possessing social, cultural and psychological dimensions. What therefore is the justification for such an insistent emphasis on what is patently a half-truth?

These logical confusions surrounding the use of the word 'social' provide even greater opportunities for variations of interpretation in order to protect the central syllogism. The assertion that meaning is social can not only be taken to mean many different things but is taken to mean them by proponents of the new orthodoxy. Far from this being a weakness, however, it is a major source of strength, since it is usually by means of a judicious shifting backwards and forwards from one interpretation to another that exponents of the 'all meaning is social' dogma are able to make it appear persuasive. Thus, as we have seen, if the meaning of an action is not social 'explicitly' then it must be so 'implicitly'; if it is not social in content, then it must be so in character; if it is patently not social in the sense of shared then it must be social in the sense of 'in common'; if it is not social in the sense of communal or interactive then it must be social in the sense that cultural phenomena, like language and knowledge, can be said to be 'social'. Finally, if all else fails, one can always fall back on the claim that all meaning is social because after all everything human is social, a claim which leads into a consideration of a central plank in the structure which is situationalist orthodoxy, the importance attached to socialisation and 'learning from others'.

10   The 'learning everything from others' thesis

One of the key arguments advanced by situationalists stresses how the meaning which informs the actions of individuals either derives from knowledge which is 'learnt from' or 'acquired via interaction with' other people, or alternatively constructed employing abilities which have themselves been acquired in this way. A claim which is seen as sufficient grounds for declaring such understandings and therefore any associated action to be 'social' in character. This assumption has become so widespread and taken-for-granted by situationalists that it is routinely made *en passant* in discussions without any attempt to justify it. Thus in the passage from Totman quoted above he states that the gardener's knowledge is 'passed through the community', when in reality much of it could have been acquired from books or through experience.[1] There are several different versions of this argument depending on what exactly it is presumed that individuals learn from others in this way. At one extreme all that is stressed is denotative meaning or simply the names for people, objects and events, whilst at the other it is the whole body of discursive and non-discursive knowledge which it is assumed is transmitted in this fashion. One commonly encounters the view that everything necessary for the individual to engage in successful action in the world is effectively 'socially derived' and 'language carried', which is to say it is acquired from others. In so far as the argument stresses the acquisition of general abilities rather than knowledge itself, then those most commonly identified tend to be the possession of a self and hence the ability to be reflexive, as well, of course, as the ability to use language.

The simplest of these arguments is the claim that since individuals learn the specific meanings of objects and events from others they must therefore share with these others a common knowledge of their 'meanings' (and consequently actions which embody these warrant the designation 'social'). Symbolic interactionists in particular commonly advance this argument. Thus Blumer claims that meaning is a social product since the meaning of objects for a person arises fundamentally out of the way they are defined to him by others with whom he interacts. Thus we come to learn through the indications of others that a chair is a chair, that doctors are a certain kind of professional, that the United States Constitution is a given kind of legal document, and so forth.[2]

Now there are two significant points about Blumer's examples. Firstly, all the items mentioned are objects or people and not actions. Secondly, the 'meanings' which Blumer claims to be social products turn out to refer to the names of things rather than to any more comprehensive interpretation of that concept. Now both of these are characteristic features of the general situationalist 'all meaning is social' argument with the result that although the crucial claim relates to the meanings of actions the examples chosen to illustrate this thesis typically merely refer to the naming of objects. Again and again one finds that a discussion of the denotative meaning of objects is a prelude to a conclusion about the social meaning of actions. This is no accident but stems from the fact that the relationship between objects and their denotative meaning or 'name' illustrates the situationalist claim in a clear and unambiguous fashion whilst the relationship between actions and their 'meaning' does not. The reasons for this are first because objects (including people) have determinate parameters in a way that actions do not (in the case of Weber's famous example, although it is exceptionally difficult to know how the woodcutter's activities should be divided up such that *an* act can be identified, there is little difficulty in identifying the axe, the woodcutter or the log). Whilst in the second place although individuals may learn many things from experience it is necessarily the case that they must learn what things are called from others; since the naming of things has to be arbitrary it is therefore *necessarily* social. However, it does not follow that the way in which individuals learn the names of objects can tell us much about the manner in which they learn the meaning of actions. Even then, if we overlook these major limitations and accept the basic premise that the meanings which objects have for individuals are acquired from others, this does only apply initially. Blumer is frank enough to suggest this, observing that the meanings which objects have for people actually 'grow[s] out of' or 'arise[s] . . . out of' the way that they are defined by others.[3] In other words, as individuals mature these meanings are likely to develop and change. Of course this development may occur as a consequence of instruction by, or interaction with, others; but then again it need not. It may simply follow from an individual's personal experience of acting or from their direct experience of the natural or man-made environment. It would still not follow even on this argument that, for adults at least, the meanings which inform their actions are 'social products' in any direct sense.

This tendency of situationalists to equate 'meaning' with denotative understanding or 'naming' also leads them to assume that 'knowledge' is equatable with the ability to identify and hence they overlook its character as 'awareness'. It is this, for example, which largely accounts for such extraordinary suggestions as Jack D. Douglas' claim that there cannot be any such thing as 'private knowledge', but that *all human knowledge is necessarily shared knowledge*.[4] But of course knowledge consists of much more than having learnt 'what things are called', or what terms and concepts one should employ in making sense of and thus in describing the world. It also consists of differential states of experiential awareness. It is obviously ridiculous to suggest that the woodcutter does not 'know' that he has cut himself with the axe until he is able to show someone else the blood, or that the sailor in the crow's-nest does not 'know' that he has sighted land until the rest of the crew have been informed; or that the insomniac does not know that she is lying awake until she has woken her partner and informed him of the fact. Because one can only learn from others that being unable to sleep is called insomnia, or that one is conventionally supposed to cry out 'Land Ho!' when sighting land, or that the sticky liquid which oozes out when the skin is cut is called 'blood', is clearly neither here nor there. Knowledge is as much a matter of awareness of oneself and one's surroundings as it is to do with assimilating the culture of a group. Even then it is not clear that all denotative meaning is necessarily shared. Robinson Crusoe had names for different parts of his island before he met Man Friday. Are we therefore meant to believe that he could not really have 'known' what these different places were called? Does a child not 'know' the name of her imaginary friend just because her parents and other children refuse to recognise the friend's existence? To grant ontological privilege to inter-subjective processes and phenomena at the expense of intra-subjective ones in this way seems quite unjustifiable.

A second popular version of the 'all knowledge is learnt from others' argument (again one widely taken-for-granted by sociologists) presumes that it is the individual's general ability to create and manipulate meaning which originates in social processes, an ability which stems from the development of a self and an associated capacity to be reflexive. This is also seen as justifying describing the meanings so created as 'social'. The stress here is therefore placed on the processes of socialisation, and, in particular, drawing on the work of George Herbert Mead, the importance which is attached to 'taking the role of the other' in childhood. Harre and Secord are among those who use this argument in order to claim that meaning is a social product. They state that 'The use of self-referring pronouns depends upon a person having been referred to as a person by other people, and so is logically posterior to the recognition that there are other people.' Whilst they also observe that 'The capability of self-commentary depends upon the commentator having a standpoint outside the field of the commentary.'[5]

Of course, if the argument is simply that self-consciousness is a prerequisite for any individual to engage in meaningful action and it is considered sufficient to point to the social origins of this ability in order to justify labelling the meanings created through its use 'social', then it would necessarily follow that all human action is social by definition. Once again one would be forced to the conclusion reached by Totman reported above to the effect that 'there would be no form of behaviour against which to contrast that which we are calling social'. In which case once again the adjective 'social' becomes redundant and the argument self-defeating. Apart from this logical difficulty the other fairly obvious objection is that the *source* of an individual's ability to act meaningfully is a very different matter from the manner in which that ability is used. Just because actors develop the ability to see themselves as objects as a consequence of interacting with others it does not follow that (either initially or thereafter) they see themselves as the same object that others see. The fact that a self-regarding faculty is essential to action tells us nothing about the *content* of an individual's self-regarding attitudes, let alone about any actions which may spring from them. It is unfortunate, but again perhaps understandable given the pervasiveness of the situationalists' imperialist paradigm, that sociologists seem to have acquired the habit of confusing the claim that the self is a social entity because it originates in social processes with the claim that the self will be social in content because at any one time its character is determined by the attitudes which others adopt towards the individual. A confusion which involves treating Mead's theory of the development of the self as if it justified equating intra- with interpersonal dialogues in adults. Thus Blumer refers to the fact that in taking the role of the other

the person is in a position to address or approach himself (*sic*) as in the case of a young girl who in 'playing mother' talks to herself as her mother would do, or in the case of a young priest who sees himself through the eyes of the priesthood. We form objects of ourselves through such a process of role-taking. It follows that we see ourselves through the way in which others see or define us.[6]

But of course it does not follow that because we possess the capacity to regard ourselves as objects that we will therefore see ourselves in the same way that others see us. For this is to confuse the manner in which a particular ability is developed with the way in which it is subsequently employed. Mead correctly notes that in order to *become* an object to ourselves we must see ourselves from the outside and that in order to do this we must place ourselves in the position of others. But the fact that our concept of self and with it our capacity for self-interaction is formed in the first place through a process of taking the role of another does not mean that all subsequent self-interactions must involve taking over the role of some specific and real social actor or actors. For once the capacity for self-interaction and internal dialogue has been created it can be used in ways which do not mirror the real interactions to which actors are a party. One might, for example, debate with culturally significant rather than socially significant 'others', such as God, Jesus Christ, the devil, or characters from fiction or the mass media.[7] Equally we may just learn that talking to ourselves is functional, enabling us to clarify our thoughts, reach decisions, negotiate our way through complex tasks, or even arouse ourselves to action. In none of these instances, however, is there any reason to assume that the intrapersonal dialogue has some inter-personal corollary or homologue in the social world. Hence to quote Mead, as many sociologists do, to the effect that 'To look upon oneself as an object is to see oneself as others do'[8] is only true if it is merely taken to mean that actors have the same ability as observers to see themselves as objects. It does not mean that actors will see themselves as the *same objects* that observers see. For individuals can and often do regard themselves in ways which no other person does.

Indeed, George Herbert Mead's name has been invoked inappropriately by social situationalists in this respect. For his own argument concerning the development of the self leads to precisely the *opposite* conclusion. It is true that Mead rejected theories of the isolated self associated with introspective philosophy and individualistic psychology and developed a theory in which social processes are necessarily prior to the development of a self-conscious self. However, such a self is certainly not a mere reflection either of the social processes which made it possible or of the views and attitudes expressed by others toward the individual. For as John D. Baldwin has indicated, Mead's theory of the development of the self helps to explain 'two complementary facets of agency: creativity and control'. Ones reflected by the 'I' and the 'me'. It is the dialectic between these two which accounts for the 'unique, creative contribution of the individual' as well as the ability to engage in self-evaluation, self-control and responsible action.[9] What is more the 'other' becomes more and more 'generalised' as the child matures, such that it ceases to represent the attitudes of given individuals or even groups. This results in an individual whose responsible decisions are far from being the outcome of a simple process of internalising or taking over the attitudes of given others. On the contrary, responsible decisions are arrived at through 'the organic and creative processes of reflective intelligence; and in these processes, the social values and control functions of the "me" are counterbalanced by the innovative functions of the "I".'[10] Hence, what Mead's theory outlines is the manner through which individuals develop the ability to be self-conscious, as by means of a process of self-indication, they control and direct their own actions. This argument does not lend any support to the view that the conduct of adults is guided or controlled by the way that others see them. Quite the contrary, it explains the origins of their ability to act independently of the actions, attitudes and opinions of others. Mead is quite explicit on this point. He writes: 'After a self has arisen, it in a certain sense provides for itself its social experiences, and so we can conceive of an absolutely solitary self.'[11] Mead's theory is valuable because it helps to account for the fact that individuals, even when in a clear 'social context', are able to act out of inner imperatives which over-ride any social pressures they might experience. In this way Mead explains how the meanings which inform an individual's actions can indeed be quite unrelated to the social settings in which they occur.

Learning from experience

As we have seen, symbolic interactionists are especially keen on arguing that learning must involve others. As Blumer says 'the meaning of any-thing and everything has to be formed, learned and transmitted through a process of indication – a process that is necessarily a social process'. But now let us consider Herbert Blumer's interesting discussion of the exam-ple of boxing. He observes that a blow may be either symbolic or non-symbolic depending on whether it is preceded by reflection or not:

> Non-symbolic interaction is most readily apparent in reflex responses, as in the case of a boxer who automatically raises his arm to parry a blow. However, if the boxer were reflectively to identify the forthcoming blow from his opponent as a feint designed to trap him, he would be engaged in symbolic interaction.[12]

Now this is a perfectly acceptable argument about how one might go about distinguishing action from behaviour. It does have its difficulties since even identifying a feint could well become an automatic response in an experienced boxer.[13] However, we can set this complication aside here. The really interesting point is the reference to the boxer *identifying the blow as a feint* and how this process of indication might relate to what Blumer has claimed above. For there he asserts that 'the meaning of a thing for a person grows out of the ways in which other persons act toward the person with regard to the thing' and that the 'meaning of anything and everything' has hence to be transmitted from one person to another. But can it really be suggested that the boxer in question has learnt to identify certain forthcoming blows as 'feints' through such processes as these? Perhaps he did; perhaps his trainer shouted out 'watch out, that is a feint' during a practice bout, or perhaps his sparring partner actually said, 'now I am going to throw a feint' before doing so. Or perhaps he learnt to identify feints by having them pointed out to him by a more experienced boxer whilst watching other fights. However, all this appears far-fetched. It seems rather more likely that it was through direct personal experience (possibly gained through fist-fights with his childhood friends) that our prospective boxer first realised that some of his antagonist's threatened blows actually were deliberately faked in order to outwit him. In other words, young boxers are likely to learn very quickly and *from experience* that some apparent blows are actually 'feints'. Hence the claim that the meaning of 'anything and everything' must be learnt from others is simply unconvincing; a great deal is learnt and probably can only be learnt, from the experience of living in the world. Of course, what we can only learn from others is that an incipient blow which is intended to deceive us is called a 'feint' in English. But that is not the point at issue here; the point is that an individual can discover how to interpret the action of another without the participation of others. Because the name 'of everything and anything' has to be learnt from others it does not follow that the 'meaning' of everything is learnt from others. For a great deal of meaning is acquired through the experiences of living, and as such is acquired independently of others. Learning that some blows are feints is, in this sense, no different from learning that you can get wet standing in the rain or that nettles can sting you.

It should be clear from this discussion that a central weakness of the situationalist position, one which arises from its very marked cognitive bias, is the tendency to assume that all individuals need in order to be competent actors is the appropriate 'knowledge'. The whole emphasis is upon knowledge, whether in the form of names, shared concepts, typifications or tacit understandings, the assumption being that in order to be able to act (or more usually interact) actors need to 'know' or 'understand'. Yet this is to misrepresent the pre-requisites for successful human action. For in order to accomplish action it is necessary, not merely to understand or 'know things', but to have acquired certain skills. In other words, the situationalist position tends to confuse learning *about actions* with learning *how to perform them*. For whilst people necessarily learn both what things are called and what their purpose is directly from others, it is questionable how far individuals can be said to learn from others how to perform the actions associated with those objects. After all, learning to ride a bicycle (that is to say, learning to perform the action of 'cycling') involves rather different processes from learning that a pedal-powered, two-wheel means of transport is called a bicycle. The latter, of necessity, one can only learn from others; but the former one could learn, at least in principle, by trial and error. Indeed, even learning *that* you ride a bike by sitting on the saddle and pedalling does not resolve the problem of learning *how* to do it without falling off. Even when learning under instruction by others, it is still the case that in the last resort one learns such things by trial and error. Some people, for example, never master the technique no matter how much instruction they receive, although most normal people have little difficulty in learning to identify a bicycle by name. At the same time, autodidacts learn such complex skills as riding a bicycle or playing a piano without any help from others. What is more, an individual's attempts to learn to ride (whether self-taught or not) may have little relation to the previous attempts of others to master this skill. Such an activity is of necessity a personal if not entirely a private matter. This is because bringing behaviour under willed control in order to turn it into action is dependent upon the subject's ability to successfully monitor feedback from his or her own movements and make the appropriate adjustments. Only the results of this process are visible to others, whilst the process itself remains invisible. Since all actions are dependent upon such a process of internal monitoring it is somewhat inaccurate to suggest that individuals learn their actions from others. They may well learn what they are supposed to do from others, whilst in addition they may well receive some form of guidance or tuition; but essentially learning how to perform tasks successfully is something which individuals are forced to do for themselves.[14]

It can be seen from this that one very good reason why individuals cannot be said to learn how to perform actions 'from others' is because the processes upon which much successful action depends are actually covert and hence not directly observable. Thus it follows that the way in which individuals accomplish their actions is not in general a social matter since only the end result is witnessed. Take the example of remembering; generally speaking it does not matter *how* an individual succeeds in remembering their cash-point number as long as they do, and, in fact, it appears that people use a variety of different methods. Some people may have learnt about such methods from others, but it is hard to see how they could have learnt how to remember by observing how others do it. It is equally inappropriate to claim, as Mills does, that 'motives' are learnt from others. Maybe, as he suggests, words and phrases are learnt in this way, along with knowledge of the appropriate occasions on which to articulate them. This, however, is different from claiming that *motives* are learned. Motives are complexes of meaning which serve to energise and control actions, and as such one of their distinctive features is that they are not open to scrutiny by others; they are part of the covert self. The monitoring by others as well as the use of sanctions by others typically relates to actions themselves not to motives. Hence, what motives individuals succeed in developing in order to help them perform their actions is generally left to them. As long as they work, others will not bother to query them. Thus although it can certainly be claimed that individuals 'learn' their motives, this is probably achieved through a process of personal trial and error which does not involve others. Whether, for example, an entrepreneur is motivated to work hard and accumulate wealth by a fear of poverty, a lust for power, or a desire to please God, is a question which only he or she can answer. Others may not know which it is and normally will have no particular reason to inquire.[15]

Of course, situationalists not only conveniently overlook both covert actions and those covert processes which are essential to the successful accomplishment of most overt actions, but they also overlook the phenomenon of the covert self. So here there is another powerful argument for assuming that when individuals regard themselves 'objectively' they cannot simply be 'taking the role of the other' in the sense of viewing themselves in the way that others see them. This is because when individuals regard themselves they take into account conduct and experience which is unknown to others. Such conduct is still, like the overt forms, viewed objectively by the actor and related to the concept of self. Indeed, this covert version of the self may be a more important determinant of conduct than the overt, public one.[16] Of course, individuals may evaluate their covert actions in ways which they imagine others would if they were aware of them. None the less, it is unconvincing to suggest that attitudes towards the covert self mirror those adopted by others towards the public self.

Many of these objections apply just as much to the phenomenological, that is to say, Schutzian, version of the 'all meaning is social' claim as they do to the symbolic interactionist one. In this case emphasis is placed on the idea that individuals learn about the meaning of their own actions from the necessity of 'describing', or making sense of, or rendering intelligible, those actions of others. Indeed it is largely on these grounds that Schutz bases his general claim that meaning is essentially 'intersubjective' or social in nature. But there are many difficulties with this thesis. First, as noted, since much human action is covert, either wholly or in part, it can only have a very limited application. Thus whilst it might be plausible to claim that individuals learn about the meaning of their own overt actions by making sense of the overt acts of others, this cannot apply to the world of covert action. All we can possibly know of this is what we can infer or what the other chooses to tell us (and of course situationalists have ruled out the possibility of learning anything from the accounts of actions which others supply).[17] It cannot be the case that an individual's knowledge of his or her own covert acts derives from the process of understanding those of others. On the other hand, knowledge of one's own covert world of action (whether acquired through self-observation or introspection) could serve as the basis for speculation or insight into the covert world of others. Consequently, it is rather more plausible to suggest that we learn to understand what others are doing as a result of knowing what we ourselves do.

Secondly, and again as noted above, since even overt actions rely for their successful accomplishment upon covert intra-personal processes it seems unlikely that individuals can even learn to understand their own overt actions simply by observing the overt acts of others. Learning to act by observing another actor is rather like learning to ride a bike by observing a cyclist. It cannot really be done; learning involves *doing it* through trial and error. In this respect 'what we do' covertly involves a technology, an ability to achieve results, which we can only develop through personal trial and error. We obviously cannot learn by watching others, or even listening to them, but only by discovering 'what works for us'. Since the range of possible strategies is limited, the solutions we devise may indeed resemble those of others, but we still arrive at them independently of the activities of others.[18]

. Thirdly, it follows from this that perceiving the acts of others to be intelligible is a quite different matter from being able to accomplish them. Whilst the actions of others might be regarded as no more than some kind of intellectual puzzle which we are required to solve, our own actions are events and as such have to be accomplished rather than merely interpreted. This means that we are very likely to 'understand' our own actions in a rather different manner from that in which we 'interpret' those of others. Or, to the extent that the two exercises are similar it must be because individuals employ their understanding of how their own actions are accomplished to understand others rather than vice versa. What an act 'means' to an actor is necessarily different from what it 'means' to an observer because the actor's meaning includes the experience of creating and performing the act. The idea that individuals could learn about their actions by first interpreting those of others derives from the mistake of assuming that action is no more than 'a complex of meaning or meaning-context',[19] whilst confusing the knowledge necessary to accomplish actions with the behavioural control skills necessary to do so. At the same time, as indicated, it reveals that cognitive bias in the analysis of human conduct which is such a marked feature of situationalism.

We are now in a position to conclude that the claim that the meanings which inform the actions of individuals are 'social' because it is necessarily the case that they are learnt from others is unconvincing. Whilst the claim that such meanings stem from the use of faculties which have themselves been acquired via interaction with others (such as the ability to be reflexive or use language) undoubtedly has some truth, it does not justify labelling the individual's actions as 'social'. In addition, the Schutzian claim that actors can only learn the meanings of their own acts by first describing those of others also seems unsupportable. The mistakes which largely account for these errors involve treating the learning of actions as if it were a process analogous to learning the names of objects; overlooking the important role which learning from experience plays in human maturation; presuming that action is based on the acquisition of knowledge when it is actually more dependent on the development of skill, and ignoring the significant phenomenon of covert action and of the part played by covert processes in the performance of overt actions as well as the covert self itself.

11   The communicative act paradigm

We have seen that the 'all meaning is social' thesis is the key to that syllogism which is central to the dominant situationalist orthodoxy in sociology and hence, in effect, the principal reason why all action is regarded as if it were indeed social action. Yet, as we have just seen, there are many grounds for believing such a thesis to be implausible. One is bound to ask why in that case it has come to have such a grip over the minds of contemporary sociologists. In part, the answer lies in the fact that this is dogma, now no more than an unquestioned assumption, equivalent in the eyes of many sociologists to the belief that sociology is a discipline which necessarily confines itself to the study of social phenomena. Yet it seems unlikely that such a belief could have gained acceptance within the discipline in the first place unless it had some empirical support; which indeed it does. For there is a certain form of conduct – communicative action – which accords with the situationalist assumptions concerning action in general. Indeed, it is largely because situationalism involves taking such actions as paradigmatic of all human conduct that sociologists have been persuaded to adopt the new orthodoxy. Unfortunately, it is not clear that most human actions are best understood by treating them as if they were forms of communication.

There is little doubt that the main strength of situationalism arises from the dominance accorded to a situationally determined communicative act paradigm. That is to say the application of a model of conduct derived from the study of a special category of communicative actions, not merely to all communicative actions, or even to all socially meaningful actions, but to all human actions. Those symbolic, expressive actions which have been designed specifically to convey meaning from one individual to another are thus the focus of analysis and are typically used to illustrate points about action in general. This fact is very clear from a glance at the situationalist literature where favourite examples include a man scratching an itch on his nose and thereby unintentionally making a bid at an auction; a motorist signalling a turn when approaching a cross-roads; a groom placing a ring on a woman's finger in a marriage ceremony, and an audience clapping at the end of a performance. What is significant about these examples is that not one of them resembles those examples employed by Weber. That is to say, none of these is an example of instrumental action of the kind which individuals might engage in whether someone else was present or not. This does not mean that they are distinctive in being 'social' acts in any conventional sense of that term, that is not what sets them apart. What is special about them is that they are unique in not having an instrumental function other than that of communication.[1]

Consequently what marks these acts off from all other human actions is the fact that they have *a* given meaning as opposed to being merely 'meaningful', which is to say, being merely 'intelligible' to others. This meaning consists of the 'message', that which is conveyed from one actor to one or more other actors. Now it is obvious that such actions will only be performed in a social situation, that is to say, when other individuals are present to receive the message. What is more, if such actions are to fulfil their communicative function then their specific meanings must be known and shared among those actors who are party to the act. In addition, since the act is a symbol this meaning can only be learnt from others. Thus it follows that such acts are necessarily 'social' in almost every sense of that word. Which is why such items of conduct are perfect illustrations of the situationalist's view of what constitutes 'social action'. However, it is important to note that situationalism's view of the 'social' is not fully exemplified by reference to communicative acts in general but requires reference to a special category of such acts. For just stressing the fact that the meaning of an act is shared and learnt from others whilst the act itself occurs in a public context is not enough to illustrate the situationalist thesis. In order to do this it is necessary to invoke those communicative acts which can be judged to be constituted by the social situations in which they occur, or rather by the rules and conventions governing the context of their occurrence. That is to say, the action must itself not only be a socially defined unit but it must be the case that, 'the conventions, rather than the agent's intentions, determine what is being done'.[2] Therefore illustrating the central point that 'Meanings are putatively assigned to actions on the basis of rules specifying the conditions under which an appropriate behaviour counts as an action'.[3] Hence, these are not just actions which have a social meaning, they are actions which are themselves socially constituted, with their very nature and parameters given by features of the context in which they occur.[4] This makes them social actions in a very fundamental sense. Consequently it is not communicative actions in general which serve to illustrate the situationalist thesis but only situationally constituted communicative acts.

As can be seen, this paradigm draws very heavily on the study of language and meaning; indeed speech acts can be seen as the very exemplars of the communicative act paradigm. Thus the widespread adoption of this paradigm is largely due to the heavy dependency on arguments drawn from the philosophy of language. Acts which are intended to convey messages are sufficiently similar to words – being effectively physical symbols – that the analogy with the study of meaning and language is seen to be highly pertinent. However, most actions are not words and regarding all human actions in this way is tantamount to treating the actions which comprise finger-spelling or signing as if they were typical of all intentional movements which deaf people might perform with their hands. Communicative acts form a small segment of all human actions, whilst socially constituted communicative acts constitute an even smaller proportion. Hence, the reality is that the communicative act paradigm actually has a very limited application.

Indeed, as we have seen, this paradigm does not even apply to the majority of communicative actions. This is because not all communicative acts are situationally constituted. Certainly all communicative acts have clear parameters and their meaning can be assumed to be widely shared. This much is largely true by definition. But this does not mean that their meaning is therefore socially constituted in the sense of being dependent on situationally embodied rules or conventions. Such acts as winking, making rude gestures, blowing a kiss, signalling to someone to follow you, nodding, or shaking one's head, do not (at least in British society) rely on the situational context for their meaning. They are identifiable in almost any context. This is because they are all culturally rather than situationally constituted. Anyone reared in the appropriate culture can successfully identify these acts and thus readily identify their meaning and what is more they can do this without reference to the social context in which the act occurs. By contrast, one cannot make a bid unless one is participating in an auction; or signal a turn unless you are in charge of a vehicle on a highway; or take a wedding vow unless participating in a wedding ceremony. Hence there is a significant difference between context-dependent communicative acts and context-independent ones. To employ the situationalist communicative act paradigm to study all communicative acts would thus once again involve conflating the cultural–social difference in favour of the latter. But then one reason why the social–context communicative act paradigm has been so widely over-applied is because sociologists have been far too ready to treat actions as communicative in character in the first place. The fact that very many human actions are performed within visual or aural range of others does not automatically mean that they are oriented to those others and hence should be studied as if they were communicative acts. What many sociologists unquestionably treat as 'social acts' are probably no such thing: they are merely actions. The presumption that any act which an actor knows to be witnessable by others must therefore be a 'social' act either in the sense of possessing communicative intent, or in the sense of being subject to interpretation by others as if it carried a message, is a persistent but unwarrantable assumption which bedevils sociology. Its most serious consequence is that the fundamentally instrumental nature of these actions becomes overlooked.

Only a small proportion of the total range of human actions appears to fit the situationalist paradigm. It has already been noted that some actions are so patently purposive and complex that it is absurd to suggest that they can be understood without reference to the subjective meanings present within the actor. To these we can now add the even larger number of basic human actions which are also patently identifiable without reference to their context. It is interesting, in relation to the auction 'bid' example, that situationalists appear to see no difficulty in referring to an individual 'scratching an itch' even though there are no situationally embedded rules or conventions which would give an individual's behaviour such a meaning. The truth is that the vast majority of actions are identified without reference to socially situated rules or conventions. For although one may have to be in an auction before one can 'bid' or driving a car on a road before one can 'signal a turn', one does not have to be in a restaurant, for example, to be judged to be 'eating', or on a concert platform to be 'singing', or in front of a camera to be 'smiling', or in a church to be 'praying', or in a library to be 'reading', or in a race to be 'running'.

However, the problem is not just that this paradigm is not applicable to most actions; it is that adoption of the paradigm causes sociologists to fail to recognise many human actions as actions. In other words it creates serious blind spots in the sociological vision. Two of these, in particular, need to be mentioned. The first concerns those items of behaviour which are in fact unsuccessful attempts by actors to perform certain acts. Since these will not conform with the social norms or rules pertaining to the situation in which they occur they will, according to the situationalist thesis, not be identifiable as acts at all. The learner driver whose attempt to signal is not recognised as such by other road users, or the person at the auction whose strange gesture is not recognised by the auctioneer as a bid, will simply not be judged to have acted. Hence there is no room in this perspective for failed actions, accidentally performed actions, or mistaken actions. The very possibility of their existence is ruled out. By attempting to exclude any reference to subjective or 'mental' states from the process of identifying actions, the rule-constituted approach is unable either to provide any way of identifying or explaining 'failed' actions or of distinguishing between those which were intended and those performed 'by accident'. If 'doing the right thing' under 'the right circumstances' qualifies the conduct in question as 'action', what do we call that conduct which is 'the wrong thing' but was nevertheless performed under 'the right circumstances'? Or 'the right thing' done under the wrong circumstances? Indeed, how could we distinguish these two categories from each other? Are all such actions to be lumped together with instinctive reactions and impulses under the general heading of 'behaviour'? Surely it defies common sense not to recognise the existence of such categories of human conduct as 'failed action', 'accidental action' and 'inappropriate action'. Yet to do so requires abandoning the situationalist paradigm.

The second significant lacunae in the situationalist position concerns the fact that there is a whole range of actions in which some aspect of the subjective state of the actor is crucial to defining the act itself. The difference between the 'giving of a gift' for example and 'the offering of a bribe' rests more upon the contrasting goals and intentions of the giver than it does upon the social situation in which it is performed. Even more obvious examples where this is the case are the acts of murder and suicide. In both these cases the actor's intention is a defining feature of the act. An individual cannot, in that sense, be deemed to have murdered someone unless an intention to cause their death was judged to be present in the mind of the actor; equally one could not be judged to have committed suicide unless it was the actor's intention to take his or her own life. It is absurd to claim in these instances that 'social conventions, rather than agent's intentions'[5] determine whether the act has been performed. For unless these intentions are established the act 'becomes' something else. The fact that there may be conventional means of determining what the agent's intentions were is beside the point.[6] Indeed, these examples, if we might adapt an argument of John Searle's, seem to suggest that the nature of the intention is, in these cases at least, actually 'constitutive' of the act. One simply cannot commit murder unless your intention is to kill the other person. Take away the intention and you have not performed the act (you have engaged in manslaughter instead).[7]

Of course, the truth is that *all* actions are really identified by reference to the actor's subjective state, the situationalists protestations notwithstanding. In other words, the murder and suicide examples are not unusual in having actors' internal states as defining features, they are typical. Let us consider one of the situationalist examples more carefully, that of the unwitting bidder at the auction. Here we have an instance of an individual who, whilst sitting in the audience at an auction, happens to scratch an itch on the side of his nose, a gesture which is mistaken by the auctioneer for a bid. Let us now imagine that this is the highest bid and that the individual now finds himself the owner of an object which he did not want. Consequently he explains to the auctioneer that actually he was just scratching his nose at the time and not bidding at all. Now the auctioneer knows that the action in question was not in fact a bid at all. Although this may not alter the situation and the hapless individual may still be required to pay for the item in question, the action has at last been correctly identified. In fact it was never correct to describe the individual's behaviour as 'making a bid' in the first place. A full and correct description of the action would have been 'attempting to alleviate an itch by scratching his nose and thereby unintentionally making a bid'.

What this example illustrates is the fact that contextual rules, where they exist, are only employed by observers as a basis for formulating *hypotheses* concerning 'what is being done'; hypotheses which observers themselves recognise as subject to correction once information concerning the subject's intentions comes to light. The auctioneer is unlikely to deny the individual's contention that he was actually scratching his nose and not bidding even if he continues to insist that the item is payed for. To claim that the meaning of an action can be *provisionally* established simply by reference to contextual rules is, at least in some instances, relatively plausible; to argue that it can be *successfully* established in this way without the necessity of checking with the agent's understanding of what he or she was doing is quite unrealistic. Yet it is this latter position which situationalists insist on. In everyday life however individuals are more sensible and operate on the assumption that situationally established assumptions about an act's meaning are merely provisional and frequently need to be confirmed through consultation with the actor or actors concerned.

Thus one finds situationalists arguing that knowledge of an individual's circumstances is a sufficient basis for deciding that they 'have a motive' of one sort or another, much in the way that sleuths are wont to do when drawing up a list of suspects in the course of investigating a murder.[8] Yet they conveniently forget that this exercise is simply a way of formulating hypotheses concerning the forces which *might* have motivated certain individuals to act in this way. Once again it refers to the construction of hypotheses and does not demonstrate that any individual identified as 'having a motive' did in reality experience the slightest urge to kill the victim. Yet if they did not experience such promptings (whether held in check or not) then they cannot be said to have 'had a motive'. Even if the term is used (somewhat incorrectly) to mean a 'reason' for acting it would still be necessary to show that the individual concerned was conscious of it. These attempts to argue that both actions and their associated meanings can be identified without any reference to the subjective world of the actor are quite unrealistic since, in the last resort, the meaning of an action can only be established by consulting the actor concerned.

On the basis of the above arguments one is forced to conclude that the situationally constituted communicative act paradigm has a very limited application. In the first place it does not apply to a wide range of simple and universal forms of conduct known to all humans such as eating, laughing, smiling, crying, walking, running, singing, and the like, or to more highly complex and mentally demanding activities such as playing chess, solving mathematical puzzles, composing music, etc. In addition, it is a perspective which is quite unable to identify deviant, innovative or failed actions or, of course, those where internal states are actually constitutive of the act. Finally even on those relatively rare occasions where there is a possibility of identifying the meaning of an act from a study of the context alone, all that is really produced is a hypothesis concerning what the act means. A speculation which still requires confirmation by reference to the actor or actors concerned before one can confidently declare that the meaning of the action is known.

Rules and meaning: the logical connection

Why in this case, has the communicative paradigm gained such a hold over the minds of sociologists? One reason would seem to be the prominence given to the views of certain post-Wittgensteinian philosophers concerning the role of rules in the constitution of meaning. Since rules or conventions play a critical role in constituting the meaning of many communicative acts there has naturally been much attention paid to the connection between rules and meaningful conduct in general. Particularly influential in this respect has been a purely logical argument, commonly advanced by post-Wittgensteinian philosophers, to the effect that meaningful propositions must imply rule-following. This argument has been widely used to boost the claims of the communicative paradigm and hence the general contention that meaning is inherently social. However, it is far from clear that this philosophical argument has any particular sociological implication.

Very briefly expressed the Wittgensteinian–Winchian claim concerning the logical dependence of categories of meaning on social rules suggests that if an act is to be distinguished from behaviour by the fact that it has a subjective sense or 'meaning' then the actor must in effect be committed to behaving in one way rather than another. That is to say his or her conduct must be characterised by the application of a rule, and the application of a rule in turn implies a social context. Thus, in Winch's words, meaning categories or concepts are '*logically* dependent for their sense on interaction between men' whilst 'the very existence of concepts depends on group life'.[9] What is more, this is an argument which applies to even 'the most private acts if, that is, they are to be meaningful'.[10] More specifically, for a word to have a given meaning then its utterer must be following a rule. This is because it is rules which guarantee the quality of 'sameness' which underpin the meaningfulness of all concepts. Behaviour can only be adjudged to be rule-following, however, if 'somebody else could in principle discover the rule which I am following' or if someone else could himself 'go on in that way as a matter of course'.[11] It is this argument which some sociologists have repeated on the assumption that it supports the general claim about the social nature of all meaning outlined above (and the wide applicability of the communicative act paradigm). However, it is hard to see how one can arrive at this conclusion, for this purely logical claim would appear to have little direct implication for the empirical investigation of social life.

In the first place, it is important to note that even if one were to accept the claim that actions gain their meaning from their relationship to a rule, it does not follow that the rule in question is to be found in the immediate social context in which the act is performed or is one which is known to the other actors present. For all that is required to satisfy the argument is that the act relates to some rule, somewhere, which is known (or could be known) to others. Sufficient research has been undertaken into the significance of role models and reference groups in influencing the nature of action to be certain that there will be many instances where the rule which gives an action its meaning does not derive from the immediate social context.[12] It may derive from social groups of which the actor is not a member (but perhaps aspires to join), or from cultural material rather than from social groups at all.[13] Hence one cannot claim that the Wittgensteinian–Winchian thesis directly supports the situationalist syllogism, as to do so would involve conflating the social–cultural distinction once again. It is interesting therefore that sociologists seem so predisposed to assume that a 'social' rule necessarily means a rule embodied in the immediate social context of the action concerned.

But then more importantly, since individuals are in practice perfectly capable of formulating their own 'social-style' rules, actions need not in practice derive their meaning from actual rules which are expressed in the social lives of groups at all, either ones of which the actor is a member or not, and at one point Winch himself admits as much. He says:

> It is, of course, possible, within a human society as we know it, with its established language and institutions, for an individual to adhere to a *private* rule of conduct. What Wittgenstein insists on, however, is, first, that it must be in principle possible for other people to grasp that rule and judge when it is being correctly followed; secondly, that it makes no sense to suppose anyone capable of establishing a purely personal standard of behaviour *if* he had never had any experience of human society with its socially established rules.[14]

In other words, although social life is a necessary prerequisite for the existence of culture and hence the meanings which characterise human action, and it is intrinsic to the very idea of a rule that other people would understand it if they knew about it, an action need not relate to any extant social rule in order to be meaningful, but could well gain its meaningfulness from an entirely private rule. Unfortunately Winch promptly proceeds to forget his own caveat, for throughout the rest of the book he continues to refer to 'social rules' as if this term necessarily referred to rules which actually prevail within social groups, rather than to rules which are formulated in such a way that they could in principle be grasped by others if they were to become aware of them. For example, further on in the book he asserts that 'all meaningful behaviour must be social, since it can be meaningful only if governed by rules, and rules presuppose a social setting'.[15] However, as we have seen, this statement is deeply ambiguous, since the existence of a rule does not presuppose an *actual* social setting to which the rule in question is related, merely the existence of human society in general and the successful socialisation of the actor. In other words, Winch would appear to be a victim of a very similar confusion to that noted above concerning Mead's theory of the development of the self, that is between observations concerning the social origins and characteristics of meaning in general and those concerning the social nature of the meaning of particular acts. As Winch so rightly notes meaning logically presupposes the existence of an human community together with the associated processes of socialisation. But it does not follow from this that there cannot be private rules and hence private meanings as he admits in the above quote. Hence there is no justification for concluding that all meaning is social. The necessary link between meaning and a 'social context' is historic (the individual must have been socialised) and logical (the rule must be in principle open to others to grasp) but not contemporary or substantive.

One reason why Winch, as well as those who have adopted his argument, tend to make this mistake is not only because they imagine that the meaning of actions can be approached in the same way as can the meaning of words, but also because they imagine that stressing the role of rules in the constitution of meaning is in keeping with a basically anti-mentalist position. As we saw earlier it is anti-mentalist views which underpin the denial of the reality of subjective meaning thesis. Hence not only are they inclined to be rather uncritical in their attitude towards any argument which appears to support the all meaning is social thesis, they are also likely to believe that individual or 'private' meanings cannot exist; which may perhaps go some way towards explaining the fact that Winch overlooks his own caveat. This tendency to dismiss the possibility of private meaning is thus closely associated with Wittgenstein's rejection of the possibility of there being such a thing as a 'private language'.

The debate which Wittgenstein instigated, over whether it is possible for there to be such a thing as a 'private' language, has dimensions which have little relevance to the sociological question which is at issue here. Thus whether a desert-islander, who has succeeded in maturing to adulthood outside of normal human society, could develop a language, or whether there was a single individual who first 'invented' language are both irrelevant to the question of whether action can embody 'private' or 'individual' as opposed to 'social' or 'shared' meanings.[16] The critical point is that the term 'private language' is ambiguous, since it can either mean that language which individuals employ when talking to themselves (especially perhaps about their 'private' and 'covert' experiences) or it can mean a language which is devised by individuals themselves and consequently cannot be understood by others. Wittgenstein himself appears to have used the term in both senses.[17] However, while there do seem to be real objections to the latter thesis there is really no difficulty in assuming the reality of the former and hence of the existence of 'private meanings'. That is to say, there is no good reason whatsoever why individuals cannot employ a publicly available language to give expression to private experiences or to make their private actions meaningful.[18]

Jürgen Habermas recounts another strand in Wittgenstein's arguments against the possibility of private rules; the suggestion that individuals cannot follow rules for themselves alone. The reason given for this is that 'to *think* one is obeying a rule is not to obey a rule. Hence it is not possible to obey a rule "privately": otherwise thinking one was obeying a rule would be the same as obeying it.'[19] The reason for this conclusion is the suggestion that an individual could never be sure whether he or she was following a rule if there were no situation in which the behaviour was exposed to the judgement of one or more observers. Habermas says that 'A rule has to possess validity intersubjectively for at least two subjects if one subject is to be able to follow the rule – that is, the *same* rule.'[20] However this claim simply does not ring true. For, in the first place, it would make 'inner' ethical conduct an impossibility. Trying to make one's emotional life conform to the rule of not lusting after one's neighbour's wife (or husband), for example, would be an impossibility, as by definition one could never actually be 'obeying' this rule but only 'thinking' that one was obeying it. But then Wittgenstein's opposition of thinking to obeying in this way is very strange in any case. For if thinking is necessarily contrasted with obeying why should the fact than an observer 'thinks' that an individual is obeying a rule count for more than the actor 'thinking' it? Or, for that matter, does the fact that an actor 'thinks' it to be true mean that it cannot be?

The prevalent view that the close connection between meaning and rules demonstrates that all meaning is essentially social has a substantive as well as a logical variant. As we saw above, some essentially communicative or expressive acts are indeed instances where meaning is constituted by the rules or conventions governing the context of their occurrence. As we have just seen, there is also an argument which logically connects meaningfulness and rules. However, neither of these arguments provides any basis for assuming that the majority of human actions have a social meaning, even though, of course, most human actions could indeed be adjudged to be 'rule-governed'. This then constitutes the final situationalist confusion over rules and social meaning, the confusion between actions which are rule-constituted and those which are merely rule-governed.[21] It may be reasonable to contend that acts which are constituted by their rules deserve the designation 'social acts'. But activities which are merely rule-governed certainly do not warrant this designation. Whilst it can be said, quite rightly, that the meaning of my action of signalling a right turn is constituted by the rules for signalling, it cannot be claimed that the 'meaning' of my driving down the road is constituted by the rule which says that I must keep to the left. Activities which are merely rule-governed or rule-guided do not obtain their meaning from such rules but from the physical activity involved.

Is there any need to know other minds?

The second major reason why the communicative act paradigm has exerted such an influence over sociologists, even though it applies to only a small proportion of all human action, is because many sociologists have come to believe that communication, or at least 'shared understandings', are essential for successful interaction to occur. As we have seen, successful communication necessarily depends on the communicants sharing a common symbol system; otherwise, messages could not be transmitted and received. Due to the powerful influence of this model, sociologists have come to believe that the same must be true of non-communicative actions – that here too successful interaction must depend on both interactors attributing the same meaning to their actions. Since in these instances it is obvious that actions do not possess a given and widely agreed meaning, it has been assumed that actors must possess some means of ascertaining the meaning (in the form of the goals or motives) which others attach to their actions. There must be a close correspondence of some sort between the meaning which an actor attributes to his or her action and the meaning which an observer or interactant attributes to it or successful interaction would not be possible. Situationalists now take it for granted that successful social action as well as successful interaction (if there is a difference) depends upon processes of *verstehen* or somehow 'knowing other minds'. Thus, although the communicative act paradigm specifically excludes the need for individuals to penetrate to the subjective meaning of actions (since the action carries its own unambiguous meaning there is no need for the recipient of the message to probe into the actor's goals or motives) its predominance has led sociologist to believe that non-communicative interaction, if it is to be successful, requires just such a discerning of the actor's subjective meaning. If actors do not 'share' an understanding of the action concerned, successful interaction will not occur.

Schutz appears to be the theorist mainly responsible for this assumption. In fact, Schutz makes a series of assumptions which can only be dubbed rather strange in this connection. These are, first, that individuals are engaged in efforts to ascertain the subjective meaning informing the actions of others whilst, secondly, employing *verstehen* to achieve this end and thirdly, that they are usually successful in this aim, with the result that, fourthly, this successful insight into the goals and motives of other actors explains their confidence in the successful outcome of their own actions.

These assumptions are strange in the first place because a substantial amount of human interaction involves treating the other as a 'thing' rather than as an experiencing subject, although clearly in these cases no interpretive understanding of the actions of the other is required. Weber's cyclists interact by colliding, and also by fighting, yet neither of these activities necessarily involves any interpretive understanding of each other's actions. Such forms of interaction are neither rare nor insignificant, for there are many instances in daily life where the mere presence of one or more other people exerts an influence on an individual's conduct and where the individual's presence influences others. Equally one may have lengthy and complex interactions with others, as for example may occur in a game of tennis or football without the majority of one's actions necessarily being oriented to others as anything other than 'things'. Obviously much orderly interaction does not require individuals to discover the subjective meaning informing the actions of others. Unfortunately, as we noted earlier, Schutz deliberately excludes such phenomena from his definition of social action.[22]

The second strange assumption is that although Schutz notes that those with whom we interact are likely to have only a vague notion of what we are doing and why, he goes on to presume that they will be engaged in the effort of trying to 'increase their chances' of finding out.[23] Indeed, Schutz devotes a great deal of effort himself to an attempt to answer the question of how it is that we 'know other minds'. One of the examples he discusses in this connection is how 'we know what is going on in the woodcutter's mind'.[24] However, whilst it is understandable that an interpretive sociologist would be interested in such a question, it is hard to see why any ordinary individual would devote much time and effort to trying to answer it. Why would any person who happens to encounter the woodcutter in a clearing have any reason to ask such a question? Equally it is hard to see why anyone who interacts with the woodcutter, say someone who asks for directions, or is interested in buying firewood from him, would be inclined to puzzle over the man's motivation. Indeed, it is difficult to understand why Schutz should assume that anyone, with the exception of the sociologist, has any interest in 'what is going on in the woodcutter's mind'. For such knowledge is needed neither in order to perceive his conduct as intelligible nor in order to interact with him successfully. Of course, should interested bystanders wish to know what is going on in the woodcutter's mind then they might resort to the simple device of asking him; a tactic which, strangely, Schutz is at pains to exclude.[25]

The third strange assumption which Schutz makes is that an individual's 'knowledge' of the social world about them normally includes knowing about the goals and motives which inform the actions of others. He says that 'We normally "know" what the Other does, for what reason he does it, why he does it at this particular time and in these particular circumstances. That means that we experience our fellow-man's actions in terms of his motives and goals.'[26] He then goes on to give an example which supposedly illustrates this claim. He writes, 'if I read an editorial stating that France fears the re-armament of Germany, I know perfectly well what this statement means without knowing the editorialist and even without knowing a Frenchman or a German, let alone without observing their overt behaviour'.[27] However, this example can hardly be said to illustrate the contention that Schutz understands 'what the Other does' for the immediate object in question – an item in a newspaper – is a cultural entity and not an action at all. Even when one turns to consider the content of that item, it transpires that this does not even describe an act but the typical state of mind of a group of people, that of fear. Clearly there is nothing remarkable about the capacity of one human being to understand the fear experienced by another. If, however, Schutz really does have an action in mind then this can only be that of the newspaper editor in writing and publishing the passage in question. Yet it is hard to accept Schutz's assertion that he *knows* what motivated the editor to write that particular editorial or that he *knows* what his purpose was in doing so. There are many possible motives for such an act, as there are too specific goals which the editor might have had in mind. Whatever could be the process of inspired intuition or telepathy which could lead Schutz to imagine that he 'knows' which they were? Yet this passage is cited as evidence that 'we experience our fellow-man's actions in terms of his motives and goals'.[28]

Schutz seems to confuse the fact that he finds the statement which he reads in the newspaper *intelligible* with the assumption that he has insight into the real goals and motives underlying the actions of others. He may well be right to insist that individuals apply their learned common-sense knowledge, in the form of typical motives, identities, goals and actions, to the conduct of others, and as a consequence are able to perceive it as intelligible. What is more, being able to perceive the actions of others as intelligible can indeed, as he claims, be regarded as a prerequisite of orderly social life. But he does not provide any convincing evidence that these observer 'understandings' bear any real correspondence with the actual meanings which inform the actions of individuals. For whilst he admits that such observer-based perceptions inevitably 'fall short' of complete understanding of the action of 'the other',[29] he presumes that a marked degree of correspondence must exist 'sufficient for coming to terms with fellow-men, cultural objects, social institutions – in brief, with social reality'.[30] Yet it is doubtful if this presumption is justified. For it rests on two none-too-convincing arguments; firstly, that there must be a high degree of overlap because such common-sense constructs are shared, and secondly, that the high degree of orderly interaction which marks social life suggests that individuals must be able to penetrate to the meaning underlying each other's actions with a high degree of success.

Elsewhere Schutz provides another example which is meant to illustrate the same contention concerning an actor's 'knowledge' of the goals and motives guiding the conduct of others. Only in this instance Schutz is also attempting to demonstrate that normal social interaction involves a successful 'interlocking' of the goals and motives of different actors. He writes:

> I take it for granted that my action (say putting a stamped and duly addressed envelope in a mailbox) will induce anonymous fellow-men (postmen) to perform typical actions (handling the mail) in accordance with typical in-order-to motives (to live up to their occupational duties) with the result that the state of affairs projected by me (delivery of the letter to an addressee within reasonable time) will be achieved.[31]

As an illustration of the fact that 'we normally know what the Other does and . . . why' this example is no more convincing than the first. For here too there seems little reason to suppose that Schutz knows what motives actually impel postmen to act as they do. Why should it be 'to live up to their occupational duties' rather than 'to earn a living' or 'to provide for their wives and families'? Obviously, Schutz has no idea what motives (typical or atypical) guide postmen in their actions, a fact which he attempts to disguise by providing a re-description of the activity itself as if it were a 'motive'. For not only is the desire 'to live up to their occupational duties' a highly conjectural and rather unconvincing account of postmen's motives, it also approximates to a tautology to suggest that postmen discharge their occupational duties because they are motivated to discharge their occupational duties.[32]

But then the real mystery here is why Schutz imagines that there is any need for him to know what motivates postmen to perform their job. For he certainly does not need this information in order to be able to post a letter. There is no more need for him to understand the actions of postmen and their motives in order to be able to use the postal service successfully than there is to comprehend the technical workings of an automatic exchange to speak to someone in the next town by telephone.[33] Such knowledge, whether judged to be discursive or non-discursive in form, is simply not a prerequisite for successful action. Schutz suggests that 'predictions based on *Verstehen* are continuously made in common-sense thinking with high success'. He follows the comment with the observation that 'There is more than a fair chance that a duly stamped and addressed letter put in a New York mailbox will reach the addressee in Chicago.'[34] But this example does not suggest that any resort to *Verstehen* has occurred. The confidence that an individual may have that any letter posted in New York will reach its destination in

Chicago owes nothing whatever to a prediction about the conduct of others 'based on *Verstehen*' (indeed it is very doubtful whether any prediction about the actions of others has been made). On the contrary, such confidence as exists is likely to owe everything to experience. *Verstehen* is no more involved than it would be in a gardener's confidence that if he sows seed in the ground plants will grow. Hence, it is only in a very limited sense the case that people have to 'understand' the actions of others in order to achieve goals which are dependent on the actions of others. It is certainly not normally necessary to correctly grasp their motives even if some understanding of their goals is occasionally required. It is not even necessary to understand the actions of others when interacting with them face-to-face in order to achieve one's goals. Most of the time all that is needed is for the actor to successfully identify the overall situation in order to know what kind of response (if any) is expected. Thus one can successfully interact with the other drivers on the motorway without knowing where they are driving to or why; or order a book from a bookseller without having the faintest idea what selling a book means to him, and even post a letter without having any notion of the goals or motives of postmen.

The simple truth is much interaction (whether face-to-face or indirect) merely requires the actor to make the same assumptions that he or she would if engaged in interaction with the physical environment. For normally there is little need to penetrate to the 'subjective meaning' of the other's actions. Not only is the communicative paradigm over-applied, but so too is the interpretive interactive one. The success of our actions may well depend upon actions performed by others but this does not mean that there is any need for us to 'understand' their actions. Much of our conduct depends for its success on the conduct of unknown actors acting out of unknown goals and motives or indeed on natural and mechanical processes of which we are ignorant. There is no more need to 'understand the subjective experiences' contained in the actions of others to interact with them successfully than there is to understand the detailed inner workings of complex machines like the internal combustion engine or computers in order to interact with them success-fully. Experience, not *verstehen*, is the key to successful interaction as it is to successful action.[35] This is not to suggest that an actor's conduct is unintelligible to an observer since actions can be meaningful without having a social meaning. For most observers (especially if they have been socialised into the same culture) will usually have little difficulty in perceiving an actor's conduct to be intelligible under one rubric or another. This is not the same, however, as penetrating to the subjective meaning which it has for the actor concerned. Hence, not only will an observer 'understand' an action without knowing the real goals and motives underlying it, but there is no good reason why different observers should even agree on their descriptions of the activity in question. If we take the example of the chess-player moving some chess pieces, different observers may designate what they see as 'playing a game', 'playing chess', or 'developing the King's side', depending on their knowledge and understanding of what is going on. If an observer has any particular reason to penetrate to the real subjective meanings lying behind the conduct of actors, then they will usually endeavour to revise their initial hypotheses concerning 'what they are doing' by asking them.

The vast majority of human actions are not symbolic, communicative acts (whether socially or culturally constituted), nor are they interactions. They are, on the contrary, instrumental actions designed primarily to achieve a change in the actor's state of being or relationship to his or her environment. These actions share none of the special features of communicative acts. Since they are not intended to convey a message they do not have *a* meaning; indeed, they do not have commonly agreed parameters and hence what constitutes *an* act is not even discernable by an observer. *An* act does not convey *a* meaning to an observer because the observer is unsure what constitutes *an* act. Hence, actor and observer cannot be said to share the meaning of the act. It follows that the majority of human actions do not deserve the designation 'social', that is to say, they neither have *a* determinate meaning which is shared between actor and observer(s) nor are their parameters and meanings constituted by the social situations in which they occur. Unfortunately these truths are often obscured because the crucial distinction between 'conveying a definite and given meaning to others' and 'being intelligible to others' is typically glossed over by the careless use of the phrase 'having social meaning'. Ordinary acts should not be described as 'having social meaning' (least of all, as having *a* social meaning) when at best all they possess is merely 'a social dimension'.

12   The linguistic turn for the worse

Since the comunicative act paradigm draws very heavily on the study of language and meaning, with speech treated as exemplifying communicative action, it is hardly surprising to discover that situationalism itself has come to prominence as part of a broader post-war interest in language. Indeed, in large measure the rise of social situationalism has happened principally because British sociologists have been persuaded that the philosophy of language had something useful to offer the discipline. In particular, they came to believe that the study of human action could profit from the conclusions reached by linguistic philosophers and philosophers of ordinary language concerning the nature and origin of meaning. Philosophers had, for their own reasons, taken a 'linguistic turn' in the early 1960s,[1] and by the 1970s and early 1980s many micro-sociologists seemed eager to follow suit. But it is now clear that this 'linguistic turn' has proved to have been a turn for the worse, if not for sociology as a whole, certainly for the sociology of action and the interpretive tradition. This is because the assumption of an extensive parallelism between language and action is deeply misleading, as there is a fundamental difference between identifying the meaning of a symbol and establishing the meaning of an event such as an act. Consequently, conclusions arrived at from the study of meaning and language cannot be safely carried over into the study of action. For although it might appear that there is a similar concern with the study of 'meaning' in both cases the many differences between the two phenomena are such as to render these totally dissimilar exercises.

Boundary disputes

One of the most critically important distinctions is that actions, unlike words, are not single discrete items about whose boundaries there is common agreement. Anyone who sets out to determine the meaning of a word like 'Everest' or 'Rover',[2] for example, can take the unity and discreteness of the word itself for granted. By contrast, those who would study the meanings of actions must first face the difficult problem of deciding where the parameters of any single action might lie. It is not simply that the investigator does not know what constitutes action, or how to recognise when individuals are acting as opposed to behaving.[3] Rather, the immediate problem is to know precisely where the breaks are to be found which might serve to divide the actor's flow of meaningful activity into individual acts and consequently the proper frame of reference to employ in describing them. The process of breaking someone's speech up into standard, discrete, units may not be all that easy; but at least the analyst has the advantage that there are recognisable and socially agreed entities called words (and also, of course, phrases, clauses and sentences). But the process of breaking up someone's conduct in the same way is not so easy as there are no such standard, recognisable units of action which correspond to non-verbal conduct in the way that words correspond to speech. However, unless one can be confident that such units have been successfully identified it is not clear what value there is in speculating about the meaning of an actor's conduct. Of course, most situationalists do not confront this problem, for by employing the communicative act paradigm, they concentrate on that limited set of actions which are necessarily communally defined and delineated. Yet the sheer inadequacy of adopting this approach to the study of all actions is revealed by the fact that although one can always look up the meaning of a word in a dictionary, there is no reference work in which one can check on the meaning of an action. Indeed in so far as such reference works do exist they necessarily refer to purely communicative acts.[4]

Now symbolic interactionists have been among those situationalists who have been particularly keen to claim that actions, like objects and words, do have clear, discrete and commonly agreed parameters. Thus Charon asserts that 'acts are social objects [which] the actor pulls out of the stream of action' and that 'Each act . . . is like all other social objects: It is named, its name is social.'[5] Whilst Warriner observes that 'The actors in a society structure their activity into unit acts which are recognized by themselves and others as units',[6] claiming that as a result there is a socially agreed and conventional understanding concerning what counts as an action and what each action is called. He then illustrates his contention with the example of an individual engaging in the action of 'sawing a board' (perhaps with Weber's more famous example in mind), claiming that this is

a unit social act which exists as an identifiable fact regardless of the unique end in view (whether it is getting a wage or constructing a tree house, dog house, or toy house), regardless of the internal state of the actor (his emotions), regardless of his physiology, handedness, musculature, or effectiveness. Others watching can identify the act regardless of variations in these dimensions.[7]

Yet the assumption made here, that what is 'an act' to an actor coincides with what is 'an act' to an observer, seems unwarranted. There are three critical issues.

First, there are always several ways of defining actions since the stream or flow of conduct is constantly being re-defined and re-divided in many different ways. No observer can be sure what system of division applies, and hence what the units are, without consulting the actor. Even if it is known that the act is primarily instrumental (it could, of course be serving expressive functions), it does not follow that an observer can know what part of the activity is a 'means' and which a 'goal', let alone what that goal is. In the above example, no observer can be confident that 'sawing a board' is the appropriate rubric under which to describe what the actor is doing. He or she *might* be using this definition, but there are many alternative possibilities. The actor could be defining the activity as 'sawing a board in half', or as 'shortening a board', or as 'sawing all these boards to the right length'. He or she could even be using a larger frame of reference and might respond to an inquiry about the activity by stating that it was 'making a kennel', or even 'preparing firewood'. An observer may even be applying a quite inappropriate frame of reference altogether, as the actor may simply be 'trying out a new saw', or even 'getting a little exercise'.[8] The second point is that what constitutes 'an action' is constantly open to re-definition depending upon the extent to which the actor encounters problems in accomplishing his or her aims. If, for example, the actor is having difficulty in 'sawing the board' (if that is indeed how the subject has defined the activity), then it could easily become re-defined as 'trying to prevent the saw from jamming in the knotted wood', or 'trying to make a clean cut and not allow the wood to splinter', or even 'trying to summon up the energy to complete this cut'. What an individual can be said to be 'doing' at any one time depends on the immediate goal which they are concentrating on achieving, something which in turn determines the actor's frame of reference. Yet due to the irredeemable unpredictability and intractability of the natural world (and indeed many aspects of the social one), individuals find that they are regularly involved in such re-definitions and hence re-formulations, of 'what they are doing'. So again, no observer could be confident that they 'know' what is going on. The third and last point is that even if there were general social agreement on what constituted units of action (such that it is 'sawing a board' in this instance) no observer can know if it really constitutes action as opposed to behaviour. The carpenter who does this kind of thing all the time will probably perform such routine tasks quite automatically whilst thinking about something else, in which case the real action consists of that which preoccupies the actor, not simply that which is apparent to an observer. Hence what he or she is 'doing' in this case may well be 'working out how much to charge for the kennel', or 'estimating if there is enough wood to do the job without fetching more'. Such a recognition that not only is much action covert, but that people can indeed 'do' more than one thing at a time, also serves to undermine the suggestion that individuals only perform socially agreed, conventionally named actions.

The second, critically important distinction between words and actions is that the former are symbols whilst the latter are events. Consequently although a word, since it is a cultural item, may be studied like any symbol apart from the human agents who employ it in speech or writing, this cannot be the case with actions. Hence it is possible to study texts, 'dead' and artificial languages, and indeed linguistic meaning generally, without necessarily investigating the language users themselves. This cannot be the case with actions, which are inseparable from actors. Actions are performed by human agents and as such their study is a part of the study of agency. However, one of the characteristics of situationalism is, as we have seen, the attempt to exclude the subject as actor from sociology and thus the representation of actions as if they were not really the accomplishments of human beings at all, but rather the 'product' of social situations.

Meaning and use

Thirdly, it follows from this that since a word is a symbol the relationship between it and any aspect of the physical world is necessarily arbitrary. However, since an action is not a symbol (or at least, it is never *merely* a symbol) but is a physical event, its relationship to other physical events is not arbitrary but is governed by natural laws. This makes for a tremendous difference when studying 'meaning'.[9] For whilst individuals cannot (as individuals) arbitrarily change the meaning of a word, the meaning which they accord to their actions will change according to the circumstances in which they find themselves and is not dependent on communal agreement. This can be illustrated by comparing the names of objects with their use. Thus an object may come with a name which carries with it a designated use; for example, an object is called an 'axe' and it is typically used for chopping wood. Consequently an individual cannot use the word 'axe' to mean 'sword' or 'spade' and still expect it to serve the purpose of accomplishing successful communication with others. This does not mean, however, that the object itself cannot be used for other purposes than chopping wood. It can, for example, be used to kill one's enemy, or even, in the absence of a spade, to scrape a hole in the soft earth in which to bury him or her. Now Schutz does his best to try and ignore this critical distinction between the meaning of words and the use of objects. For, after correctly noting that the way in which any one person uses a word must relate to its use by others, he also tries to suggest that this is true for objects. He writes that 'A tool . . . is experienced . . . in terms of the purpose for which it was designed by more or less anonymous fellow-men and its possible use by others'.[10] However, as we have just seen, objects can be and often are used for purposes other than those for which they were designed. An axe can be used to kill, a book to prop up the leg of a table, or an umbrella to ward off a savage dog. When it comes to objects, unlike the case with words, the maxim 'meaning is use', actually leaves the individual with a considerable degree of freedom to create their own meaning. For it is the physical properties of objects which determine their use; whilst it is the symbolic nature of words which determines theirs. But then it is important to remember that *all* actions, even those such as speech which serve expressive or communicative purposes, are also physical events. It follows from this, fourthly, that the search for the meaning of a word is usually ended once its referent (together with its place in the overall linguistic system) has been successfully identified. An action by contrast is a physical, biological, and psychological event, and hence establishing its meaning involves much more than simply identifying a referent. It involves identifying the conditions which led to its occurrence, the manner of its accomplishment, as well as its possible consequences; all of which can be said to comprise its 'meaning'. It follows from this that whilst the meaning of a word can be studied purely synchronically in relation to the language system of which it is a part, actions must necessarily be understood diachronically as they unfold over time.

Denotative meaning

It is here that situationalism has made the biggest mistake in using the study of language as its model because this has led to the mistake of assuming that the 'meaning' of an act, like that of a word, is essentially denotative in character. Consequently investigating meaning is regarded as equivalent to trying to discover what the act represents, or denotes, and hence that success is to be equated with the correct *identification* of the act in question. This is abundantly clear from the way in which the meaning of action is discussed both by philosophers such as Schutz and Winch, but also by such founders of sociological situationalism as C. Wright Mills and Herbert Blumer. All refer to the question of how acts are successfully identified or 'named' (or more usually, as we have seen, of how objects are named) as if this was what 'meaning' was all about. Again and again, the examples chosen concern either the meaning of words or the naming of objects.[11] Now this would not matter so much if the establishment of such denotative meanings were merely the first stage of a process aimed at establishing the full meaning of an act (and if, in addition, the denotative referent was established by asking the actor). For to know what an act 'is' can reasonably be regarded as a necessary preliminary in such an exercise, much as Weber regarded 'direct observational understanding' as a first step towards the end of proper 'motivational understanding' of actions. But unfortunately this is not how it is conceived. Rather, it is regarded as both the beginning and the end of the search for meaning. To establish what the act 'is' or what it 'stands for' is regarded by situationalists as effectively exhausting its 'meaning'. It is for this reason of course that any additional information which is brought to light, whether it relates to 'reasons', 'goals', 'motives' or the like, is not considered to be a significant addition to understanding but is treated as simply amplifying the primary denotative meaning or 'description', such that all information relating to non-denotational meaning is forced into the denotative, that is to say the purely descriptive, mould. The reason for this is that one does not 'explain' a word or a symbol, one merely 'defines' it. On the other hand it is not sufficient merely to 'define' an event; it is also necessary to 'explain' it.

Talk is (not really) action too

Now of course situationalists, in drawing attention to what they consider to be the close parallel between the study of language and the study of action, have been quick to observe that the analogy does not only lead in one direction. For, not only have they examined actions as if they were words or symbols but they have been quick to observe (as we saw in the discussion of accounts), that 'words', or at least 'talk', is action too. Indeed one very important influence on the development of contemporary sociology has been that perspective which treats words as if they were deeds. This tradition can be traced back to speech act theory and, in particular, the work of Austin.[12] His stress on the fact that one can 'do something' through 'saying something' would appear to complement the more usual situationalist emphasis on the way in which actors 'say something' through 'doing something' (as in Harre and Secord's example of clapping at the end of a performance). However, contrary to what one might expect, this development has not resulted in an extension of the action perspective, but paradoxically worked in favour of situationalism. This is because talk, as was noted earlier, is a distinct and special form of action, one which is atypical of human action in general. Firstly, the fact that it is communicative action means that talk is that one form of action which can be divided into units by the observer, just as it is also that form where it is feasible to assume that the denotative meaning can be known without consulting the actor. But there is also another important point. Talk is also a form of action which can be discussed without the analyst needing to confront the fact that it is a physical event involving effort and energy. For talk is not so much 'cheap', as 'easy' to accomplish (at least for the majority of normal adults). It is not, in that respect, conduct which normally leads to an awareness of issues of motive either in the mind of the actor or indeed in those of observers. Hence treating talk as action has not resulted in talk being appropriated into a proper action framework. Rather it has led to a confirmation of the misleading view of action as a predominantly cognitive phenomenon. So despite the situationalist slogan, words have not actually been analysed as if they were indeed fully-fledged actions at all. They have merely been studied in accordance with the communicative act paradigm: one which is not applicable to the majority of actions.

One can see, in hindsight, how a tendency to replace the study of what people do with the study of what they say they do is implied in the very assumptions of situationalism. For by rejecting actors' accounts as a source of information about their conduct and insisting on granting priority to the social situation, sociologists are bound to end up studying talk about action in place of action itself. The only alternative would appear to be a move toward behaviourism. The fact that talk has itself been studied 'as action' does not make this process any the less inevitable. However, once this substitution has been acceded to, then it is hard to see how the tendency to reduce everything to language can possibly be opposed. In this respect, the rejection by sociologists of self-reports as a means of studying action is likely to prove as disasterous for sociology as the rejection by behaviourists of self-reports and introspection as a means of studying mental processes proved to be for psychology.[13]

Already the study of social and psychological phenomena and processes is being replaced by the study of the language employed to talk about such phenomena. Indeed this is the explicit programme of social constructivism.[14] In this sense the history of what has happened with 'motive' is merely the beginning of what is planned for all significant social and psychological terms. Hence, any sociological interest in the self as an entity or even more usefully, in intra-personal processes in general, is displaced by a concern with how the self is talked about or theorised in discourse. Any idea of studying the 'self' behaving in an environment is cast aside in favour of analysing 'the language practices and discourses prevalent in different contexts'.[15] Potter and Wetherell continue by suggesting that the phenomenon of mind is 'intersubjectively constituted' through interaction with others and that the 'language of the self' is publicly available,[16] thereby echoing Mills' 1940s comment to the effect that 'there is no need to invoke "psychological" terms like "desire" or "wish" as explanatory, since they themselves must be explained socially'.[17] This would appear to be less the 'social imperialism' of traditional situationalism so much as the 'linguistic imperialism' which is inherent within it.

To reject such linguistic reductionism is not to suggest that sociologists should not study language. This is a perfectly proper topic for sociological investigation. Indeed, its study is an essential part of the interpretive tradition. The error has been in studying action as if it were language and, in particular, treating its quality of 'meaningfulness' as if it resembled that which is embodied in language, whilst also taking communicative actions to be paradigmatic of action as a whole. The problem is not so much that sociologists have payed too much attention to language; rather, it is their commitment to particular philosophical theories of language and meaning. This has led to the view that language is exclusively a medium of communication. Consequently, actors' accounts of their actions are always regarded as produced for an audience and as functioning to explain, justify, cajole, or persuade others. But language also performs functions other than that of communicating with others, some of which are vital if action is to occur in the first place. It is not the study of language as action which is needed; it is the study of the role which self-directed language plays in enabling individuals to accomplish their actions which should be the focus of study.

13   The myth of social action

As long as sociologists persist in regarding social action as their predominant subject-matter, there can be little hope of reviving interest in the subjective viewpoint and with it the action theory perspective as a whole. Consequently the key question which sociologists have to ask themselves is the one posed by the philosopher Don Locke. He asked whether there is 'anything distinctive about social action which warrants a special theory'.[1] In the present chapter we may also ask whether there is anything distinctive about social action which warrants a special concept. For if one accepts that 'action' is significantly different from 'behaviour' (as it would appear many sociologists are happy to do) then all the crucial questions do concern the concept of 'social action'. For example, does the fact that action is 'oriented to others', or occurs 'in a social situation', or 'embodies social meaning', actually have any theoretical significance? Does it really follow that this form of action differs in any significant way from 'non-social' action? In order to answer these questions it is necessary to engage in a brief review of the various definitions of the term which have been proposed.

Firstly, there is the view that action should be considered to be social in so far as it embodies the intention of influencing others. Thus Duncan Mitchell declares that action is social when it 'is intended to influence the actions of one or more other persons'.[2] He seems to have acquired this interpretation from Florian Znaniecki who similarly defined social actions as those 'which have as objects conscious beings, individually or collectively, and which purpose to influence those beings'.[3] Secondly, and in stark contrast, there is the view that action is social if it is indeed influenced *by* others. For example, Cohen writes that an action is social 'when (among other things) . . . the situation is such that . . . others possess facilities, objects or characteristics which enable them in some way to influence the conduct of the actor'.[4] Jonathan H. Turner, at the end of his useful review of theories of social action, concludes that the term refers to action that is 'circumscribed' or 'constrained' by the behaviour of others.[5] Thirdly, there is the tendency to simply identify social action as that which is performed in the company of others. Thus, J. E. Goldthorpe asserts that 'most of the things we do in the company of other human beings . . . are obviously social actions',[6] later commenting that action is social if 'other people are involved'.[7] Fourthly, in a similar vein yet somewhat more vaguely, there is the definition of social action as that which occurs in a 'social context' or a 'social situation', or in Goffman's more precise formulation, 'within [the] . . . visual and aural range' of another person or persons.[8] Fifthly, there is the suggestion that action is social if the orientation which guides it (in the form of the governing goals, beliefs, attitudes or values) is shared with others. In Cohen's words, one of the criterion of social action is that 'the actor shares with [these] others certain sets of expectations and, possibly certain values, beliefs and symbols'.[9] Sixthly, and with increasing frequency, one encounters the contemporary version of this position which is that action is social if it embodies 'social meaning'. Finally we need to note that some sociologists have found it necessary to combine two or more of these ingredients in order to satisfy themselves that they have succeeded in specifying the nature of 'social action'.[10]

Let us consider these possibilities in turn and ask in each case whether there is any good reason to assume that the phenomenon identified is sufficiently different from the concept of action to warrant the use of a new term. The first possibility, action which seeks to 'influence others', would seem no different from actions which seek to exert an influence over non-human but animate creatures, or indeed aspects of the inanimate environment, *unless* that is, the form of influence implied is that exerted by means of symbolic communication. In that case, such instances of 'social' action would actually be instances of communicative action. As for the suggestion that social action is that form of action which is influenced by or constrained by others, here too there seems no reason why this should differ in any significant manner from action unless, once again, communication is the medium involved. Otherwise, once communication of the symbolic kind exemplified by language is excluded, then 'influence' would seem to mean no more than 'conditioned' or 'constrained' or, where intention is known to underlie the constraint, manipulation of some sort; something equally applicable to non-human phenomena.[11] Then we have the suggestion that social action refers to action undertaken 'in the company of others' or, at least, within sight or sound of them. Once again we have to ask why such acts should differ in any way from acts performed when the individual is alone or concealed from others, and the only answer which seems plausible is that the presence of others *might* prompt the actor to seek to communicate with them, or indeed vice versa (including perhaps unintentional or unconscious communication although the existence of such forms clearly needs to be established not assumed). In that case, once again, social action dissolves into the two possibilities of action or communicative action. Finally we have the suggestion that action is social if it embodies orientations, values or beliefs which are shared with others, or contains meanings which are in some other way 'social'. This position, which was discussed at length earlier, also amounts in effect either to the use of the term 'social action' to mean human action in general or to refer to that specific form of symbolically mediated action which is communication between humans.

As far as Weber's original conception is concerned Schutz would appear to be quite correct in arguing that conduct oriented to other people as 'things', or even to their behaviour rather than their action, does not really differ in any significant way from conduct oriented to the non-human environment. Similarly, Weber's actual usage – in which it is decisions relating to others which is the critical defining feature – would similarly not appear to constitute any particularly significant distinction. At the same time, Schutz's own suggestion that the actions of individuals become social when they are oriented towards the Other in the sense of the 'consciousness and the subjective experiences being constituted therein'[12] does not seem any more useful. Although it suggests that there might be a fundamental difference between action and social action, Schutz does not provide the sociologist with any way of recognising which actions are actually orientated in this fashion. Instead, he seems to assume that all actions 'involving others' will, of necessity, be of this kind. However, whilst it may be the case that some individuals do attempt to relate to others in this way at times, there is no evidence to suggest that such an orientation is essential for successful interaction and thus might be commonplace. Once again, only in those instances where one attempts to communicate with others via symbolic means, which in effect mainly implies language use, are there some grounds for assuming that the actor might be oriented to the other's 'subjective experience' (although even here this need not be the case).

If we turn, finally, to consider Habermas' four types of 'social action', it would seem that these too fall into the same two basic categories. It is clear, for example, that teleological action would simply represent action under any conventional understanding of that term, even though Habermas tries to insist that its 'strategic' version is a form of social action on the grounds that the individual's decisions are influenced by those taken by others.[13] But then, as we have already seen, there would appear to be no grounds for believing that action influenced by human agencies differs significantly from action influenced by non-human agencies. That leaves 'normatively regulated' and 'dramaturgical action'. Now one would have thought that all action, even the teleological, is 'normatively regulated' to some degree, and hence, as Parsons has argued, this could be considered a necessary characteristic of action in general. Dramaturgical action is simply another form of communicative action, since in essence it involves an attempt to convey a particular 'impression' (or message) to others. Finally communicative action largely speaks for itself, although the way in which Habermas develops this concept suggests that he is actually using it to refer to a form of interaction. What is more Habermas, rather like Schutz, builds in to his concept the presumption that successful interaction necessarily involves individuals in establishing an 'understanding' or rapport with those with whom they interact. Habermas describes all four of these types as 'social action' although it is not clear what they have in common apart from the fact that they are forms of *action*; what makes them all 'social' is not explained.

We can conclude from this very brief summary that the case has yet to be made for the concept 'social action', as it has too, therefore, for a 'theory of social action'. To date, no theoretically significant criterion for distinguishing social action from action has been identified. Consequently, the adjective 'social' is typically redundant. The phenomenon referred to differs in no theoretically significant manner from action – or rather, that portion of it which may do appears to relate to communicative action rather than what has traditionally been encompassed by the term social action. Thus 'action' and 'communicative action' would seem to be the only theoretically significant terms. Otherwise, the remaining possibility is that the adjective 'social' is being used as a synonym for 'interaction', a phenomenon which might be considered to possess some characteristics not displayed by action itself.[14] However, it would not seem to help the cause of conceptual clarity to use the term 'social action' when 'interaction' is the phenomenon under discussion.

Logically, viable definitions of social action are most likely to be those which refer directly to some activity which humans can engage in only with respect to other humans. It then follows that these will successfully distinguish such conduct from non-social forms. The obvious candidates here would seem to be either the use of language or of some faculty such as empathy or *verstehen* and it is therefore the incorporation of such ingredients which makes both Schutz' and Habermas' definitions more promising than most. Unfortunately, both writers seem reluctant to abandon the common-sense notion of the social as that which 'involves others' or involves 'interacting with others' in some way. As a result, they are forced into a position of arguing that action which involves others will also *and of necessity*, require the use of this special human faculty or skill. Thus, Schutz presumes that actors have to discern the contents of other minds, whilst Habermas presumes that they must 'reach an understanding' through language in order to co-ordinate their actions. Both theorists presume that orderly interaction must be due to the employment by actors of these distinctive abilities. But this is none too convincing. There is no good reason to assume that all contact between humans, even that which is prolonged, orderly and 'successful', *must* involve the participants in using their special human faculties to relate to each other. The logically justifiable definitions of social action and the common-sense ones remain unconnected, with the consequence that the sociologist is forced to choose between a definition which relates to normal usage but has no theoretical justification or a theoretically sound definition which (if it applies at all) probably covers only a small portion of what is conventionally thought of as 'social action'. The disjunction between these two alternatives is somewhat obscured by the need to explain how orderly interaction is possible. This need tempts theorists into 'inventing' the phenomenon encompassed by the theoretically significant term.

Finally, whatever feature is made the defining characteristic of 'social' action, it is necessary to know whether it is conceived of as a subjective or objective measure. Weber wrote that social action was action which involved an 'orientation to others' as opposed to that which is oriented solely to 'the behaviour of inanimate objects'.[15] But he does not make it clear whether he means action which the actor believes to be oriented to others or which an observer believes to be so oriented. Is it social action if the conduct is oriented to objects, animals or entities which the actor believes to be 'others' in the sense of gods, spirits, ghosts or other 'personal-style' actors? Is it not social action, even though oriented to 'others', if the actor refuses to recognise the humanity of those others, but insists instead in treating them as animals? Whose, in other words, is the critical perspective, the actor's or the observer's? Now although as suggested above, language and *verstehen* can be taken as distinctive of human–human interaction, they can be employed by humans in any context in which they believe themselves to be interacting with humans or human-style agents, in which case 'social action' might not involve more than one (real) human actor. This issue is very pertinent to the approaches of both Schutz and Habermas, both of whom seem to presume a natural correspondence between the employment of a distinctly 'human' orientation and the actual presence of other human beings.

Three important points emerge from the above discussion. Firstly, since there is no viable way of conceptualising social action the temptation to use it to displace the concept of action should be resisted. As we have seen, not only do the various definitions of this term lack any theoretical significance but the claim that all meaning is necessarily social is both logically self-defeating and empirically false. What is more, conduct which is intelligible to others should be described as action and not social action, whilst there is little justification for employing the term social action to cover those phenomena of interest to sociologists but which lack meaning for the actors concerned. Secondly, there would appear to be good grounds for distinguishing communicative action from the more general category of action and it could be that the term 'social action' might be reserved for this phenomenon. To do this, however, and still retain the definition of the subject-matter of sociology as 'social action' would be unfortunate, since it would restrict the discipline to a relatively small, if interesting, part of human conduct. Finally and as a corollary to this, there continues to be a need for the general concept of action (defined in terms of behaviour which possesses subjective meaning), together with an associated theory of action. Indeed it would seem that in reducing the classic trichotomy to a dichotomy sociologists have abandoned the wrong concept and consequently the wrong theoretical tradition. For it is the concept of action which lies at the centre of sociological thought and which should be retained, whilst social action would seem to be a largely empty and superfluous term.

14 The obstacle which is social situationalism

Social situationalism is the major obstacle to any further development of the theory of action. Its very existence obscures the need to revitalise such a perspective because it gives the impression that theories of action are already flourishing. Thus, although it really has little connection with that interpretive tradition of sociological analysis which takes 'action' as its primary focus, the fact that its subject-matter is given as 'social action' and that it is commonly labelled a 'social action perspective' means that it is easy for sociologists to mistake it for part of that tradition; whereas in reality the subject-matter of situationalism is situated conduct, not action. However, because of the widely taken-for-granted status of its anti-mentalist assumptions, together with the hold which the social action syllogism has over the minds of many British sociologists, this point is not widely appreciated. Social situationalism also obstructs the development of a proper theory of action in other ways. For example, the social imperialism which it embodies leads to a denial of the independent realms of the cultural and the psychological, thereby hindering the investigation of the manner in which these dimensions interact to form the phenomenon which is action.[1] In addition, the use of the term 'social action' to refer to what is in effect merely communicative action and interaction serves to deflect attention away from the problem of understanding how action is itself accomplished and on to the more hypothetical 'problem of intersubjectivity'. Finally by espousing a purely synchronic analysis and adopting an anti-naturalist philosophy, situationalism leads to the complete neglect of the aetiology of actions and hence creates an unnecessary rift with the work of those psychologists and social scientists who do study the causes of human behaviour. Indeed it is clear in hindsight that sociologists of action would have been better advised to pay more attention to psychologists and less attention to philosophers. It is odd, in this respect, that they have been so ready to accept the arguments of philosophers on matters relating to action when their 'data' typically consist of fictional examples, whilst at the same time ignoring the empirical findings on human conduct gathered by psychologists. But then many sociologists, although sometimes well briefed about recent developments in social psychology, often know little about the recent history of individual psychology and are consequently prone to believe that it is still a discipline in which behaviourist orientations predominate. Were they more aware of the fact that a 'cognitive revolution' has occurred in the discipline,[2] and hence that contemporary psychologists have few of their predecessors' inhibitions about studying 'mental' processes, they might overcome both their routine dismissal of psychology and their anti-mentalism. But then situationalism undoubtedly owes some of its current influence within sociology to the fact that it has attached itself to the coat-tails of what are undoubtedly important developments in the philosophical study of language and meaning, something which has undoubtedly helped to enhance its legitimacy and prestige in the eyes of many sociologists. So perhaps it is not so surprising that it is the names of philosophers rather than those of psychologists which one encounters most often in situationalist works.

The other main source of situationalism's strength and influence in the discipline derives from the fact that it is not recognised as a distinct position. Rather, it is the taken-for-granted framework of assumptions within which many contemporary sociologists actually carry out their work. What seems to have made this possible is the fact that several of situationalism's major tenets have become confused with statements about the nature and parameters of the discipline as a whole. As we have seen, the claim that social action is the central subject-matter of the discipline is not commonly perceived to be the contentious statement which it is. The consequence of this is that asserting this claim, together with the associated belief in the social nature of meaning, is easily confused with attempts to maintain the independence and autonomy of the discipline. This in turn makes proclaiming the dogmas of situationalism equivalent in the eyes of some sociologists to defending not just the prevailing orthodoxy but sociology itself. Consequently such established figures in the pantheon of sociological demonology as behaviourism, idealism, psychological reductionism and methodological individualism are often seen as, in effect, capable of being exorcised through the ritual incantation of the magic words 'social action' and 'social situation'.

The lost soul of interpretivism

The truth is that social situationalism actually denies the very principle which lies at the heart of the interpretive action theory tradition. Genuine

theories of action, those which embody the spirit of the original
Wissenschaft tradition of inquiry, take as their premise the belief that
human life must be understood in terms of those features which
distinguish it from that 'mere existence' which is experienced by other
animals. For whereas inhabitants of the animal kingdom have their
behaviour determined for them, either by drives and instincts acting from
within, or by environmental stimuli impinging on them from without (or
more usually a combination of the two), human beings are different.
They are relatively free from these constraints; or at least, they are free in
the sense of being able to use their special faculties to modify and alter
both the nature of their response and the extent to which their conduct
is no more than such a response. What makes this possible is the
existence of a culture and the consequent ability of individuals to
communicate symbolically through language and to be reflexive. Yet,
from the perspective of the Weberian action theory tradition it is
important to note that it is not these trademarks of humanity in themselves which are of critical importance. Rather it is the fact that these
make it possible for human beings to consciously direct and control their
own behaviour, which is to say, to engage in voluntary, purposive action.
This is the most central feature of the action perspective and it involves
recognising that human beings, unlike animals, not only 'could have
acted otherwise', but are *aware* that they 'could have acted otherwise'
and consequently are able to accept responsibility for their actions. In
other words, action is voluntary, willed, responsible behaviour and not
simply behaviour which is 'meaningful'.

Thus, it is rather sad and more than a little ironic that what are
designated as theories of 'social action' effectively involve the abandonment of this central premise. For one looks in vain for evidence that the
modern orthodoxy involves any recognition that the human actor might
be a free, purposive, meaning-creating agent who is not bound by the
constraints of the immediate environment in the way that is the lot of
other living creatures. Admittedly, situationalism ostensibly embraces
this tradition, for it too makes 'meaning' its central concern (indeed the
concern with meaning is so excessive that it tends to be at the expense of
action). Yet because meaning creation and manipulation is no longer
regarded as located in the individual, but is always represented as a
'social' possession, the vision of a free, meaning-creating and hence
action-creating, individual has vanished. By transferring such processes
from an intra-subjective to an inter-subjective or social setting, the
individual human being is effectively deprived of the ability to engage
in willed responsible action. For although situationalism involves
recognising that individuals possess both discursive and non-discursive

knowledge and that this is employed in such processes as 'reaching understandings' with others, or 'justifying' their actions to others, or in simply 'making sense of', or 'rendering accountable' the situation in which they find themselves, individuals are never presented as using their meaning-creating capability to actually accomplish an action, let alone transcend the situation in which they find themselves, or even, single-handedly, to transform it for others. Rather, the distinctive human capabilities which individuals are credited with possessing are portrayed as merely enabling individuals to order their experiences, or otherwise 'cope' with the social situation as given. In other words, conduct is always presented as bounded or limited by the social situation.

But then this is hardly surprising, since the terms of this paradigm only allow conduct to become action when it is situationally defined; an axiom which naturally has the effect of denying human beings any creative power. After all, if action is situationally defined then so too is the actor and hence the human being. Individuals cannot 'transcend' their situation because in doing so they would necessarily cease to be 'actors'. Consequently, one can only be human as long as one occupies a social situation. Even then, of course, being 'human' does not involve engaging in willed, responsible action, since what counts as 'action' has no connection with the actor's efforts, intentions, goals or values, being decided simply by whether the behaviour in question accords with certain social conventions or rules. From this perspective, actors who 'behave' are commonly judged to have 'acted', whilst responsible, willed actions (if they do not accord with situationally-defined expectations) are not recognised as action at all. Indeed, by defining action as conduct which possesses a 'social meaning', situationalists are almost bound to end up singling out behaviour which has little real significance for the individuals engaged in it. For, with the exception of major ritual events such as weddings, it is most unlikely that the small group of com-municative actions which have an agreed and widely-known 'social meaning' or 'message' will be regarded by those who perform them as of any particular significance. Indeed, their very status as conventional responses suggests that they are probably undertaken in such a routine and habitual fashion that actors do not even bother to register that they have performed them. It certainly seems unlikely that actors will bother to report, in answer to a query concerning 'what they had done today', that they had 'signalled a turn' when driving home, or later in the evening 'clapped at the end of a concert'. On the other hand, actions which are especially meaningful to the actors performing them will, since they are likely to involve projects of such scope and duration as to transcend many specific 'social situations', simply go unrecognised as 'actions'.

With the consequence, as Giddens has observed,[3] that whole areas of human experience are literally dubbed 'meaningless' from the situationalist perspective.

Indeed, situationalism would appear to present human beings as just as much in thrall to their environment as any animal. Admittedly the environment is portrayed as a socially constructed one and hence 'man-made', but it is not clear that, from the perspective of the individual, it is therefore experienced as any the less constraining. Certainly, situationalism does not grant individuals the power to alter it. How could it? For to imply that this was possible would amount to admitting that there was somewhere 'outside' social situations where individuals could 'stand' and yet still be able to engage in recognisable 'actions'. Consequently, situationalism denies the most important fact about actors, which is that they possess the ability to create and manipulate meaning in such a way that their conduct is *not* simply an automatic response to the situation in which they find themselves. Hence situationalism, ironically in the context of all the talk of rejecting the cultural dope model, itself promotes something resembling a social situational dope model of the actor. Actions are not simply regarded as defined by the social situations in which they occur; they are regarded as produced by them. Indeed, the situations' connection with the individual's response (incorrectly dubbed an 'action') has strange echoes of the old S-R model associated with crude behaviourism; although in this case, of course, the S stands for situation rather than stimulus. Surely there can hardly be a greater irony in contemporary sociology than the fact that movements which had their origins in reactions against positivism and behaviourism, have become, purely as a consequence of treating meaning as essentially a property of social situations and thereby separating it from individual consciousness, essentially similar to precisely that which they were designed to replace.[4] Just in case it should be felt that such an analogy constitutes an unjustified and exaggerated assessment, let us consider the model of the human actor which situationalism contains.

The image of the actor

Social situationalism can be described as located at that point in the modern history of the social sciences where anti-mentalism meets anti-behaviourism to constitute what can only be described as anti-human actor-ism. On the one hand, as Habermas has observed, an analytic philosophy of language and a psychological theory of behaviour have combined to undermine not merely the concept of 'mind' but any concern with individual consciousness.[5] This would have been serious enough in itself, but when coupled with the long-standing prejudice on the part of many sociologists against behaviourism and consequently any acceptance of the essentially biological basis of human conduct, the consequences can only be judged to be bizarre. For it means that under the situationalist paradigm human actors typically possess neither mind nor body. While it has become an axiom of faith for many contemporary situationalists that, as Garfinkel expresses it, there is nothing to interest the sociologist 'under the skull' of actors, their inherited anti-behaviourism also means that they are effectively debarred from investigating 'under the skin';[6] that is to say, from studying the behavioural basis of human conduct in so far as it constitutes responses (voluntary or otherwise) to stimuli. As a direct consequence the individual human being, who as a living, thinking actor was once at the very centre of the sociological stage, has been completely dissolved away, stripped of both mind and body, now no more than a ghost in the social machine. What is more, since anti-mentalism has led to the discounting of actors' reports of their conduct, it means that, according to the situationalist creed, the actions of individuals are to be studied without reference to what they think, feel, or say (about their actions, that is).

It would seem that, having rejected the psychological and the biological, sociologists have truly taken Durkheim's injunction about the reality *sui generis* of the social to heart, representing the individual as nothing more than co-ordinates in social space, which is to say, as an object in the eyes of others. Indeed, reading the writings of contemporary micro-sociologists it is possible to believe that human beings live out their lives in continual interaction with others. For there is hardly a mention in the course of hundreds and thousands of words of the possibility that people may spend a good deal of their time in private or, even if in the presence of others, engaged in purely self-directed acts. Indeed, many sociologists, if one was to judge by their writings, appear to subscribe to Bishop Berkeley's denial of the existence of matter, at least as far as human beings are concerned. That is to say, they appear to believe that people only exist when they are the object of observation by other human beings (or consider themselves to be so) only to disappear into thin air when not so regarded. But then this belief does accord with one of the central features of situationalism, which is the privileging of the individual as observer over that of the individual as actor. Something which explains why even though social actionists frequently represent themselves as adopting the point of view of ordinary people or 'members', as opposed to that of the 'scientific observer', their work still has such a strong behaviourist flavour.[7]

This privileging of the observer stems directly from the paradox of purporting to study 'meaning' yet rejecting the suggestion that this might be located inside 'the mind of the actor'. This is a paradox since in reality all 'meaning' necessarily implies the existence of one or more 'minds' to 'comprehend' it. In this basic sense it is obvious that all claims to the effect that 'action X means Y' invites the natural response, 'means Y to whom?'. Now one only has to examine situationalist discussions of action to see very clearly in which minds that meaning is actually located, for when reference is made to items of conduct being 'defined' as actions, or as having 'meanings assigned to them' or as 'given meaning' and hence 'identified as actions', it is clear that these phrases refer to activities engaged in by observers of the conduct concerned. Hence, despite the repeated situationalist assertions that meaning is located 'in the situation', what is actually meant is that it is located in the minds of those observers who are present. We can see this clearly if we consider the example of the individual at the auction who seeks to alleviate the itch on his nose. We are told that what 'determines' the meaning of his conduct are the 'social conventions' which prevail at auctions. Now although these may 'determine' the meaning, it is clearly located in the mind of the auctioneer (plus, presumably all others present acquainted with the conventions who happened to witness the scratching). It might indeed be the case that he or she makes use of his knowledge of the conventions governing the conduct of auctions to arrive at this conclusion. But that is hardly the point; for when situationalists claim that the 'movements' made by the actor 'mean' a 'bid' to the auctioneer they are necessarily saying that the auctioneer mentally registers that as the 'meaning of the act'. This is the meaning which is located in his mind and which consequently accounts for his subsequent response.[8] But then this appears to lead to the peculiar paradox of suggesting that meaning is to be found 'within' the minds of human beings in so far as they constitute the audience for actions performed by others, yet is absent from their minds as soon as they themselves become actors. Of course, 'actors' are also reflexively able to 'observe' their own 'actions' and it is precisely this image of the individual as a self-observer, someone who views his or her own conduct as if from the perspective of another, which prevails within situationalism. However, it is precisely this individual-as-self-observer model which has replaced the individual-as-actor, since the actor is not presented as actually *engaging* in action, but is represented as regarding its 'having-been-accomplished' reality with as much bemused fascination as if awakening from a hypnotic trance. In general, one can say that situationalism involves replacing the model of the individual as an actor with the individual as observer and interpreter of actions, whether self-accomplished or performed by others.[9]

This stress on the individual as an observer rather than an actor also helps to account for the marked cognitive bias which is such a feature of situationalism. For in taking 'the linguistic turn' situationalists have also taken 'the cognitive turn'. One only has to look at the way in which the aim of sociology is defined to see this overwhelming cognitive emphasis. Thus for Schutz the primary goal of interpretive sociology is 'the greatest possible clarification of what is *thought* about the social world by those living in it';[10] whilst for Garfinkel and for ethnomethodologists in general it is to discover how actors come to share and exhibit common *understandings* of the world and hence 'make sense' of it, or render it 'accountable'. Symbolic interactionism, on the other hand, is concerned with how individuals 'name' objects, people and events, 'negotiate meanings' and generally 'interpret' their situations. In each case, the only human faculties implied by the activities stressed are cognitive ones. Now this, of course, makes sense if individuals only feature as 'observers' rather than 'actors', as one only needs to employ cognitive faculties when attempting to understand or make sense of what one witnesses. However, if situationalism was to actually confront the problem of how people manage to act then they would be required to recognise the relevance of the fact that people feel, desire, dream and imagine, let alone struggle. It is hardly surprising that in situationalist interpretations of social life, such individuals also never act and that action is actually as invisible in social situationalist theories as in the Parsonian action schema.

This substitution by situationalism of the image of the individual as an inactive, situationally located and purely-cognitively-equipped disinterested observer of conduct (whether self-undertaken or performed by others) for the creative, living, responsible and striving human actor, also helps to explain the absence of any interest in explaining action. Situationalism typically fails to address the crucial question of why actions happen at all. For there is no room in this perspective for any consideration of the crucial issue of why an individual acted rather than remained inactive, or even more critically performed one act rather than another. There is no possibility, once one has adopted a situationalist perspective, of explaining why some of those people present at the auction did bid whilst others did not, or why some started bidding and then stopped before the item was sold. All situationalists can tell us is that 'bidding' and 'not bidding' are both permitted according to the social conventions which govern auctions. Equally, they can offer no explanation of why some road users might fail to signal before turning, or some members of an audience neglect to clap at the end of a performance. Consequently, it is all very well for situationalists to reject the 'springs of action' position which assumes that there is some form of internal mental state or process 'from which acts spring as from a reservoir' (to use Wittgenstein's words), but this does mean that some other theory of what causes action and what makes an actor choose one course rather than another is required. But then none is supplied, for situationalists simply turn their backs on the issue of explanation altogether. But, as Martin Albrow has observed, explanation is central to the Weberian conception of not just action theory but sociology itself, for he was attempting to erect a discipline around the very question, 'Why do people do things – anything or everything?'[11] The general lack of interest in explanation, characteristic of many micro-sociological perspectives, is another indication of the widespread influence of situationalism.[12] This failure to confront the issue of explanation, especially when combined with a social imperialism which refuses to recognise the independence of the cultural or psychological realms, results in a form of what can only be called methodological situationalism, or the belief that all attempts to account for social phenomena are to be rejected unless they refer exclusively to facts about social situations.

Social situationalism is a perspective which, although overwhelmingly concerned with cognition, actually eschews the study of mind. It is ostensibly concerned with meaning yet eschews the study of consciousness; it disparages the 'scientific' causal-style form of analysis and yet has clear behaviouristic and deterministic overtones. It also involves privileging the public over the private, the overt over the covert, the inter-subjective over the intra-subjective, the observer over the actor, and the denotative over all other forms of meaning. Whilst the model of the human being contained in social situationalism is of someone who has learned everything from others but nothing from experience, who has a social location but not a biography, who is an object to himself or herself only in so far as they are already one to others, whose only knowledge about themselves derives from their prior efforts to understand others, who learns everything about the world and themselves from observing others but nothing whatever from the accounts of their actions which others provide. It follows from all this that social situationalism or 'the social action perspective', has little or nothing to do with the traditional action theory form of sociological analysis, but is on the contrary antithetical to it. What situationalists mean by 'social action' has little to do with 'action', being merely situated behaviour, whilst the situationalist's 'actor' bears no relation at all to the actor of traditional action theory. Until such time as situationalism is displaced from its current position as the prevailing sociological orthodoxy, there is unlikely to be a revival in the fortunes of either action theory or interpretivism more generally.

15   Epilogue: bringing action back in

This book has taken the form of an extended critique of what is currently orthodox opinion within micro-sociology, if not the discipline more generally. As such it has been necessarily negative in tone and content. However, this critique has not been undertaken for its own sake, but in order to 'clear away the undergrowth' which has been allowed to grow up and choke the still-delicate sapling which is the interpretive action theory tradition. That task undertaken (with what degree of success, if any, is a matter for others to judge), it is appropriate to end the book on a more positive note by indicating something of the direction which any 'green shoots' of new growth might take. In order to do this it is necessary to reflect on what a truly successful and viable theory of action might look like and consequently how best to avoid some of the mistakes which have characterised theorising about action to date.

It should be obvious to the reader that the attack on social situationalism has not been a prelude to the advocacy of a rationalistic or even empiricist paradigm for studying action such as is represented by rational actor or rational choice theories.[1] These perspectives have increased greatly in popularity among sociologists in recent years and are not so easily dismissed by their critics as once they were. But then, as suggested earlier, this development must be seen as closely related to the success of social situationalism itself. The rise of the latter has clearly served to prompt new interest in the former and thus effectively worked to polarise the profession. Sociology has long been a schismatic discipline and observers have commented before on the existence of two or more sociologies.[2] Indeed, it is possible to think of several possible divisions, such as that between conflict and consensus theories, between functionalism and interpretivism, or even between macro and micro approaches, but the divide which it seems is rapidly coming to displace these in significance is that between two essentially 'micro' perspectives: an interactionalist social situationalism on the one hand and a methodologically individualistic rationalism on the other.[3] Increasingly, the work of contemporary sociologists seems to fall under one or other of the two mutually exclusive paradigms of *action* or '*social action*'. Thus, one half of the profession advocates rational choice and strategic modelling in order to address the phenomenon of individual action and choice (or *why* people choose to act as they do) whilst appealing to what they treat as real (if ideal-typical) intra-personal mental processes in the course of their explanations. By direct contrast, the other advocates a 'social action' approach which, as we have seen, deals only with communicative action or interaction, neglects the question of choice (concentrating instead on *how* people manage to interact) whilst ignoring intra-personal processes of any kind. Since these two really are the only extant perspectives which purport to deal with action, it is hardly surprising that the rise to prominence of social situationalism should have sparked off a subsequent growth of interest in rational actor theories among those sociologists who either do not wish to study interaction or have an interest in why people act as they do. What is so sad is that these are the only alternatives on offer. Clearly what is desperately needed is a 'third way' of some kind, and it is possible, on the basis of the critique developed here, to suggest what this might look like.

Singularly absent from the current sociological scene is a theory of action which is not in the first instance a theory of social action (that is to say, a theory of communicative action or interaction), and yet which both fully embodies the principle of voluntarism and recognises the reality and significance of intra-subjective processes – without, however, being so completely intellectualist as to regard its subject-matter as composed entirely of decision-making processes (or indeed of 'meaning-making' processes). In the social sciences at present, the only traditions of thought which recognise the critical role of emotion, feeling, imagination or effort in the accomplishment of action are those, like Freudianism or behaviourist psychology, which either directly reject or are ambiguous about the issue of voluntarism. At the same time, neither of these perspectives adopts a truly interpretive approach since the real viewpoint of the actor is either simply never taken into account or subject to extensive re-interpretation. The strange assumption which appears to prevail is that to take account of emotive or conative aspects of conduct is necessarily to adopt the observer's rather than the actor's viewpoint. But of course this does not follow and there is no reason why there cannot be a dynamic as opposed to a purely cognitive or rational form of interpretivism.

But then merely to identify such a 'third way' is to recognise that most theories of action have failed, to date, to address what is necessarily a most fundamental question. Whilst a theorist of action is understandably concerned with why people perform the acts they do, when they do, this is not sufficient in itself. For it is also necessary for such a theorist to address the problem of how people manage to act at all.[4] In this respect an action theory also needs to be a theory of agency. However, to date, most theories have simply taken the actor's power of agency for granted and concentrated instead on the question of how that agency is employed (or indeed constrained). Yet it is clearly important to recognise the problematic nature of action-accomplishment itself. Individuals do not always succeed in their attempts to implement decisions and complete their planned programmes of action, yet this failure is not necessarily anything to do with opposition from others or a deficiency in knowledge or understanding. Rather, it stems from the inherently problematic nature of action itself. We need to ask how it is that individuals frequently do manage to implement their will and therefore 'act'. In other words, what are the conditions necessary for accomplishing individual practical action? Now, it is no answer to stress the importance of socialisation. Such questions concern how it is that individuals remain actors even though they are faced with ever-present pressures which threaten to reduce their actions to behaviour. Socialisation may indeed be relevant to an understanding of the *pre*-requisites for action, in the sense of those things which must have already come to pass before a person can become a effective agent. But it cannot be assumed that successfully socialised adults are therefore fully competent and effective agents whose power to perform actions can simply be taken as given. Even fully socialised human beings commonly come up against the limits to their own power of agency. Consequently, the 'requisites' for action, or conditions necessary for individuals to maintain their effective status as actors, still have to be identified.[5]

It is hard to imagine a more fundamental question in sociological theory than that of how action itself is possible, since this is equivalent to asking how order is maintained at the most basic level of social life. Indeed, the term 'action' means no more than behaviour which manifests signs of having been consciously 'ordered'. More than one commentator has noted how theory in the social sciences inevitably focuses on the problem of order,[6] and that trying to explain its existence, at all levels from the person to the nation state, constitutes the natural starting point for all social theory. Yet the problem of order at the most basic of all levels, that of individual action, has not received the attention which it warrants. Sociologists have mistakenly interpreted this question either to refer to the relationship of means to an end and hence become caught up in discussions over the role of norms and the criterion of rationality, or alternatively have perceived it to be connected with problems of meaning and hence the nature of the cognitive order. However, both these perspectives still involve taking the individual's *ability* to act for granted, yet it is the very fact that the conduct of individuals is predictable, consistent or displays persistent patterns, in other words, that it constitutes action, which itself has to be explained. How is it that actors are able to impose that order which is action upon the natural disorder which is behaviour? This is the question which must be addressed. To date, the focus has largely been elsewhere, mainly on the nature of the actions performed and not on the conditions necessary for their performance. Typically action theorists have concentrated upon classifying types of acts (as Weber does) or orientations to action (as Parsons does), or in seeking to specify and elucidate the processes through which the meaning informing action is constructed (as Schutz does). What they have not done has been to inquire into the practical workings of agency itself, with the result that theories of action seem to have very little to say about 'doing'.[7] In other words, although the phenomenologists have explored the way in which 'meaning' can be said to be a construct, there has been no similar effort to understand the way in which 'action' is also a construct.

Such an omission also constitutes a serious failure to adopt the subjective viewpoint. Truly to adopt the actor's perspective is to regard action as an accomplishment and to recognise that it is the outcome of a struggle: something which has to be achieved against resistance, being in effect the end product of a willed effort involving certain given processes of 'determination'. Now, actors know that there is no certainty that any projected act or programme of actions will ever be carried through to completion. They are aware that action is problematic and never take their own powers of agency for granted, as theorists commonly do. Strangely, sociologists rarely seem to take the competence of individuals as interactors for granted but are usually eager to subject this to detailed examination, so why one wonders do they routinely appear to take their competence as actors for granted?

Once again it is the prevalence of the disembodied image of the actor, combined with the cognitive bias which marks so much contemporary theorising, that has led to the error of assuming that the real life problems experienced by individuals are purely intellectual in character. Even when these are not identified as the purely ratiocinative ones of calculating and deciding such that the actor is presented as some kind of game theory exponent (as with rational actor and rational choice theories), the tendency is still to stress general intellectual processes such as the creation, manipulation and negotiation of meaning (as with phenomenology and symbolic interactionism). No doubt most human beings spend some time (consciously or sub-consciously) engaging in just such activities, whilst some may spend much of their time doing so.

It is to be doubted, however, whether this is a very accurate picture of the nature of the predominant concerns of the majority of mankind.[8] It seems more than likely that for most people the central problems that they face in the course of their everyday lives require neither the cognitions of a game theoretician nor the perceptions of a philosopher; for the simple reason that they are neither beset by a continual need to make choices nor a desperate desire to understand the phenomenal ground of their actions. On the contrary, their pressing problems tend to be of a much more practical nature and are less likely to centre around the question of what actions to undertake than *how* to do them. Traditionally, action theory has focused on the ability of individuals to make choices; this, indeed, is the basis of its claim to be a voluntaristic theory. However, this has been taken to refer to either the individual's choice of goals or, more usually, of means to the attainment of given goals. But voluntarism is as much to do with the willed accomplishment of actions as it is with the choice of means or ends. Individuals faced with no choice over means or ends still face the problem of how to will into being those actions which they accept they have to perform.

One could say that individuals are, in this sense, marked by a pre-dominantly practical or pragmatic attitude to life. How to 'do what has to be done' is what concerns them. Action theorists have from the time of Hobbes and Locke onwards, had a tendency to tell 'just-so' stories in which individuals are 'at rest' or 'inactive' until pressed by some need, want or desire into action. But the reality is that human beings grow to maturity only to 'find themselves' committed to certain programmes of action, since as members of society, they have expectations to meet and obligations to fulfil. Consequently, their pressing problem is not likely to be what to do or why, or even in a purely instrumental sense, how to do it, since in all probability the means are as prescribed as the goals. What exercises them is precisely how they are going to manage to accomplish those tasks which they recognise they are obliged to undertake. This is the 'problem of action' as ordinary people experience it and it is the problem of how to 'carry on' or 'keep going' in the face of the pressure which threatens to erode all programmes of action. Hence the primary problem is not how to 'make sense of' things or 'make them intelligible', or even 'render them accountable', but how to maintain agency; and of course it is not necessary in order to act successfully to assume that others would see things as you do were they in your position, or that the reality you encounter is the same reality that they encounter. Indeed, quite the contrary, actors need to be sensitive to their own personal tastes, motives and incentives if they are to achieve their goals.[9] For their principal concern must be to discover what 'works' for them, what practices, devices or mechanisms effectively enable them to prevent their actions from deteriorating into behaviour, and consequently to accomplish their chosen projects.

To date the interpretivist tradition of inquiry has been marked by too great a cognitive concern. The injunction to understand action in terms of its 'subjective meaning' for the actor has been interpreted as necessitating a search for the 'intentions', 'goals' or 'motives' (usually in the sense of reasons) which it is assumed 'caused' it to be performed. In particular, there has been a focus on the 'means–end' schema and the norm of 'rationality'. Consequently, 'understanding' has been taken to imply either placing the act within the logical context of a means–end chain or eliciting the logic underlying the actor's reasoning in deciding to perform that action at that time. Yet penetrating to the real 'subjective meaning' of an action to the extent necessary to understand its occurrence involves more than ascertaining the reasons why particular means were selected or decisions taken. It means attempting to establish how the accomplishment of the action was itself made possible, something which involves ascertaining the role played by emotion, imagination, effort, attention and will. To do this does not involve stepping outside of an interpretive framework or abandoning the subjective viewpoint. Quite the reverse, since actors actually experience actions in this manner, as complex events in which they need to engage in a variety of complex sub-actions or control-actions if they are indeed to be carried through to completion. Sociologists, if they are to claim that they have 'understood' the actions, need to be in a position to describe these intra-personal processes, their relationship to extra-personal ones and the manner in which they contribute to the accomplishment of action. For it is impossible to account for human action without reference to this dimension. Not only does a dynamic interpretivism come closer to the fundamental reality of the subjective viewpoint than the artificiality of logical interpretivism, but it seeks to discover the very preconditions of action itself. What is looked for in the actor is not some 'entity' (be it an intention, reason, value, emotion or belief) but rather the complete range of human voluntary processes through which the act itself was accomplished. In this respect the actor's capacity to create and manipulate meaning has to be regarded as a critical resource employed to accomplish acts and not simply that which 'gives' actions their meaning. Action and meaning have to be seen as critically inter-dependent and whilst interpretivists might struggle to discover what actions 'mean', unless individuals themselves have the capacity to manipulate this meaning in ways independent of that 'given' in the social situation, they could never be performed.

It is critical in this respect that sociologists abandon not merely their prejudice against studying intra-personal processes but their refusal to recognise the essentially covert nature of action itself. Sociologists have tended to employ a model of action which presumes that acts are identifiable (if only provisionally) through observation alone, and that it is the meaning of such acts which being covert is not available to the observer, who is thus required to employ some kind of intuitive or *verstehen* method to discern it. Yet such a model is misleading. For it is action itself, which if not actually covert, commonly possesses a covert dimension and is thus not immediately discernible. It is unusual for sociologists to be in a position to observe 'actions'; what they typically observe are the overt behavioural manifestations (where there are any) of actions. This can be illustrated by one of Weber's own examples, that of the person engaged in the calculation 'twice two equals four' in the course of 'balancing a ledger'.[10] Now, Weber refers to such a person 'stating' this proposition or 'writing it down', but of course the 'action' of engaging in the calculation is not itself overt (in the case of a clerk completing a ledger), for it is only the actual writing of the entry in the book which can be witnessed. Such actions are not unusual, but rather constitute the norm. In which case the concept of action needs to be revised to take into account the fact that it is essentially a covert (or at least a co-overt) phenomenon.

At the same time, there is a need to recognise that action theory needs to be concerned with meaningfulness and not merely with meaning. For action is best represented as that portion of an individual's conduct which is meaningful to the actor: that is to say, has significance for the actor given his or her current commitments and action state. This is true subjective meaning and it clearly indicates that only actors can possibly know what their action consists of. But then that should not be surprising because all action is ultimately performed alone, undertaken by the individual as the sole agent. No matter whether the action in question is 'social' in the sense of occurring in the company of others, or even if it is part of an ongoing system of 'interaction', it is still an individual and largely covert accomplishment. This is because all true actions are the outcome of an 'act of will', a covert and personal event which actors can only perform for themselves. Hence understanding action must involve grasping the character and nature of this process of 'willing', and whilst recognising that it is not translatable into either metaphysics or biology, appreciate that it centres around the individual's ability to create and manipulate meaning. Those 'meanings' which are most pertinent to the occurrence of an act do not stem from any pool of 'inter-subjective' understandings or shared typifications, least of all from any social rules and conventions, but are created *de novo* by individuals as and when they are needed to meet the immediate exigencies of their action situation, and although they will probably draw heavily on cultural material, this will probably be closely woven into the actor's past experiences and future hopes to comprise the effective inner 'life-world' of the actor. It is these essentially personal, intra-subjectively created meanings which are the immediate and direct 'causes' of actions.

Notes

2. ACTION REPORTED MISSING IN ACTION THEORY

1 See, among others, Alan Dawe's comment that 'the very concept of action itself has gone', in 'Theories of Social Action', in T. Bottomore and R. Nisbet, eds., *A History of Sociological Analysis* (New York: Basic Books, 1978), pp. 362–417, p. 405. Also Giddens observes that '*There is no action in Parsons' "action frame of reference"*' (Anthony Giddens, *New Rules of Sociological Method* (London: Hutchinson, 1976), p. 16; italics in the original). Whilst James S. Coleman in 'Social Theory, Social Research, and a Theory of Action', *American Journal of Sociology*, 91, 6 (1986), 1,309–35, refers to Parsons having 'progressively abandoned a theory of action' during the 1950s and 1960s (p. 1,310), with the consequence that there was a 'loss of a theory of action' within the discipline (p. 1,312). John Heritage, in his discussion of the emergence of ethnomethodology observes that 'Parsons had failed to construct a theory of *action* at all but had instead constructed only a theory of dispositions to act' ('Ethnomethodology', in Anthony Giddens and Jonathan H. Turner, eds., *Social Theory Today* (Oxford: Polity Press, 1987), pp. 224–72, p. 228; italics in original).

2 There are a variety of meanings which can be given to the concept of *verstehen*; see William Outhwaite, *Understanding Social Life: The Method Called Verstehen* (Lewes; Jean Stroud, 1975).

3 Nicholas Abercrombie, Stephen Hill, Stephen and Bryan S. Turner, *The Penguin Dictionary of Sociology* (London: Penguin, 1985) *s.v.* 'action theory'. Alexander also refers to two forms of action theory, identifying them as the 'instrumental-objective' and the 'interpretive-subjective'. See *Theoretical Logic in Sociology Vol. 3.* (Berkeley: University of California Press, 1982), pp. 24f.

4 For evidence of the apparent inability of Parsons and Schutz to have a valuable and productive exchange of views, see Richard Grathoff, ed., *The Theory of Social Action: The Correspondence of Alfred Schutz and Talcott Parsons* (Bloomington and London: Indiana University Press, 1978).

5 Roscoe C. Hinkle, 'Antecedents of the Action Orientation in American Sociology Before 1935', *American Sociological Review* 28 (1963), 705–15. For a somewhat different account of the development of the 'empirical study of action', mainly in psychology, in both Germany and the USA up to the 1950s, see Paul F. Lazarsfeld, 'Historical Notes on the Empirical Study of Action: An Intellectual Odyssey', in Paul F. Lazarsfeld, *Qualitative*

Analysis: Historical and Critical Essays (Boston: Allyn and Bacon, 1972), pp. 50–100.

6 See for example, Brian Barry, *Sociologists, Economists and Democracy* (Chicago, IL: University of Chicago Press, 1970); Anthony Oberschall, *Social Conflict and Social Movements*, (Englewood Cliffs, NJ: Prentice-Hall, 1973); Anthony Heath, *Rational Choice and Social Exchange* (Cambridge: Cambridge University Press, 1976); Jon Elster, ed., *Rational Choice* (Oxford: Blackwell, 1986); James S. Coleman, *The Foundations of Social Theory* (Cambridge, MA: Belknap Press of Harvard University Press, 1990); and James S. Coleman and Thomas J. Fararo eds., *Rational Choice Theory: Advocacy and Critique* (London: Sage, 1992).

7 See, for example, the collection of papers in Michael Chapman, ed., 'Intentional Action as a Paradigm for Developmental Psychology: A Symposium', *Human Development*, 27 (1984), 113–44; especially that by Lutz H. Eckensberger and John A. Meacham, 'The Essentials of Action Theory: A Framework for Discussion', *Human Development*, 27 (1984), 166–72.

8 Jochen Brandtstadter distinguishes three forms of action theory in psychology: motivational, system-analytic and structuralist; see, 'Action Development and Development through Action', in Michael Chapman, ed., 'Intentional Action as a Paradigm for Developmental Psychology: A Symposium', *Human Development*, 27 (1984), 115.

9 Lutz H. Eckensberger and John A. Meacham, 'The Essentials of Action Theory: A Framework for Discussion', *Human Development* 27, (1984), 166–72.

10 R. Harre and P. F. Secord, *The Explanation of Social Behaviour* (Oxford: Blackwell, 1972); Rom Harre, *Social Being: A Theory for Social Psychology* (Oxford: Blackwell, 1979); R. Harre, D. Clarke and N. de Carlo, *Motives and Mechanisms: An Introduction to the Psychology of Action* (London: Methuen, 1985).

11 See Kenneth J. Gergen, 'The Social Constructionist Movement in Modern Psychology', *American Psychologist*, 40, 3 (1985), 266–75; G. R. Semin, in G. R. Semin and K. J. Gergen eds., *Everyday Understanding* (London: Sage, 1990). For additional references, see Helga Dittmar, *The Social Psychology of Material Possessions* (Hemel Hempstead: Harvester Wheatsheaf, 1992).

12 See G. E. M. Anscombe, *Intention* (Oxford: Blackwell, 1957); A. Melden, *Free Action* (London: Routledge & Kegan Paul, 1964); Donald Davidson, *Essays on Actions and Events* (Oxford: The Clarendon Press, 1980). See also the introduction by Myles Brand and Douglas Walton, to *Action Theory: Proceedings of the Winnipeg Conference on Human Action* (Dordrecht: D. Reidel, 1976), pp. 3–10; Berent Enc, 'On the Theory of Action', *Journal for the Theory of Social Behaviour* 5, 2 (1975), 145–67.

13 For material on the revival of interest in the work of Talcott Parsons, see J. C. Alexander, 'The Parsons Revival in German Sociological Theory', *Sociological Theory*, 2 (1984), 394–412; David Sciulli, 'Social Theory and Talcott Parsons in the 1980s', *Annual Review of Sociology*, 11 (1985), 369–87; Richard Munch, 'Parsonian Theory Today: In Search of a New Synthesis', pp. 116–55 in Anthony Giddens and Jonathan H. Turner, eds., *Social Theory Today* (Oxford: Polity Press, 1987).

14 See especially J. Habermas, *The Theory of Communicative Action*, vol. 1: *Reason and the Rationalization of Society*, trans. T. M. McCarthy (Boston, MA: Beacon Press, 1984), and *The Theory of Communicative Action*, vol. 2: *The Critique of Functionalist Reason* (Cambridge: Polity Press, 1987).

15 Cited by J. C. Alexander in his review of *The Theory of Communicative Action*, vol. 1., in the *American Journal of Sociology*, 91, 2 (1985), 422.

16 See William H. Sewell Jr, 'Theory of Action, Dialectic, and History: Comment on Coleman', *American Journal of Sociology*, 93, 1 (1987) 166–72, footnote to p. 169. Also James S. Coleman, 'Social Theory, Social Research, and a Theory of Action', *American Journal of Sociology*, 91, 6 (May 1986), 1,309–35. James S. Coleman, 'Actors and Actions in Social History and Social Theory: Reply to Sewell', *American Journal of Sociology*, 93, 1 (1987) 172–5. Among Giddens' many works, see especially *Central Problems in Social Theory* (London: Macmillan, 1979); *The New Rules of Sociological Method* (London: Hutchinson, 1976); and *The Constitution of Society* (Cambridge: Polity Press, 1984).

17 Anthony Giddens, *New Rules of Sociological Method* (London: Hutchinson, 1976), p. 16.

18 Giddens, *New Rules*, p. 16.

19 *New Rules*, pp. 16–17.

20 John Heritage, 'Ethnomethodology', in Giddens and Turner, eds., *Social Theory Today*.

21 *New Rules*, p. 16; italics in original.

22 Ibid., p. 96.

23 Goran Therborn, 'Social Practice, Social Action, Social Magic', *Acta Sociologica*, 16, 4 (1972), 157–74, p. 168.

24 Ibid., p.161.

25 See, for example, J. H. Turner and L. Beeghley, 'Current Folklore in the Criticism of Parsonian Action Theory', *Sociological Inquiry*, 4 (1974) 47–55.

26 Anthony Giddens, *Constitution of Society* (Cambridge: Polity Press, 1984), p. xxxvii.

27 *New Rules*, p. 53.

28 Ibid.

29 John Heritage, *Garfinkel and Ethnomethodology* (Cambridge: Polity Press, 1984), p. 73.

30 *New Rules*, p. 40; italics in the original.

31 Ibid.

32 Paul Atkinson, 'Ethnomethodology: A Critical Review', *Annual Review of Sociology*, 14 (1988), 414–65, p. 447. Indeed, it is not at all clear that ethnomethodologists should really be regarded as part of the interpretive tradition at all. The interest shown in language, for example, is not really that of the interpretive sociologist. This is because talk is not of interest as a medium which embodies and transmits meaning but rather as a 'form of collaborative conduct' (Atkinson, 'Ethnomethodology', p. 449).

33 Blumer, Herbert, 'Action vs. Interaction', *Society*, April 1972.

34 Habermas, *Theory of Communicative Action*, I, p. 85.

35 Ibid., p. 85.

36 Ibid., p. 90.

37 Ibid., p. 96.
38 Ibid., pp. 95–6.
39 Ibid., p. 377.
40 Ibid., p. 281.
41 Jonathan H. Turner, *A Theory of Social Interaction*, (Stanford: Stanford University Press, 1988), p. 3; italics in original.
42 For details of Giddens' theory of structuration see Giddens, *Central Problems in Social Theory* (London: Macmillan, 1979).
43 Ian Craib, *Anthony Giddens* (London: Routledge, 1992), p. 35.
44 *New Rules*, p. 53.
45 *New Rules*, p. 75; italics in original.
46 *Constitution of Society*, p. 19.
47 One worrying feature of Giddens' otherwise imposing contribution to the theory of action and agency helps to illustrate this point. This is the fact that he does not use Weber's distinction between behaviour and action. Given that this lies at the very heart of Weber's formulation this is rather disturbing. It is not entirely clear why Giddens does not use this distinction, but it would appear that his inclination to dismiss it stems from his dissatisfaction with arguments advanced by philosophers concerning the contrast between descriptions of individual conduct couched in 'actional' terms and those which refer to 'movements'. Whilst Giddens is undoubtedly correct to reject the suggestion that the language of movements and the language of actions represent 'alternative, *and equally correct*, modes' (*New Rules*, p. 73; italics in original) of describing the same item of conduct, this does not mean that the contrast between action and *behaviour* should be abandoned. For this contrast is rooted in the psycho-biological basis of the human condition. To contrast action with behaviour does not necessarily carry with it the implication that one is employing contrasting descriptive schemes or paradigms (let alone incompatible epistemologies and methodologies), it is merely to refer to *empirically differentiated* forms of conduct. To state that the proper unit of reference for the analysis of action 'has to be the *person*, the *acting self*' (ibid. p. 74; italics in original) does not imply that sociologists must abandon the conceptual distinction between behaviour and action. This would appear to be a concrete instance of the way in which allowing philosophers to set the agenda for discussions of action leads to a focus on issues which have little significance or relevance for the sociology of action. If material from other disciplines is to be introduced into discussions of matters of human conduct and agency it would be more valuable to use psychology and thus relate debate to empirical data and not merely logic and argumentation.
48 Jürgen Habermas, 'Remarks on the Concept of Communicative Action' in Gottfried Seebass and Raimo Tuomela, eds., *Social Action* (Dordrecht: D. Reidel, 1985), pp. 151–78, p. 151.

3. ACTION AND SOCIAL ACTION

1 John Rex, *Key Problems of Sociological Theory* (London: Routledge & Kegan Paul, 1961), p. 78.

2 Percy S. Cohen, *Modern Social Theory* (London: Heinemann, 1968).
3 David Martin, *50 Key Concepts in Sociology* (London: Lutterworth Press, 1970), p. 1.
4 G. Duncan Mitchell, ed., *A New Dictionary of Sociology* (London: Routledge & Kegan Paul, 1979); Panos D. Bardis, *A Dictionary of Quotations in Sociology* (New York: Greenwood Press, 1985).
5 Gibson Burrell and Gareth Morgan, *Sociological Paradigms and Organisational Analysis: Elements of the Sociology of Corporate Life* (London: Heinemann, 1979), p. 189; italics added.
6 Mitchell, ed., *A New Dictionary of Sociology*, p. 2.
7 Alan Dawe, 'Theories of Social Action', in T. Bottomore and R. Nisbet, eds., *A History of Sociological Analysis* (New York: Basic Books, 1978), pp. 362–417, p. 379.
8 David Lee and Howard Newby, *The Problem of Sociology: An Introduction to the Discipline* (London: Hutchinson, 1983).
9 Stephen Mennell, *Sociological Theories: Uses and Unities* (London: Thomas Nelson, 1974; 2nd edition (Walton-On-Thames: Nelson, 1980).
10 See Michael Haralambos, *Sociology: Themes and Perspectives* (Slough: University Tutorial Press, 1980) and Michael Haralambos, and Martin Holborn, *Sociology: Themes and Perspectives* (London: Unwin Hyman, 1990).
11 David Jary and Julia Jary, *Collins Dictionary of Sociology* (London: Harper Collins, 1991), *s.v.* 'action', 'social action'.
12 Ibid., p. 4; italics added.
13 For example, Weber's discussion of types of *social* action would seem in practice to be no more than a typology of action. See Max Weber, *The Theory of Social and Economic Organization*, trans. A. M. Henderson and Talcott Parsons, ed. with an intro. Talcott Parsons (New York: The Free Press, 1964).
14 A good example would be John Heritage and Max Atkinson, eds., *Structures of Social Action* (London: British Sociological Association and The Social Science Research Council, 1984).
15 See Alfred Schutz, *The Phenomenology of the Social World*, trans. George Walsh and Frederick Lehnert, with intro. by George Walsh (Evanston, IL: Northwestern University Press, 1967); Florian Znaniecki, *Social Actions* (New York: Russell and Russell, 1967); Mitchell, ed., *A New Dictionary of Sociology*; Cohen, *Modern Social Theory*.
16 One can find instances where the contrast between action and behaviour is used merely as a means of introducing what is presented as the more important concept of social action in R. Harre and P. F. Secord, *The Explanation of Social Behaviour* (Oxford: Blackwell, 1972), and in Tony Bilton et al., *Introductory Sociology* (2nd edn; Basingstoke: Macmillan, 1987.
17 Weber, *The Theory of Social and Economic Organization*, p. 88.
18 Ibid., p. 114.
19 Ibid.
20 David Lee and Howard Newby, *The Problem of Sociology: An Introduction to the Discipline* (London, Hutchinson, 1983), p. 174; italics in the original.
21 Mike O'Donnell, *A New Introduction to Sociology* (London: Harrap, 1981), p. 15; italics in the original.

22 Michael Haralambos and Martin Holborn, *Sociology: Themes and Perspectives* (1990), p. 19, italics added; Tony Bilton et al., *Introductory Sociology*, p. 589, italics added.

23 Mike O'Donnell, *A New Introduction to Sociology*, p. 13; italics added. See also Norman Goodman, *Introduction to Sociology*, (New York: Harper-Collins, 1992) p. 6.

24 See Bilton et al., *Introductory Sociology*, pp. 589f.

25 Macmillan, 1987.

26 Ibid., p. viii.

27 1981 edn, contents page.

28 1987 edn, contents page.

29 Ibid. p. 22; italics in the original. It is only fair to observe, however, that in both editions there is a similar entry in the table of contents under chapter 12, 'Sociological Theories', headed, 'Social Action Perspectives', in which Symbolic Interactionism, Weber's Theory of Social Action, Phenomenological Sociology and Ethnomethodology all appear.

30 See K. Knorr-Cetina and A. V. Cicourel, eds., *Advances in Social Theory and Methodology, Toward An Integration of Micro- and Macro-sociologies* (Boston: Routledge & Kegan Paul, 1981).

4. ACTION VERSUS SOCIAL ACTION

1 David P. Levine and Lynn S. Levine, 'Social Theory and Social Action' *Economy and Society*, 4 (1975), 165.

2 See discussion in chapter 9 below.

3 Max Weber, *The Theory of Social and Economic Organization*, trans. A. M. Henderson and Talcott Parsons, ed. with intro. Talcott Parsons (New York: The Free Press, 1964), p. 88.

4 This would also seem to have been Parsons' position, at least in principle, for he wrote that his action schema was inherently subjective in the sense that 'normative elements can be conceived of as "existing" only in the mind of the actor' (Talcott Parsons, *The Structure of Social Action* (New York: The Free Press, 1948) p. 736.

5 David Lee and Howard Newby, *The Problem of Sociology: An Introduction to the Discipline* (London: Hutchinson, 1983) p.174.

6 Tony Watson, *Sociology, Work & Industry* (2nd edn; London: Routledge & Kegan Paul, 1987), p. 14; italics in the original.

7 C. Wright Mills, 'Situated Action and the Vocabulary of Motives', *American Sociological Review*, 15 (December 1940), 904–13.

8 Mills, 'Situated Action', pp. 906–7.

9 Ibid. p. 907; italics in original.

10 Alfred Schutz, *The Phenomenology of the Social World*, trans. George Walsh and Frederick Lehnert, with intro. George Walsh (Evanston, IL:Northwestern University Press, 1967), p. 15.

11 Ibid.

12 Ibid., p. 145.

13 Ibid., p. 149.

14 Ibid., p. 145.

15 Ibid., p. 144.
16 Ibid., p. 145.
17 Ibid., p. 16.
18 Ibid., p. 109.
19 Weber, *The Theory of Social and Economic Organization*, p. 113.
20 Ibid., p. 113.
21 Ibid., p. 114.
22 Ibid., p. 113; italics added.
23 Ibid., p. 88; italics added.
24 Schutz, *The Phenomenology of the Social World*, p. 146. See also comments on p. 142 on the value of Weber's definition of social action.
25 Of course Schutz also makes significant changes to Weber's conception of *action*, but this is not the point at issue here.
26 Tony Bilton et al., *Introductory Sociology* (2nd edn; Houndsmill, Basingstoke: Macmillan, 1987), p. 24; italics added.
27 James Heap, 'Reconceiving the Social', *Canadian Review of Sociology and Anthropology*, 13, 3 (1976), 272.

5. THE RISE OF SOCIAL SITUATIONALISM

1 J. E. Goldthorpe. *An Introduction to Sociology* (3rd edn; Cambridge: Cambridge University Press, 1985), p. 9.
2 R. Harre and P. F. Secord, *The Explanation of Social Behaviour* (Oxford: Blackwell, 1972), p. 39; italics in original.
3 Heap, 'Reconceiving the Social', *Canadian Review of Sociology and Anthropology*, 13, 3 (1976), 272.
4 Goldthorpe, *An Introduction to Sociology*, p. 9; italics added.
5 Thomas S. Kuhn, *The Structure of Scientific Revolutions* (Chicago, IL: University of Chicago Press, 1962).
6 P. Berger, 'Identity as a Problem in the Sociology of Knowledge', *Archives Europénnes de Sociologie: European Journal of Sociology*, 7 (1966), 105–15; P. Berger and T. Luckmann, *The Social Construction of Reality* (Harmondsworth: Penguin, 1966); T. W. Goff, *Marx and Mead: Contributions to a Sociology of Knowledge* (London: Routledge & Kegan Paul, 1980).
7 K. D. Knorr-Cetina and Michael Mulkay, eds., *Science Observed: Perspectives on the Social Study of Science* (London and Beverly Hills, California: Sage, 1982).
8 On the social constructionist movement in psychology, see Kenneth J. Gergen, 'The Social Constructionist Movement in Modern Psychology', *American Psychologist*, March 1985, 266–74. Both the 'ethogenic' and the 'social constructionist' movements within psychology would appear to have benefited from the existence and themselves served to strengthen the situationalist movement within sociology. The 'ethogenic' movement associated with Rom Harre and colleagues was quite explicitly based on the model of the human actor contained in the works of post-Wittgensteinian British philosophers. The social constructionist movement is, as Helgar Dittmar observes 'best viewed as consisting of converging orientations which

have historical links to such diverse fields as the sociology of knowledge . . . phenomenological sociology . . . , philosophy of language . . . , Soviet socio-cultural psychology . . . , and particularly the social behaviourism of the Chicago school later termed symbolic interactionism' (*The Social Psychology of Material Possessions* (Hemel Hempstead: Harvester Wheatsheaf, 1992), p. 67). With the exception of the reference to Soviet socio-cultural psychology, this is the same list as that identified above as giving rise to social situationalism in sociology.

9 See Nigel Gilbert and Michael Mulkay, *Opening Pandora's Box: A Sociological Analysis of Scientists' Discourse* (Cambridge: Cambridge University Press, 1984); Jonathan Potter and Margaret Wetherell, *Discourse and Social Psychology* (London: Sage, 1987).

10 See H. Sacks, E. Schegloff and C. Jefferson, 'A Simplest Systematics for the Organization of Turn-taking in Conversation', *Language*, 50 (1974), 696–737; P. Atkinson, *The Clinical Experience: The Construction and Reconstruction of Medical Reality* (Farnborough: Gower, 1981); John C. Heritage, 'Ethnomethodology' in Anthony Giddens and Jonathan Turner, eds., *Social Theory Today* (Oxford: Polity Press, 1987), pp. 224–72.

11 See *Studies in Ethnomethodology* (Englewood Cliffs, NJ: Prentice-Hall, 1967), p. 70.

12 Marvin B. Scott and Stanford M. Lyman, 'Accounts', *American Sociological Review* 33 (1968), 112.

13 Alan F. Blum and Peter McHugh, 'The Social Ascription of Motives', *American Sociological Review*, 36 (February 1971), 101.

14 C. Wright Mills, 'Language, Logic, and Culture', *American Sociological Review*, 4 (1939), 671–80, p. 676.

15 Mills' principal sources for this view seem to have been Grace DeLaguna, Bronislaw Malinowski and, to a lesser extent, L. S. Vygotsky; see Mills, 'Language, Logic and Culture'.

16 John Heritage, *Garfinkel and Ethnomethodology* (Cambridge: Polity Press, 1984), p. 50.

17 Anthony Giddens, *New Rules of Sociological Method* (London: Hutchinson, 1976), p. 17.

18 Ibid., p. 34.

19 Ibid., p. 52.

20 Jonathan H. Turner, 'The Concept of "Action" in Sociological Analysis', in Gottfried Seebass and Raimo Tuomela, eds., *Social Action* (Dordrecht: D. Reidel, 1985), p. 78.

21 C. Wright Mills, 'Situated Action and the Vocabulary of Motives', *American Sociological Review*, 5 (1940), p. 906.

22 Douglas V. Porpora, 'On the Post-Wittgensteinian Critique of the Concept of Action in Sociology', *The Journal for the Theory of Social Behaviour*, 13 (1983), 132.

23 Garfinkel, cited by John Heritage, 'Ethnomethodology', in Anthony Giddens and Jonathan H. Turner, eds., *Social Theory Today* (Oxford: Polity Press, 1987), p. 233.

24 Erving Goffman, *Forms of Talk* (Oxford: Blackwell, 1981), p. 84.

25 Mills, 'Situated Action and the Vocabulary of Motives. This includes the title

but ignores synonyms or phrases which are used in place of the single word 'situation'.

26 Jonathan Potter and Margaret Wetherell, *Discourse and Social Psychology* (London: Sage, 1987), p. 58; italics added.

27 See Gordon Marshall, 'Accounting for Deviance', *International Journal of Sociology and Social Policy*, 1 (1981), 17–45, p. 35.

28 Mills, 'Situated Action and the Vocabulary of Motives', p. 905; italics added. See discussion in the following chapter.

29 Nicholas Abercrombie, Stephen Hill and Bryan S. Turner, eds., *The Penguin Dictionary of Sociology* (London: Penguin, 1985), p. 16.

30 Jack D. Douglas, ed., *Understanding Everyday Life* (London: Routledge & Kegan Paul, 1971), p. 4; first italics in text: second italics added.

31 Maria Sifianou, *Politeness Phenomena in England and Greece: A Cross-Cultural Perspective* (Oxford: The Clarendon Press, 1992), pp. 91–2.

32 Max Weber, *The Theory of Social and Economic Organization*, trans. A. M. Henderson and Talcott Parsons, ed. with intro. Talcott Parsons (New York: Free Press, 1964), p. 90.

33 Goldthorpe, *An Introduction to Sociology*, p. 9.

34 Ibid., pp. 9–10.

6. THE ARGUMENT BY DENIAL

1 See, for example, the 'Rescuing motives' debate in the pages of *The British Journal of Sociology*: S. Bruce and R. Wallis, 'Rescuing Motives', *The British Journal of Sociology*, 34, 1 (1983), 61–72; W. W. Sharrock and D. R. Watson, 'What's the Point of "Rescuing Motives"?', *The British Journal of Sociology*, 35, 3 (1984), 435–51. Steve Bruce and Roy Wallis, ' "Rescuing Motives" Rescued: A Reply to Sharrock and Watson', *The British Journal of Sociology*, 36, 3 (1985), 467–70. W. W. Sharrock and D. R. Watson, 'Relocating Motives', *The British Journal of Sociology*, 37, 4 (December 1986), 581–3.

2 D. Rubenstein, 'The Concept of Action in the Social Sciences', *Journal for the Theory of Social Behaviour* 7 (1977), 209–36, p. 214.

3 Of course this does raise the intriguing question of why all ordinary people (including situationalist sociologists when 'off duty' so to speak) appear to believe, and indeed go so far as to act on the belief, that these internal factors are the real causes of their conduct. However, this is not a question which situationalists show much interest in addressing.

4 Cited by Oswald Hanfling, *Wittgenstein's Later Philosophy* (Basingstoke: Macmillan, 1989), p. 80.

5 G. E. M. Anscombe, *Intention* (Oxford: Blackwell, 1957); R. S. Peters, *The Concept of Motivation* (London: Routledge & Kegan Paul, 1958), and Peter Winch, *The Idea of a Social Science and its Relation to Philosophy* (London: Routledge & Kegan Paul, 1958); A. I. Melden, *Free Action* (London: Routledge & Kegan Paul, 1961). See, in addition, S. Hampshire *Thought and Action* (New York: Viking Press, 1959); Richard Taylor, *Action and Purpose* (Englewood Cliffs, NJ: Prentice-Hall, 1966), and A. R. Louch, *Explanation and Human Action* (Oxford: Blackwell, 1966).

6 Hanfling, *Wittgenstein's Later Philosophy* (London: Macmillan, 1989), p. 86.

7 Ibid., p. 79.

8 Ibid., p. 86.

9 Ibid., p. 80.

10 Potter and Wetherell attempt to justify their dismissal of actors' accounts by drawing upon the post-Wittgensteinian theory of language to suggest that mentalistic terms like belief and memory have no 'inner referent' at all and that 'instead of being merely descriptions of mental states these words are *themselves* an autonomous part of particular social practices' (*Discourse and Social Psychology*, p. 179; italics in the original). But this is not the issue. The question is not whether understanding the meaning of a word or term requires reference to the contexts of its use rather than the discovery of some internal mental entity to which it might refer. The question is whether understanding the nature and occurrence of an action requires reference to the actor's accomplishment of covert or intra-personal processes; ones which actors can only report to others through the medium of accounts which employ such terms.

11 D. Rubenstein, 'The Concept of Action in the Social Sciences', *Journal for the Theory of Social Behaviour*, 7 (1977), 226.

12 Weber, *The Theory of Social and Economic Organisation*, trans. A. M. Henderson and Talcott Parsons, ed. with intro. Talcott Parsons (New York: The Free Press, 1964), p. 116.

13 In fact it does not follow that just because much action is habitual it must necessarily be the case that the action framework is only applicable to a small part of an individual's overall conduct. Since individuals are capable of 'doing' more than one thing at a time, the habitual performance of routine acts is frequently accompanied by consciously monitored and deliberated actions.

14 Weber, *The Theory of Social and Economic Organisation*, p. 116.

15 Melden, *Free Action*, p. 92.

16 For, as William James observed, 'In any action grown habitual, what instigates each new muscular contraction to take place is . . . the sensation occasioned by the muscular contraction just finished . . . the only impulse which the intellectual centres need send down is that which carries the command to start.' Cited by Gregory A. Kimble and Lawrence C. Perlmuter, 'The Problem of Volition', *Psychological Review*, 77 (1970), 361–84, p. 369.

17 Melden, *Free Action*, would appear to be the main source of this argument.

18 See Kimble and Perlmuter, 'The Problem of Volition'.

19 Thoughts about an action are often accompanied by minute activation of the muscles that would have been involved in the action had it been overtly performed. This activity can be detected with an electromyograph. See E. Jacobson, 'The Electrophysiology of Mental Activities', *American Journal of Psychology*, 44 (1932), 677–94. Intense problem-solving thought or silent reading, for example, may produce detectable muscle activity in the lips and tongue; see A. N, Sokolov, *Inner Speech and Thought* (New York: Plenum Press, 1972).

7. ACCOUNTS AND ACTIONS

1 Ethnomethodologists are particularly prone to advance this argument. See Paul Atkinson, 'Ethnomethodology: A Critical Review', *Annual Review of Sociology*, 14 (1988), 441–65, p. 449.

2 C. Wright Mills, 'Situated Actions and the Vocabulary of Motives', *American Sociological Review*, 5 (1940), p. 907.

3 See for example, John Heritage, 'Accounts in Action', in G. Nigel Gilbert and Peter Abell, eds., *Accounts and Action: Surrey Conferences on Sociological Theory and Methods* (Aldershot: Gower, 1983), pp. 117–31.

4 See for example, G. Nigel Gilbert and Michael Mulkay, *Opening Pandora's Box: A Sociological Analysis of Scientists' Discourse* (Cambridge: Cambridge University Press, 1984).

5 For a useful review of this work, see G. R. Semin and A. S. R. Manstead, *The Accountability of Conduct: A Social Psychological Analysis* (London: Academic Press, 1983).

6 It should be noted that some sociologists and social psychologists have simply opted out of any attempt to even address the issue of how actors' accounts and their actions are related. They disdain to consider the problem, contenting themselves with asserting that this is a 'non-issue'. In Potter and Wetherell's words, 'The descriptive accuracy of discourse and its adequacy as a map or chart of private, subjective, mental experience is the non-issue from our perspective' (*Discourse and Social Psychology*, p. 179).

7 Alexander Rosenberg, *Philosophy of Social Science* (Oxford: The Clarendon Press, 1988) pp. 36ff.

8 A. McIntyre, 'The Idea of a Social Science', pp. 95–114 in *The Aristotelian Society*, supplementary volume 41 (1967), 99.

9 Douglas V. Porpora, 'On the Post-Wittgensteinian Critique of the Concept of Action in Sociology', *The Journal for the Theory of Social Behaviour*, 13 (1983), 129–46.

10 The phrase 'reasons for doing A' is ambiguous. It could refer either to an individual's intentions or purposes in embarking on the course of action which is A, or it could refer to the reasons for *deciding* to do A rather than B or C. In addition, it is also sometimes used to refer to an individual's *motive* for doing A.

11 This is not, however, the position held by the author. For, as should be clear from the discussion of the concept of motive (see pp. 67f) neither reasons nor decisions can possibly be the immediate 'cause' of an action. Since action is a physical event its direct 'cause' must be another such event, and in the case of voluntary intentional actions this could be said to consist of an 'act of will'.

12 See Semin and Manstead, *The Accountability of Conduct*. The term 'vocabulary of motives' is quite inappropriate for although Mills did originally advocate the study of *vocabularies*, what sociologists and social psychologists actually examine tends to be *talk* itself. See, in this respect Colin Campbell, 'Re-examining Mills on Motives: A Character Vocabulary Approach', *Sociological Analysis*, 52 (1991), 89–98.

13 Jeremy Bentham, 'Of Motives', in Jeremy Bentham and John Stuart Mill, *The*

Utilitarians (reprint of 1823 edn; New York: Doubleday Anchor Books, 1970), p. 98.

14 Bentham, 'Of Motives'.

15 J. A. Hadfield, *Psychology and Morals: An Analysis of Character* (London: Methuen, 1955), p. 200; italics in the original.

16 Ibid., p. 200; italics in the original.

17 Weber, *The Theory of Social and Economic Organization*, p. 95.

18 Ibid., pp. 98–9.

19 Ibid., p. 95.

20 Ibid., p. 95.

21 Ibid., p. 96

22 Max Weber, *The Protestant Ethic and The Spirit of Capitalism*, trans. Talcott Parsons (London: Unwin University Books, 1930), p. 231; italics added.

23 Ibid., p. 282.

24 Alfred Schutz, *The Phenomenology of the Social World*, trans. George Walsh and Frederick Lehnert, intro. George Walsh (Evanston, IL: Northwestern University Press, 1967), p. 89.

25 Ibid., p. 91.

26 Ibid., p. 92.

27 Richard J. Bernstein, *The Restructuring of Social and Political Theory* (New York: Harcourt, Brace, Jovanovich, 1976), p. 162.

28 Ibid.

29 Hans Gerth and C. Wright Mills, *Character and Social Structure: The Psychology of Social Institutions* (London: Routledge & Kegan Paul, 1954), p. 113; italics in original.

30 R. S. Peters, *The Concept of Motivation* (London: Routledge & Kegan Paul, 1958), p. 28.

31 Ibid., p. 37.

32 Ibid., p. 38.

33 Peter Winch, *The Idea of a Social Science and its Relation to Philosophy* (London: Routledge & Kegan Paul, 1958), p. 78.

34 Ibid., p. 82; italics in original.

35 Melden, *Free Action*, pp. 21–2.

36 Ibid., p. 90.

37 Ibid., p. 83.

38 Mills, 'Situated Action and the Vocabulary of Motives', p. 905.

39 Peters, *The Concept of Motivation*, p. 29.

40 Ibid., p. 31.

41 Ibid., p. 35.

42 Stanford M. Lyman and Marvin B. Scott, 'Accounts', *American Sociological Review*, 33 (1968), 46–62, p. 112.

43 Lyman and Scott do admit, however, that their concept of an 'account' bears only a 'family resemblance' to the verbal component of a 'motive' in Weber's sense of that term, and that their principal concern is with the 'sociology of talk' (p. 112).

44 Alan F. Blum and Peter McHugh, 'The Social Ascription of Motives', *American Sociological Review*, 36 (1971), 98–109, p. 55.

45 Harre and Secord, *The Explanation of Social Behaviour*, p. 149.

46 Semin and Manstead, *The Accountability of Conduct*, pp. 71–2.
47 Mills, 'Situated Action and the Vocabulary of Motives', p.905.
48 In fact, Lyman and Scott, 'Accounts', do note this fact yet omit to take it up.
49 Mills, 'Situated Action and the Vocabulary of Motives', p. 907.
50 It should perhaps be observed at this point that the ethnomethodological approach to motive differs considerably from the vocabulary of motives tradition. For the concern is not with the function which accounts serve in 'justifying' or 'excusing' actions but merely with the way that orderly sequences of talk are produced. Thus Blum and McHugh describe the concept of motive as a 'rule of relevance' ('The Social Ascription of Motives', p. 99), regarding it as a term employed by actors in public contexts in order to render the conduct of themselves and others 'intelligible'. As they say, 'to give a motive is not to locate a cause of the action, but it is for some observer to assert how a behavior is socially intelligible by ascribing a socially available actor's orientation . . . To talk motives is to talk grammar' (ibid., p. 100).
51 John Heritage, 'Accounts in Action' in G. Nigel Gilbert and Peter Abell, eds., *Accounts and Action, Surrey Conferences on Sociological Theory and Methods* (Aldershot: Gower, 1983), p. 118.
52 See Richard E. Nisbett, and Timothy DeCamp Wilson, 'Telling More Than We Can Know: Verbal Reports on Mental Processes', *Psychological Review*, 84, 3 (1977), 231–59. Also John McClure, 'Telling More than They can Know: The Positivist Account of Verbal Reports and Mental Processes', *The Journal for the Theory of Social Behaviour* 13 2 (1983), 111–27.
53 See for an example of the argument that individuals provide not just different but 'contradictory' accounts of the same action, G. Nigel Gilbert and Michael Mulkay, *Opening Pandora's Box: A Sociological Analysis of Scientists' Discourse* (Cambridge: Cambridge University Press, 1984).
54 Some of the many problems surrounding this argument concern the difficulties of specifying what constitutes a 'different account'. We can assume that 'an account' is not just any verbalisation but one which specifically resembles a description or narration of some action or event. As such an account is a statement which refers to something beyond itself, that something being its referent. Then in addition to the referent an account must contain some descriptive material such that 'something is said' about the referent. Now problems arise in English when people refer to 'two different accounts' because it is not clear whether the_ mean two accounts which have different referents or two accounts which have the same referent but include different descriptive material. That is to say, between two accounts of the same thing and two different accounts of the same thing. This ambiguity is then compounded by the fact that 'differ' may simply mean dissimilar or it may be taken to mean 'contrasting' or 'contradictory'. Furthermore, 'account' is also sometimes used as a synonym for an item of talk or statement such that 'two different accounts' may mean two identical statements made at different times.
55 This would appear to be the position adopted by Semin and Manstead, *The Accountability of Conduct*.
56 Of course, it could then be argued that all the sociologist could be sure of was that they were interviewing people under those conditions in which actors

(and/or their audience) *believe* that they are telling the truth. But then 'justifications', 'excuses' and 'disclaimers' only refer to forms of account which the actor (or others) 'believes' fulfil this function.

8. THE ARGUMENT BY EXCLUSION

1 Julian Freund, *The Sociology of Max Weber* (London: Allen Lane The Penguin Press, 1968), p. 103.

2 Ibid.

3 Mario von Cranach, summarising Harre's position. 'The Psychological Study of Goal-Directed Action: Basic Issues', in Mario von Cranach and Rom Harre, eds., *The Analysis of Action: Recent Theoretical and Empirical Advances* (Cambridge: Cambridge University Press, 1982), pp. 35–74.

4 Ibid., p. 38.

5 Jurgen Habermas, *The Theory of Communicative Action*, vol. 2 *The Critique of Functionalist Reason* (Cambridge: Polity Press, 1987), p. 285.

6 The dispute here is over the naturalist thesis 'to the effect that social actions can be sufficiently accounted for by the ordinary processes of causal explanation'. See Quentin Skinner, ' "Social meaning" and the Explanation of Social Action', in Peter Laslett, W. G. Runciman et al., eds., *Philosophy, Politics and Society*, 4th Series (Oxford: Blackwell, 1972), pp. 136–57, p. 136).

7 We can note that both Harre and Secord (*The Explanation of Social Behaviour*), and Habermas (*The Theory of Communicative Action*, vol. 2), describe the action framework in this way.

8 George C. Homans, 'Behaviourism and After', in Anthony Giddens and Jonathan H. Turner eds., *Social Theory Today* (Cambridge: Polity Press, 1987), pp. 58–81, p. 65.

9 This does not mean that science is irrelevant to the understanding of conduct, merely that the nature of the actor's knowledge does not have to be judged against this standard.

10 Weber, *The Theory of Social and Economic Organization*, trans. A. M. Henderson and Talcott Parsons, ed. with intro. Talcott Parsons (New York: Free Press, 1964), p. 88; italics added.

11 Jonathan H. Turner, *A Theory of Social Interaction* (Stanford: Stanford University Press, 1988), p. 41.

12 C. Wright Mills, 'Situated Action and the Vocabulary of Motives', p. 909.

13 Ibid.

14 Ibid., p. 904.

15 Michael Chapman, 'Conclusion: Action, Intention and Intersubjectivity', in Michael Chapman, ed., 'Intentional Action as a Paradigm for Develop mental Psychology: A Symposium', *Human Development*, 27 (1984), p.140), 113–14. But then sociologists have tended to display a strangely ambiguous attitude toward the study of 'internal' or 'mental' processes. For, on the one hand, they have been very dismissive of the psychological study of these phenomena whilst at the same time being apparently more than ready to give a hearing to those philosophers, such as Schutz, who discuss them at length.

16 See, for example, Anthony Giddens' useful discussion in *The Constitution of Society* (Cambridge: Polity Press, 1984), pp. 213ff.

17 See Steven Lukes, 'Methodological Individualism Reconsidered', pp. 177–86 in Steven Lukes, *Essays in Social Theory* (London: Macmillan, 1977).

18 As Runciman observes, sociology is dependent upon psychology but not reducible to it (W. G. Runciman, *The Methodology of Social Theory*: vol. 1, *A Treatise on Social Theory* (Cambridge: Cambridge University Press, 1983), p. 29).

19 Harre and Secord, *The Explanation of Social Behaviour*, p. 159.

20 Ibid.

21 Goran Therborn, 'Cultural Belonging, Structural Location and Human Action: Explanation in Sociology and Social Science', *Acta Sociologica*, 34 (1991), 177–91, p. 177.

9. THE ARGUMENT THROUGH INCORPORATION

1 Mary F. Rogers, 'Everyday Life as Text', in Randall Collins, ed., *Sociological Theory* (San Francisco: Jossey-Bass, 1984), pp. 165–86, p. 60.

2 Mike O'Donnell, *A New Introduction to Sociology* (3rd edn; London: Thomas Nelson, 1992), p. 11.

3 Alfred Schutz, *Collected Papers* vol. 1, *The Problem of Social Reality*, ed. with intro. Maurice Natanson (The Hague: Nartinus Nijhoff, 1973), p. 32.

4 P. L. Berger and T. Luckmann, *The Social Construction of Reality* (Harmondsworth: Penguin, 1966), p. 37.

5 Ibid.

6 Ibid., p. 43.

7 See p. 124 below.

8 Richard Totman, *Social and Biological Roles of Language: The Psychology of Justifications* (London: Academic Press, 1985), p. 69.

9 Ibid.

10 Totman's alternative definition, that action is social 'when it involves alternative possible ways of acting and when at least one of these alternatives can be relied on to evoke criticism and require justification' (*Social and Biological Roles of Language*, p. 70) presents its own difficulties. The main one being his presumption that actions are always overt and hence open to criticism by others.

11 Alfred Schutz, *The Phenomenology of the Social World*, trans. George Walsh and Frederick Lehnert, intro. George Walsh (Evanston, IL: Northwestern University Press, 1967), p. 10.

12 Ibid., 32.

13 Ibid.

14 Schutz, *Collected Papers*, p. 56.

15 Schutz, *Phenomenology of the Social World*, p. 32; italics added.

16 It is interesting in this respect that Heritage should comment that phenomenologists *assume* that 'type concepts' are shared or at least they characteristically treat them as shared 'until demonstrated otherwise' ('Ethnomethodology', in Anthony Giddens and Jonathan H. Turner, eds., *Social Theory Today* (Oxford: Polity Press, 1987), p. 49.)

17 Talcott Parsons is the one action theorist who has paid attention to this important feature of action. See the space allotted to discussion of psycho-biological systems in T. Parsons and E. A. Shils eds., *Toward a General Theory of Action* (Cambridge, MA: Harvard University Press, 1951); as well as his incorporation of material from Freud (see Talcott Parsons, Robert E. Bales, James Olds, Morris Zelditch and Philip E. Slater, *Family, Socialization and Interaction Processes* (Glencoe, IL: The Free Press, 1955).

18 Rogers, 'Everyday Life as Text', p. 60.

19 Harre and Secord, *The Explanation of Social Behaviour*, p. 39.

20 It would not be too difficult to construct a case for claiming that action is psychological because it rests on language, given that language acquisition requires intra-personal and not merely inter-personal processes to occur.

10. THE 'LEARNING EVERYTHING FROM OTHERS' THESIS

1 Richard Totman, *Social and Biological Roles of Language: The Psychology of Justification* (London: Academic Press, 1985), p. 69.

2 Herbert Blumer, 'Society as Symbolic Interaction', in Jerome G. Manis and Bernard N. Meltzer, eds., *Symbolic Interaction: A Reader in Social Psychology* (2nd edn; Boston: Allyn and Bacon, 1972), pp. 145–51, p. 145.

3 Ibid., pp. 145–6.

4 Jack D. Douglas, *Understanding Everyday Life* (London: Routledge & Kegan Paul, 1973), p. 27; italics in original.

5 Harre and Secord, *The Explanation of Social Behaviour*, p. 85.

6 Blumer, 'Society as Symbolic Interaction', p. 153.

7 See, for example, some of the material cited by Caughey (John L. Caughey, *Imaginary Social Worlds: A Cultural Approach* (Lincoln, NB: University of Nebraska Press, 1984).

8 E. C. Cuff and G. C. F. Payne, eds., *Perspectives in Sociology* (London: Allen & Unwin, 1981), p. 90.

9 John D. Baldwin, 'Mead's Solution to the Problem of Agency', *Sociological Inquiry*, 58, 2 (1988), 139–62.

10 Ibid., p. 157.

11 George Herbert Mead, *Mind Self & Society* (Chicago: Chicago University Press, 1934), p. 140.

12 Blumer, 'Society as Symbolic Interaction', p. 148.

13 See discussion in chapter 6 above concerning action and habit.

14 It seems that some ethnomethodologically inspired sociologists have begun to study 'embodied knowledge' or the ways in which an actor's competence resides in physical capacities rather than prescribed rules. For details see Paul Atkinson's 'Ethnomethodology: A Critical Review', *Annual Review of Sociology*, 14 (1988), 441–65, pp. 460f.

15 Both Mills ('Situated Action and the Vocabulary of Motives'), and Parsons ('The Motivation of Economic Activities', in Talcott Parsons, *Essays in Sociological Theory* (Glencoe, IL: The Free Press, 1940), pp. 50–68), seem to assume that the motives which will 'guide' an individual's conduct will be those offered to them, as it were, by their culture. But then both of them tend to confuse goals with motives in this sense (for example, profit is not a

'motive' in the normal sense, but a goal; what might motivate someone to pursue profit is quite another matter. It might be greed, perhaps, acquisitiveness or a desire for economic security).

16 This I take to be a central part of Weber's argument in *The Protestant Ethic and the Spirit of Capitalism*, with its emphasis on the 'inner-directed' nature of conduct.

17 In fact there is no way, within the constraints of a situationalist paradigm, of explaining how individuals come to learn covert actions. For individuals cannot learn by observing others and they cannot learn from the accounts which others provide of their conduct (because accounts cannot tell us anything about the acts to which they refer). No wonder covert actions are never referred to by situationalists.

18 See Roy's comments on how workers devise play strategies to cope with boredom and monotony (D. Roy, 'Banana Time', *Human Organization*, 18 (1959–60), 158–68).

19 Schutz, *The Phenomenology of The Social World*, p. 216.

11. THE COMMUNICATIVE ACT PARADIGM

1 The example of the marriage ceremony may appear to be the exception here, yet it is not unrealistic to see such a ritual as a special form of communicative act.

2 A. I. Melden, *Free Action* (London: Routledge & Kegan Paul, 1964), p. 92.

3 Douglas V. Porpora, 'On the Post-Wittgensteinian Critique of the Concept of Action in Sociology', *The Journal for the Theory of Social Behaviour*, 13 (1983), 131.

4 See the argument presented by J. R. Searle in *Speech Acts* (Cambridge: Cambridge University Press, 1969).

5 Melden, *Free Action*, p. 92.

6 The fact that there may be 'official' or 'social' ways of establishing the nature of actors' subjective states (as happens in courts of law), although accorded some significance in situationalist literature, is irrelevant. The point is that such information is recognised as necessary in order to identify the act.

7 Charles Taylor argues that rules are *constitutive of* the acts to which they relate (see 'Interpretation and the Sciences of Man', in *Understanding and Social Inquiry*, ed. Fred Dallmayr and Thomas McCarthy (Notre Dame: University of Indiana Press, 1977, p. 25). The example he gives is playing chess, in the sense that without the rules of chess one cannot 'play' chess, that is to say, 'make a move'. Hence, the action is inseparable from the rules. Rubinstein gives another example, that of acting bravely, in which he claims that a man or woman can not be judged to have acted bravely unless certain objective conditions are fulfilled no matter what the individual's subjective intentions ('The Concept of Action in the Social Sciences', p. 215). He claims that this meaning cannot be wrong and that no one can be brave if these conditions are not met. Interestingly enough, however, this statement can be repudiated by an example which Weber himself cites concerning the Spartan practice of differentiating between acts of bravery which stemmed from 'the totality of [a person's] personality' and those performed for specific reasons – such as an

attempt to atone for an earlier manifestation of cowardice – and the fact that the Spartans judged the second category of actions to be much inferior to the first (*The Sociology of Religion*, trans. Epraim Fischoff, with an introduction by Talcott Parsons (London: Methuen), p. 156). So here too we have an example of how the motive for the act is crucial in determining how the act itself is named and judged.

8 Rubinstein, 'The Concept of Action', p. 215.
9 Peter Winch, *The Idea of a Social Science and its Relation to Philosophy* (London: Routledge & Kegan Paul, 1958), p. 44; italics in original.
10 Ibid., p. 50.
11 Ibid., pp. 30–1. His examples, interestingly, involve the correct use of words.
12 Reference group theory actually takes as its premise the assumption that an individual's conduct can *not* be understood in terms of situational norms. See the discussion of reference groups in R. K. Merton, *Social Theory and Social Structure* (New York: Free Press, 1957).
13 For example, the teenager who refuses to retaliate when struck by another is likely to have her non-response judged as evidence of 'cowardice' by her peers, in accordance with the social norms governing conduct among adolescent youth groups. The individual concerned, however, may see herself as acting out her pacifist, Christian duty to 'turn the other cheek'.
14 Winch, *The Idea of a Social Science*, pp. 32–3.
15 Ibid., p. 116.
16 See Warren B. Smerud, *Can There be a Private Language? An Examination of some Principal Arguments* (Mouton: The Hague 1970); also O. R. Jones, ed., *The Private Language Argument* (Macmillan: London, 1971).
17 See C. W. K. Mundle, 'Behaviourism and the Private Language Argument', in O. R. Jones, ed., *The Private Language Argument* (London: St Martin's Press, 1971), pp. 103–17, pp. 105f.
18 Lovers, for example, frequently employ a publicly available language to reveal desires and feelings to each other which are entirely private in the sense that they had not previously been communicated to anyone else.
19 Ludwig Wittgenstein, *Philosophical Investigations* (Oxford: Blackwell, 1963), p. 81. Cited by Habermas in *The Theory of Communicative Action*, vol. 2: *The Critique of Functionalist Reason* (Cambridge: Polity Press, 1987), pp. 17–18.
20 Ibid., p. 18.
21. Anthony Giddens provides an excellent discussion of the different part played by rules in these two types of action in *The Constitution of Society* (Cambridge: Polity Press, 1984), pp. 18ff. Giddens is also one the few sociologists of action to distinguish clearly between communicative and non-communicative actions. See *New Rules of The Sociological Method* (London: Hutchinson, 1976), p. 86ff.
22 The fact that individuals need to share a common definition of the situation (for example, that this is a game of tennis) is a different issue. For there is no reason to assume that because two people share a common overall definition of a situation that they therefore know (let alone share) the meaning of each other's individual actions.
23 Alfred Schutz, *Collected Papers*, vol. 1: *The Problem of Social Reality*, ed. and intro. Maurice Natanson (The Hague, Martinus Nijhoff, 1973), p. 24.

24 Schutz, *Phenomenology of the Social World*, p. 114.
25 Ibid.
26 *Collected Papers*, I, p. 56.
27 Ibid., p. 55.
28 Schutz confuses motive with intention, as Bernstein notes (*Restructuring of Social and Political Theory* (New York: Harcourt, Brace, Jovanovitch, 1976), p. 162). That is, his concept of an 'in-order-to motive' really refers to an intention and not a motive at all.
29 Schutz, *Collected Papers*, I, p. 24.
30 Ibid.
31 Ibid., p. 25.
32 But there is another mystery here. How is it that Schutz is able to identify the actions of the newspaper editor and the postmen in the first place? For on his own admission, only actors themselves know where their actions begin and end (see his assertion that 'The unity of the action is . . . *subjective*', *Phenomenology of the Social World*, p. 63; italics in the original). If this is the case, then surely only actors know what their actions consist of? Hence it is quite impossible for another person to know what their goals and motives might be for the simple reason that they do not know what their actions are in the first place. This is suggested by Schutz's own examples, where 'handling the mail' looks suspiciously like an observer's definition of what postmen's actions consist of, rather than an actor's definition.
33 Interestingly Schutz gives using the telephone as an example in a discussion later in the book (p. 88), yet fails to draw this conclusion.
34 *Collected Papers*, I, p. 56.
35 It is accepted that, as Giddens puts it, *verstehen* is not a special sociological method but an 'ontological condition of human society as it is produced and reproduced by its members' (*New Rules of the Sociological Method*, p. 151.) This is clearly true in the sense that the social world which sociologists study is already 'pre-interpreted' and hence cannot merely be observed but also has to be understood. Consequently sociologists necessarily draw on their members' knowledge. Although this is a reasonable argument, sociologists have exaggerated the extent to which ordinary people need to understand the actions of others in order to be able to interact with them, and hence the extent to which it is actually necessary to understand this pre-interpreted world. Thus the 'problem' of intersubjectivity addressed by Schutz, which is 'how can two or more actors share common experiences of the natural and social world and, relatedly, how can they communicate about them?' (Heritage, *Garfinkel and Ethnomethodology* (Cambridge: Polity Press, 1984), p. 54), is an interesting question to struggle with but it is not germane to the issue of how individuals manage to act successfully. Rather it already presupposes not just a social action but a communicative act paradigm. Whether actors believe that they share common experiences with others has little to do with accomplishing action. It arises as an issue because Schutz has already defined action as necessarily involving the actor in ascertaining the subjective meanings of another's actions. Hence what Schutz is really concerned with is 'mutual understanding', not the successful accomplishment of action.

12. THE LINGUISTIC TURN FOR THE WORSE

1 For an account of the linguistic turn in philosophy see Richard Rorty, ed., *The Linguistic Turn: Recent Essays in Philosophical Method* (Chicago: University of Chicago Press, 1967).

2 These examples are used by Winch in *The Idea of a Social Science and its Relation to Philosophy* (London: Routledge & Kegan Paul, 1958), pp. 30–1, and by Schutz in *Collected Papers*, I, p. 21.

3 Although this is not the straightforward question which it is often assumed to be; see the comments in chapter 15.

4 Thus in order to discover that the driver's movements constitute 'signalling a right turn' it is necessary to consult *The Highway Code*.

5 Joel M. Charon, *Symbolic Interactionism: An Introduction, An Interpretation, An Integration* (4th edn; Englewood Cliffs, NJ: Prentice-Hall, 1992), p. 121; italics in original.

6 Charles K. Warriner, 'Social Action, Behavior and *Verstehen*', *The Sociological Quarterly*, 10 (1969), 501–11, p. 503.

7 Ibid., p. 505.

8 The point to note here is that the contrasting terminology relates to a difference in the nature and extent of the frame of meaning which actor and observer are imposing on the activity in question. It is certainly not that what is intelligible to the actor is unintelligible to the observer. Nor is it a question of the observer imposing a completely inapplicable frame of meaning on the actor's conduct (though that may happen). Where the actor's conduct is overt and the observer and actor both share the same cultural or sub-cultural traditions, then there is a fair chance that the observer will be able to define the actor's conduct using a frame of meaning which the actor may acknowledge as applicable. However, this does not mean that the observer is using the *same* frame as the actor.

9 The fact that actions are not primarily arbitrary symbols also explains why, unlike words, they cannot be combined syntactically to convey yet more complex messages. On the contrary, the more that specific actions are combined to make longer programmes of action the less easy it is for an observer to discern the 'meaning' which they contain whilst the information which they carry decreases rather than increases.

10 Schutz, *Collected Papers*, I, p. 56.

11 As we have noted Schutz concentrates on the name 'Rover' for a dog, Winch on the name 'Everest' for a mountain, whilst both Mills and Blumer focus specifically on the process of 'naming'.

12 J. L. Austin, *How To Do Things With Words* (Oxford: The Clarendon Press, 1962).

13 Indeed, one can note that both movements were inspired by a similar anti-mentalist sentiment.

14 Kenneth J. Gergen, 'The Social Constructionist Movement in Modern Psychology', *American Psychologist*, 40 (1985), 266–74. See also John Shotter, *Cultural Politics of Everyday Life: Social Constructionism, Rhetoric and Knowing of the Third Kind* (Buckingham: Open University Press, 1993).

15 Jonathan Potter and Margaret Wetherell, *Discourse and Social Psychology* (London: Sage, 1987), p. 103.
16 Ibid., p. 178.
17 C. Wright Mills, 'Situated Action and the Vocabulary of Motives', *American Sociological Review*, 5 (1940), 906.

13. THE MYTH OF SOCIAL ACTION

1 Don Locke, 'Action and Social Action: Comments on J. H. Turner', pp. 95–102 in Gottfried Seebass and Raimo Tuomela, eds., *Social Action* (Dordrecht: D. Reidel, 1985), p. 96.
2 G. Duncan Mitchell ed., *A New Dictionary of Sociology* (London: Routledge & Kegan Paul, 1979), p. 2.
3 Panos D. Bardis, *Dictionary of Quotations in Sociology* (New York: Greenwood Press, 1985), p. 7.
4 Percy S. Cohen, *Modern Social Theory* (London: Heinemann Educational Books, 1968), p. 95.
5 Jonathan H. Turner, 'The Concept of "Action" in Sociological Analysis', pp. 61–88 in Gottfried Seebass and Raimo Tuomela eds., *Social Action* (Dordrecht: D. Reidel, 1985), p. 83.
6 J. E. Goldthorpe, *An Introduction to Sociology* (New York: Harper Collins, 1992), p. 9.
7 Ibid., pp. 25–6.
8 Erving Goffman, *Forms of Talk* (Oxford: Blackwell, 1981), p. 84.
9 Cohen, *Modern Social Theory*, p. 95.
10 Cohen is the best case in point. For him action is social when one or more of the three following conditions are fulfilled:

> first, the situation of the actor includes other actors whose presence is taken into account when the action is performed; second, the situation is such that these others possess facilities, objects or characteristics which enable them in some way to influence the conduct of the actor; third, the actor shares with these others certain sets of expectations and, possibly certain values, beliefs and symbols. (*Modern Social Theory*, p. 95)

11 The word 'influence' here is very ambiguous. It could simply mean 'affected by', as in the example where my decision whether to walk to work or go by car is 'influenced by' the weather. Or it could be that the word is used to mean a situation where my conduct has been modified as a result of someone else's deliberate effort to affect the nature of my conduct, as in the example where my decision to walk to work and not go by car was 'influenced' by my wife's efforts to persuade me of the benefits of taking more exercise.
12 Schutz, *Collected Papers*, I, p. 14.
13 Habermas, *The Theory of Communicative Action*, vol. 1: *Reason and the Rationalisation of Society* (Boston: MA: Beacon Press, 1984), p. 285.
14 This is not a convincing argument for typically these are those features which distinguish systems of one sort or another. But then, as Parsons has argued,

action itself can be regarded as a 'system' (see, not only Talcott Parsons, *The Social System* (London: Routledge & Kegan Paul, 1951, but also *Economy and Society* (Glencoe, IL: Free Press, 1956).

15 Weber, *The Theory of Social and Economic Organisation*, trans. A. M. Henderson and Talcott Parsons, ed. and intro. Talcott Parsons (New York: The Free Press, 1964), p. 112.

14. THE OBSTACLE WHICH IS SOCIAL SITUATIONALISM

1 This tendency to collapse the independent dimensions of the psychological and the cultural into the social is also a form of social reductionism. Thus whilst sociologists are quick to object to any psychologist who seeks to explain social phenomena in psychological terms, they seem to have no hesitation in 'reducing' psychological terms to social ones. See, for example, Mills's comment that 'there is no need to invoke 'psychological' terms like 'desire' or 'wish' as explanatory, since they themselves must be explained socially' ('Situated Action and the Vocabulary of Motives', *American Sociological Review*, 906).

2 See William N. Dember, 'Motivation and the Cognitive Revolution', *American Psychologist* March 1974, 161–8.

3 Anthony Giddens, *New Rules of Sociological Method* (London: Hutchinson, 1976), pp. 40f.

4 The ethogenic and social constructivist movements in social psychology are excellent examples of this irony.

5 Habermas, *The Theory of Communicative Action*, vol. 2: *Reason and the Rationalisation of Society* (Boston, MA: Beacon Press, 1984), p. 3.

6 Cited by John C. Heritage, 'Ethnomethodology' in Giddens and Turner, eds., *Social Theory Today* (Oxford: Polity Press, 1987), p. 233.

7 In some contemporary strands of sociological inquiry a further 'slippage' has occurred in the sense that 'activity' or 'activities' has even replaced 'social action' as the central focus of analysis. This, in Atkinson's view, is true of some currents of work in ethnomethodology. He notes that 'What is clear is that contemporary ethnomethodology . . . has shifted dramatically from a concern with social action in any classical sense of that term. The move from *action* to *activity* is indicative of an ambivalent relationship with phenomeno-logical or *verstehende* antecedents'. Noting that, as a consequence of this development, the contemporary writing of some ethnomethodologists has a distinct 'structuralist and behaviorist flavor [*sic*]'. (Paul Atkinson, 'Ethnomethodology: A Critical Review', in *Annual Review of Sociology*, 14 (1988), 447.)

8 It is revealing in this connection to note Alan F. Blum and Peter McHugh's description of motives as '*observers' rules*' ('The Social Ascription of Motives', *American Sociological Review*, 26 (1971), p. 99; italics added.)

9 The situationalist position would be plausible if it merely stated that the interpretation placed on an act *varied* with the social context in which it was performed. Hence the 'scratching of an itch' meant something different to the auctioneer who witnessed it when performed in the context of an auction to its meaning to his wife when performed by the same individual in his own

home. In neither case, however, is it true to say that the 'meaning' is *located* in the social context. For in both instances the meaning of the act is located in the minds of individuals.

In fact it is very difficult to work out precisely what the situationalist position is with respect to the agent's understanding of the meaning of his or her action. Some examples cited, like the auction, suggest that individuals are assumed to be quite unaware of the meaning of 'what they are doing' – a conclusion which is rather undermined by the fact that the auctioneer is an actor who obviously does know what he or she is doing. The signalling car driver example, on the other hand, suggests that actors are probably aware of what they are doing but that its meaning is not present in their mind while they are doing it as it is done habitually or 'automatically'. The groom at the wedding ceremony on the other hand is not only clearly aware of what he is doing but is unlikely to be placing a ring on his soon-to-be-wife's finger in an habitual or automatic manner. Since, as noted, meaning cannot be located 'in' a context, only in human consciousness, the only sensible interpretation of situationalism would seem to be to assume that individuals interpret the meaning of actions by means of the social conventions which are themselves 'embedded' in a given social situation or context. But even though meanings are assigned to behaviour on the basis of rules, these meanings must still reside in the minds of actors and observers, and cannot be said to be 'in' the situations themselves. But then it cannot seriously be contended that the majority of members of society regularly perform actions 'unwittingly' without any subjective understanding of what they are doing (as in the auction example). For then it would be impossible to explain how social life comes to possess its manifest structure and order. Whether an auctioneer would have any bids at all at his auction, for example, would be entirely a matter of chance; that is to say, whether any of the random 'movements' performed by those present happened to coincide with those prescribed by the rules to constitute a 'bid'.

10 Quoted by Giddens, *New Rules of the Sociological Method*, p. 31; italics added.
11 Martin Albrow, *Max Weber's Construction of Social Theory* (London: Macmillan, 1990), p. 138.
12 Goran Therborn has noted how interest in explanation is missing from contemporary sociological theory in general, not just the theory of social action. He writes: 'Absent in or marginal to currently prevailing general sociological theorizing is any ambition to *explain*. Little interest can be found in contributing to answering questions like: Why do these people act in this way? Why does that social order change in that way?' ('Cultural Belonging, Structural Location and Science', *Acta Sociologica* 34 (1991), 177–91, p. 178; italics in the original.)

15. BRINGING ACTION BACK IN

1 Still less is this assault on social action in preparation for a plea for methodological individualism or psychological reductionism.
2 Alan Dawe, 'The Two Sociologies', in K. Thompson and J. Tunstall, eds., *Sociological Perspectives* (Harmondsworth: Penguin , 1971).

3 To some extent, of course, this division is equatable with the contrast between quantifiable and qualitative methods.

4 Unfortunately, the situationalist preoccupation with the assumed 'problem' of inter-subjective understanding and ordered interaction has served to obscure the importance of this question. For example, Schutz suggests that Weber's stress on subjective understanding obscures the inter-subjective nature of social reality and makes it difficult to understand how successful interaction is possible. Yet Schutz's stress on the inter-subjective nature of meaning makes it equally difficult to understand how individual action is possible, especially since 'reality' is not equatable with 'social reality' any more than action is equatable with conduct which is overt and witnessed by others.

5 Only Talcott Parsons – in his discussion of pattern-maintenance and tension management (see the discussion of system pre-requisites and requisites in *Economy and Society* (1956)) – seems to have regarded this as a continuing issue, one relevant to an individual's ability to act throughout life. Yet unfortunately Parsons treats this as if it were a question which could be re-translated into issues concerning the action system of the 'personality'. But the question of how individuals manage to act at all is certainly not equatable with the workings of the personality, for this is not a system of 'action' but a combined system of action and behaviour; 'character' would correspond to the system of action.

6 See Talcott Parsons, *The Structure of Social Action* (New York: Free Press, 1948), chs. 1–3, and Percy S. Cohen, *Modern Social Theory* (London: Heinemann Educational Books, 1968), pp. 18–33.

7 Giddens is a notable exception in this respect in so far as he stresses the need to focus on 'doing'. It is debatable, however, whether he actually succeeds in 'doing' this himself.

8 What is more, individuals cannot possibly *just* be doing this otherwise no action would ever be performed. Action is necessarily motivated which means that some element of desire or feeling must also be present.

9 For example, being successful in 'staying awake' when one is very sleepy, or 'controlling one's temper' when very angry requires that individuals discover what 'works' for them, just as they have to find out for themselves what it is that succeeds in motivating them to do things in general. To a large extent this is a personal matter and does not relate directly to the conduct of others.

10 Weber, *The Theory of Social and Economic Organization*, p. 95.

Bibliography

Abercrombie, Nicholas, Stephen Hill and Bryan S. Turner, *The Penguin Dictionary of Sociology* (London: Penguin, 1985).

Albrow, Martin, *Max Weber's Construction of Social Theory* (London: Macmillan, 1990).

Alexander, Jeffrey C., 'Formal and Substantive Voluntarism in the Work of Talcott Parsons: A Theoretical and Ideological Reinterpretation', *American Sociological Review*, 43 (1978), 177–98.

'Review Essay: Habermas's New Critical Theory: Its Promise and Problems', *American Journal of Sociology*, 91, 2 (1985), 398–424.

Action and Its Environments: Toward a New Synthesis (New York: Columbia University Press, 1988).

Anscombe, G. E. M., *Intention* (Oxford: Blackwell, 1957).

Atkinson, P., *The Clinical Experience: The Construction and Reconstruction of Medical Reality* (Farnborough: Gower, 1981).

'Ethnomethodology: A Critical Review', *Annual Review of Sociology*, 14 (1988), 441–65.

Austin, J. L., *How to Do Things With Words* (Oxford: The Clarendon Press, 1962).

Baldamus, W., *Efficiency and Effort* (London: Tavistock Publications, 1961).

Baldwin, John D., 'Mead's Solution to the Problem of Agency', *Sociological Inquiry*, 58, 2 (1988), 139–62.

Bardis, Panos D., *A Dictionary of Quotations in Sociology* (New York: Greenwood Press, 1985).

Barry, Brian, *Sociologists, Economists and Democracy* (Chicago, IL: University of Chicago Press, 1970).

Benedict, R., *Patterns of Culture* (London: Routledge & Kegan Paul, 1935).

Benhabib, Seyla, 'Rationality and Social Action: Critical Reflections on Weber's Methodological Writings', *The Philosophical Forum*, 12, 4 (1981), 356–74.

Bentham, Jeremy, 'Of Motives', in Jeremy Bentham and John Stuart Mill, *The Utilitarians*, (1823 edn; New York: Doubleday Anchor Books, 1970).

Berger, P., 'Identity as a Problem in the Sociology of Knowledge', *Archives Européennes de Sociologie: European Journal of Sociology*, 7 (1966), 105–15.

Berger, P. L. and T. Luckmann, *The Social Construction of Reality* (Harmondsworth: Penguin, 1966).

Bernstein, Richard J., *The Restructuring of Social and Political Theory* (New York: Harcourt, Brace, Jovanovich, 1976).

Betts, Katherine, 'The Conditions of Action, Power and the Problem of Interests', *Sociological Review*, 34, 1 (1986), 39–64.

Bevis, Richard W., ed., *Eighteenth-Century Drama: Afterpieces* (London: Oxford University Press, 1970).

Bilton, Tony, Kevin Bonnett, Philip Jones, Michelle Stanworth, Ken Sheard and Andrew Webster, *Introductory Sociology* (2nd edn; Basingstoke: Macmillan, 1987).

Blum, Alan F. and Peter McHugh, 'The Social Ascription of Motives', *American Sociological Review*, 36 (1971), 98–109.

Blumer, Herbert, 'Action vs. Interaction', *Society*, 20 (April 1972).

'Society as Symbolic Interaction', pp. 145–51 in Jerome G. Manis and Bernard N. Meltzer, eds., *Symbolic Interaction: A Reader in Social Psychology* (2nd edn; Boston: Allyn & Bacon, 1972).

'Sociological Implications of the Thought of George Herbert Mead', *American Journal of Sociology*, 71 (1966), 535–48.

Bourdieu, P., *Distinction: A Social Critique of the Judgement of Taste* (London: Routledge & Kegan Paul, 1984).

Brand, Myles, and Walton, Douglas, eds., *Action Theory: Proceedings of the Winnipeg Conference on Human Action* (Dordrecht: D. Reidel, 1976).

Brandtstadter, Jochen, 'Action Development and Development through Action', in Michael Chapman, ed., 'Intentional Action as a Paradigm for Developmental Psychology: A Symposium', *Human Development*, 27 (1984), 113–44.

Bruce, S. and R. Wallis, 'Rescuing Motives', *The British Journal of Sociology*, 34, 1 (1983), 61–72.

'"Rescuing Motives" Rescued: a Reply to Sharrock and Watson', *The British Journal of Sociology*, 36, 3 (1985), 467–70.

Burke, Kenneth, *A Rhetoric of Motives* (Berkeley: University of California Press, 1969).

Burrell, Gibson and Gareth Morgan, *Sociological Paradigms and Organisational Analysis: The Elements of the Sociology Corporate Life* (London: Heinemann, 1979).

Camic, Charles, 'The Matter of Habit', *American Journal of Sociology*, 91 (1986), 1039–87.

Campbell, Colin, 'A Dubious Distinction? An Inquiry into the Value and Use of Merton's Concepts of Latent and Manifest Function', *American Sociological Review*, 47 (1982), 29–44.

The Romantic Ethic and the Spirit of Modern Consumerism (Oxford: Blackwell, 1987).

'Re-examining Mills on Motive: A Character Vocabulary Approach', *Sociological Analysis*, 52, 1 (1991) 89–98.

'In Defence of the Traditional Concept of Action in Sociology', *Journal for the Theory of Social Behaviour*, 22 (1992), 1–23.

Caughey, John L., *Imaginary Social Worlds: A Cultural Approach* (Lincoln, NB: University of Nebraska Press, 1984).

Chapman, Michael, 'Intentional Action as a Paradigm for Developmental Psychology: A Symposium', *Human Development*, 27 (1984), 113–44.

'Conclusion: Action, Intention, and Intersubjectivity', in Michael Chapman, ed., 'Intentional Action as a Paradigm for Developmental Psychology: A Symposium', *Human Development*, 27 (1984), 113–44.

Charon, Joel M., *Symbolic Interactionism: An Introduction, An Interpretation, An Integration* (4th edn; Englewood Cliffs, NJ: Prentice Hall, 1992).

Cohen, Percy S., *Modern Social Theory* (London: Heinemann Educational Books, 1968).

Coleman, James S., 'Social Theory, Social Research, and a Theory of Action', *American Journal of Sociology*, 91, 6 (1986), 1309–35.

'Actors and Actions in Social History and Social Theory: Reply to Sewell', *American Journal of Sociology*, 93, 1 (1987), 172–5.

The Foundations of Social Theory (Cambridge, MA: Belknap Press of Harvard University Press, 1990).

Coleman, James S. and Fararo, Thomas J., eds., *Rational Choice Theory: Advocacy and Critique* (London: Sage, 1992).

Coulter, Jeff, *The Social Construction of Mind* (London: Macmillan, 1979).

Craib, Ian, *Anthony Giddens* (London: Routledge, 1992).

Csikszentmihalyi, M. and E. Rochberg-Halton, *The Meanings of Things: Domestic Symbols and the Self* (Cambridge: Cambridge University Press, 1981).

von Cranach, Mario, 'The Psychological Study of Goal-Directed Action: Basic Issues', pp. 35–74 in Mario von Cranach and Rom Harre, eds., *The Analysis of Action: Recent Theoretical and Empirical Advances* (Cambridge: Cambridge University Press, 1982).

von Cranach, Mario and Harre, Rom, eds., *The Analysis of Action: Recent Theoretical and Empirical Advances* (Cambridge: Cambridge University Press, 1982).

Cuff, E. C. and G. C. F. Payne, eds., *Perspectives in Sociology* (London: Allen & Unwin, 1981).

Davidson, Donald, 'Agency,' pp. 3–37 in Robert Brinkley et al., eds., *Agent, Action, and Reason* (Oxford: Blackwell, 1971).

Essays on Actions and Events (Oxford: The Clarendon Press, 1980).

Dawe, Alan, 'The Two Sociologies', pp. 542–55 in K. Thompson and J. Tunstall, eds., *Sociological Perspectives* (Harmondsworth: Penguin, 1971).

'Theories of Social Action', pp. 362–417 in T. Bottomore and R. Nisbet, eds., *A History of Sociological Analysis* (New York: Basic Books, 1978).

Denzin, Norman K., *Interpretive Interactionism* (London: Sage, 1989).

Dember, William N., 'Motivation and the Cognitive Revolution' *American Psychologist* (17 March 1974), 161–8.

Dittmar, Helga, *The Social Psychology of Material Possessions* (Hemel Hempstead: Harvester Wheatsheaf, 1992).

Dixon, Keith, *Sociological Theory: Pretence and Possibility* (London: Routledge & Kegan Paul, 1973).

Douglas, Jack D., ed., *Understanding Everyday Life* (London: Routledge & Kegan Paul, 1971).

Eckensberger, Lutz H. and John A. Meacham, 'The Essentials of Action Theory: A Framework for Discussion', *Human Development*, 27 (1984), 166–72.

Elster, Jon, *Sour Grapes: Studies in the Subversion of Rationality* (Cambridge: Cambridge University Press, 1983).

Elster, Jon, ed., *The Multiple Self* (Cambridge: Cambridge University Press, 1985).

Rational Choice (Oxford: Blackwell, 1986).

Enc, Berent, 'On the Theory of Action', *Journal for the Theory of Social Behaviour*, 5, 2 (1975), 145–67.

Farber, Leslie H., *Lying, Despair, Jealousy, Envy, Sex, Suicide, Drugs, and the Good Life* (New York: Basic Books, 1976).

Foote, Nelson N., 'Identification as the Basis for a Theory of Motives', *American Sociological Review*, 16 (1951), 14–21.

Freund, Julian, *The Sociology of Max Weber* (London: Allen Lane The Penguin Press, 1968).

Garfinkel, Harold, *Studies in Ethnomethodology* (Englewood Cliffs, NJ: Prentice-Hall, 1967).

Gergen, Kenneth J., 'The Social Constructionist Movement in Modern Psychology', *American Psychologist*, 40, 3 (March 1985), 266–74.

Gerth, Hans and C. Wright Mills, *Character and Social Structure: The Psychology of Social Institutions* (London: Routledge & Kegan Paul, 1954).

Giddens, Anthony, *New Rules of Sociological Method* (London: Hutchinson, 1976).

Central Problems in Social Theory (London: Macmillan, 1979).

The Constitution of Society (Cambridge: Polity Press, 1984).

Giddens, Anthony and Jonathan H. Turner, eds., *Social Theory Today* (Oxford: Polity Press, 1987).

Gilbert, Nigel G. and Michael Mulkay, 'In Search of the Action', in G. Nigel Gilbert and Peter Abell, eds., *Accounts and Action: Surrey Conferences on Sociological Theory and Method* (Aldershot: Gower, 1983), pp. 8–34.

Opening Pandora's Box: A Sociological Analysis of Scientists' Discourse (Cambridge: Cambridge University Press, 1984).

Goff, T. W., *Marx and Mead: Contributions to a Sociology of Knowledge* (London: Routledge & Kegan Paul, 1980).

Goffman, Erving, *The Presentation of Self in Everyday Life* (1959; Harmondsworth: Penguin, 1971).

Forms of Talk (Oxford: Blackwell, 1981).

Goldthorpe, J. E., *An Introduction to Sociology* (3rd edn; Cambridge: Cambridge University Press, 1985).

Goodman, Norman, *Introduction to Sociology* (New York: Harper-Collins, 1992).

Grathoff, Richard, ed., *The Theory of Social Action: The Correspondence of Alfred Schutz and Talcott Parsons* (Bloomington and London: Indiana University Press, 1978).

Gross, Edward, 'The Rationality of Symbolic Actors', *The British Journal of Sociology*, 38, 2 (1987) 152–67.

Habermas, J., *The Theory of Communicative Action*, vol. 1: *Reason and the Rationalization of Society* (Boston, MA: Beacon Press, 1984).

'Remarks on the Concept of Communicative Action', pp. 151–78 in Gottfried Seebass and Raimo Tuomela, eds., *Social Action* (Dordrecht: D. Reidel, 1985).

The Theory of Communicative Action, vol. 2: *The Critique of Functionalist Reason* (Cambridge: Polity Press, 1987).

Hadfield, J. A., *Psychology and Morals: An Analysis of Character* (London: Methuen, 1955).

Hampshire, S., *Thought and Action* (New York: Viking Press, 1959).

Hanfling, Oswald, *Wittgenstein's Later Philosophy* (Basingstoke: Macmillan, 1989).

Haralambos, Michael, *Sociology: Themes and Perspectives* (Slough: University Tutorial Press, 1980).

Haralambos, Michael and Martin Holborn, *Sociology: Themes and Perspectives* (3rd edn; London: Unwin Hyman, 1990)

Harre, Rom, *Social Being: A Theory for Social Psychology* (Oxford: Blackwell, 1979).

'Theoretical Preliminaries to the Study of Action', pp. 5–34 in Mario von Cranach and Rom Harre, eds., *The Analysis of Action: Recent Theoretical and Empirical Advances* (Cambridge: Cambridge University Press, 1982).

Personal Being: A Theory of Individual Psychology (Oxford: Blackwell, 1983).

Harre, R., D. Clarke and N. de Carlo, *Motives and Mechanisms: An Introduction to the Psychology of Action* (London: Methuen, 1985).

Harre, R. and P. F. Secord, *The Explanation of Social Behaviour* (Oxford: Blackwell, 1972).

Hasher, Lynn and Rose T. Zacks, 'Automatic and Effortful Processes in Memory', *Journal of Experimental Psychology* 108 (1979), 356–88.

Heap, James, 'Reconceiving the Social', *Canadian Review of Sociology and Anthropology*, 13, 3 (1976), 271–81.

Heath, Anthony, *Rational Choice and Social Exchange* (Cambridge: Cambridge University Press, 1976).

Heritage, John, 'Accounts in Action', pp. 117–31 in G. Nigel Gilbert and Peter Abell, eds., *Accounts and Action: Surrey Conferences on Sociological Theory and Methods*, (Aldershot: Gower, 1983).

Garfinkel and Ethnomethodology (Cambridge: Polity Press, 1984).

'Ethnomethodology', pp. 224–72 in Anthony Giddens and Jonathan H. Turner, eds., *Social Theory Today* (Oxford: Polity Press, 1987).

Heritage J. and M. Atkinson, eds., *Structures of Social Action* (London: British Sociological Association and The Social Science Research Council, 1984).

Hindess, Barry, 'Interests in Political Analysis', pp. 112–31 in John Law, ed., *Power, Action and Belief: A New Sociology of Knowledge? Sociological Review Monograph 32* (London: Routledge & Kegan Paul, 1986).

Choice, Rationality and Social Theory (London: Unwin Hyman, 1986).

Hinkle, Roscoe C., 'Antecedents of the Action Orientation in American Sociology Before 1935', *American Sociological Review*, 28 (1963), 705–15.

Homans, George C., 'Behaviourism and After', pp. 58–81 in Anthony Giddens and Jonathan H. Turner, eds., *Social Theory Today* (Cambridge: Polity Press, 1987).

Jacobson, E., 'The Electrophysiology of Mental Activities', *American Journal of Psychology*, 44 (1932) 677–94.

Jary, David and Julia Jary, *Collins Dictionary of Sociology* (London: Harper Collins, 1991).

Jones, O. R., ed., *The Private Language Argument* (London: Macmillan, 1971).

Kimble, Gregory A. and Lawrence C. Perlmuter, 'The Problem of Volition', *Psychological Review*, 77 (1970), 361–84.

Klinger, Eric, *Meaning & Void: Inner Experience and the Incentives in People's Lives* (Minneapolis: University of Minnesota Press, 1977).

Knorr-Cetina, K. D. and A. V. Cicourel, eds., *Advances in Social Theory and Methodology, Toward An Integration of Micro- and Macro-sociologies* (Boston: Routledge & Kegan Paul, 1981).

Knorr-Cetina K. D. and Michael Mulkay, eds., *Science Observed: Perspectives on the Social Study of Science* (London and Beverly Hills, California: Sage, 1982).

Kuhl, Julius and Jurgen Beckmann, eds., *Action Control: From Cognition to Behavior* (Berlin: Springer-Verlag, 1985).

Kuhn, Thomas S., *The Structure of Scientific Revolutions* (Chicago, IL: University of Chicago Press, 1962).

Lazarsfeld, Paul F., 'Historical Notes on the Empirical Study of Action: An Intellectual Odyssey', pp. 50–100 in Paul F. Lazarsfeld, *Qualitative Analysis: Historical and Critical Essays* (Boston: Allyn and Bacon, 1972).

Lee, David and Howard Newby, *The Problem of Sociology: An Introduction to the Discipline* (London: Hutchinson, 1983).

Levine, David P. and Lynn S. Levine, 'Social Theory and Social Action' *Economy and Society*, 4 (1975), 173–93.

Locke, Don, 'Action, and Social Action. Comments on J. H. Turner' pp. 95–102 in Gottfried Seebass and Raimo Tuomela, eds., *Social Action* (Dordrecht, Boston, Lancaster: D. Reidel, 1985).

Louch, A. R., *Explanation and Human Action* (Oxford: Blackwell, 1966).

Lukes, Steven, 'Methodological Individualism Reconsidered', pp. 177–86 in Steven Lukes, *Essays in Social Theory* (London: Macmillan, 1977).

Lyman, Stanford M. and Marvin B. Scott, 'Accounts', *American Sociological Review*, 33 (1968), 46–62.

A Sociology of the Absurd (New York: Appleton-Century-Crofts, 1970).

McClure, John, 'Telling More than They Can Know: The Positivist Account of Verbal Reports and Mental Processes', *The Journal for the Theory of Social Behaviour*, 13, 2 (1983), 111–27.

McCracken, G., *Culture and Consumption: New Approaches to the Symbolic Character of Consumer Goods and Activities*, (Bloomington, IN: Indiana University Press, 1988).

MacIntyre, A., 'The Idea of a Social Science', *The Aristotelian Society*, supplementary vol. 41 (1967), 95–114.

McSweeney, Bill, 'Meaning, Context and Situation', *Archives Europeenes de Sociologie*, 14 (1973), 137–53.

Maguire, John M., *Marx's Theory of Politics* (Cambridge: Cambridge University Press, 1978).

Mann, Michael, ed., *The Macmillan Student Encyclopedia of Sociology* (London: Macmillan, 1983).

Mannheim, Karl, *Man and Society in an Age of Reconstruction: Studies in Modern Social Structure* (1935; rev. and enlarged edn London: Routledge and Kegan Paul, 1940).

Marshall, Gordon, 'Accounting for Deviance', *International Journal of Sociology and Social Policy*, 1 (1981) 17–45.

Martin, David, ed., *50 Key Words in Sociology* (London: Lutterworth, 1970).

Mead, G. H., *Mind, Self and Society* (Chicago: Chicago University Press, 1934).

The Philosophy of the Act (Chicago: Chicago University Press, 1938).

Melden, A. I., *Free Action* (London: Routledge & Kegan Paul, 1964).

Mennell, Stephen, *Sociological Theories: Uses and Unities* (London: Thomas Nelson, 1974).

Sociological Theories: Uses and Unities (2nd edn; Walton-on-Thames: Thomas Nelson, 1980).

Merton, Robert K. *Social Theory and Social Structure*. (Glencoe, IL: The Free Press, 1957).

Social Theory and Social Structure (rev. and enlarged edn; Glencoe, IL: The Free Press, 1968).

Mills, C. W., 'Language, Logic, and Culture', *American Sociological Review*, 4, 5 (1939), 671–80.

'Situated Action and the Vocabulary of Motives', *American Sociological Review*, 5 (1940), 904–13.

Mitchell, G. Duncan, ed., *A New Dictionary of Sociology* (London: Routledge & Kegan Paul, 1979).

Mundle, C. W. K., 'Behaviourism and the Private Language Argument', pp. 103–17 in O. R. Jones, ed., *The Private Language Argument* (London: Macmillan, 1971).

Newcombe, Theodore M., *Social Psychology* (London: Tavistock Publications, 1952).

Nisbett, Richard E. and Timothy DeCamp Wilson, 'Telling More Than We Can Know: Verbal Reports on Mental Processes', *Psychological Review*, 84, 3 (1977), 231–59.

Oberschall, Anthony, *Social Conflict and Social Movements*, (Englewood Cliffs, NJ: Prentice-Hall, 1973).

O'Donnell, Mike, *A New Introduction to Sociology* (London: Harrap, 1981).

A New Introduction to Sociology (3rd edn; London: Thomas Nelson, 1992).

Outhwaite, William, *Understanding Social Life: The Method Called Verstehen* (2nd edn; Lewes, East Sussex: Jean Stroud, 1986).

Parsons, Talcott, 'The Motivation of Economic Activities', pp. 50–68 in Talcott Parsons, *Essays in Sociological Theory* (Glencoe, IL: The Free Press, 1940).

The Structure of Social Action (New York: The Free Press, 1948).

The Social System (London: Routledge & Kegan Paul, 1951).

Parsons, T. and E. A. Shils, *Toward a General Theory of Action* (Cambridge, MA: Harvard University Press, 1951).

Parsons, Talcott, Robert F. Bales, James Olds, Morris Zelditch and Philip E. Slater, *Family, Socialization and Interaction Process* (Glencoe, IL: The Free Press, 1955).

Parsons, Talcott and Neil Smelser, *Economy and Society* (Glencoe, IL: The Free Press, 1956).

Peters, R. S., *The Concept of Motivation* (London: Routledge & Kegan Paul, 1958).

Pope, K. S. and J. L. Singer, eds., *The Stream of Consciousness* (New York: Plenum, 1978).

Porpora, Douglas V., 'On the Post-Wittgensteinian Critique of the Concept of Action in Sociology', *The Journal for the Theory of Social Behaviour*, 13 (1983) 129–46.

'A Response to Jeffrey Alexander's *Theoretical Logic in Sociology* Concerning the Alleged Unidimensionality of Marxian Theory', *The Sociological Quarterly*, 27 (1986), 75–90.

Posner, M. I. and C. R. R. Snyder, 'Attention and Cognitive Control', pp. 71–100 in R. L. Solso, ed., *Information Processing and Cognition: The Loyola Symposium* (Hillsdale, NJ: Erlbaum, 1975).

Potter, Jonathan and Margaret Wetherell, *Discourse and Social Psychology* (London: Sage, 1987).

Rex, John, *Key Problems of Sociological Theory*, (London: Routledge & Kegan Paul, 1961).

Riesman, D. et al., *The Lonely Crowd: A Study in the Changing American Character* (Doubleday: New York, 1966).

Rogers, Mary F., 'Everyday Life as Text', pp. 165–86 in Randall Collins, ed., *Sociological Theory* (San Francisco: Jossey-Bass, 1984).

Ronsenberg, Alexander, *Philosophy of Social Science* (Oxford: The Clarendon Press, 1988).

Rorty, Richard, ed., *The Linguistic Turn: Recent Essays in Philosophical Method* (Chicago: University of Chicago Press, 1967).

Roy, D. 'Work Satisfaction and Social Reward in Quota Achievement: An Analysis of Piecework Incentive', *American Sociological Review*, 18 (1953), 507–14.

'Banana Time' *Human Organization*, 18 (1959–60), 158–68.

Rubinstein, D., 'The Concept of Action in the Social Sciences', *The Journal for the Theory of Social Behaviour*, 7 (1977), 209–36.

Runciman, W.G., *The Methodology of Social Theory: Vol. 1 A Treatise on Social Theory* (Cambridge: Cambridge University Press, 1983).

Schneider, W. and R. M. Shiffrin, 'Controlled and Automatic Human Information Processing: I. Detection, Search, and Attention', *Psychological Review*, 84 (1977), 1–66.

Schutz, Alfred, *The Phenomenology of the Social World*, trans. George Walsh and Frederick Lehnert, intro. George Walsh (Evanston, IL: Northwestern University Press, 1967).

Collected Papers, vol.1: *The Problem of Social Reality*, ed. and intro. Maurice Natanson (The Hague: Martinus Nijhoff, 1973).

Sciulli, David, 'Social Theory and Talcott Parsons in the 1980s', *Annual Review of Sociology*, 11 (1985), 369–87.

Scott, Marvin B. and Stanford M. Lyman, 'Accounts', *American Sociological Review*, 33 (1968), 46–62.

Searle, J. R., *Speech Acts* (Cambridge: Cambridge University Press, 1969).

Seebass, Gottfried and Raimo Tuomela, eds., *Social Action* (Dordrecht: D. Reidel, 1985).

Semin, G. R. and A. S. R. Manstead, *The Accountability of Conduct: A Social Psychological Analysis* (London: Academic Press, 1983).

Sewell, William H. Jr, 'Theory of Action, Dialectic, and History: Comment on Coleman', *American Journal of Sociology*, 93, 1 (1987), 166–72.

Sharrock, W. W. and Watson, D. R., 'What's the point of "rescuing motives"?', *The British Journal of Sociology*, 35, 3 (1984), 435–51.

'Relocating Motives', *The British Journal of Sociology*, 37, 4 (1986), 581–3.

Shotter, John, *Cultural Politics of Everyday Life: Social Constructionism, Rhetoric and Knowing of the Third Kind* (Buckingham: Open University Press, 1993).

Sifianou, Maria, *Politeness Phenomena in England and Greece: A Cross-Cultural Perspective* (Oxford: The Clarendon Press, 1992).

Silverman, D., *The Theory of Organisations* (London: Heinemann Educational Books, 1970).

Singer, J. L., *The Inner World of Daydreaming* (New York: Harper and Row, 1975).

Skinner, Quentin, '"Social meaning" and the Explanation of Social Action', pp. 136–57 in Peter Laslett et al., eds., *Philosophy, Politics and Society*, 4th series (Oxford: Blackwell, 1972).

The Foundations of Modern Political Thought, Vol 1: The Renaissance (Cambridge: Cambridge University Press, 1978).

Smerud, Warren B., *Can There be a Private Language? An Examination of Some of the Principal Arguments* (The Hague: Mouton, 1970).

Sokolov, A. N., *Inner Speech and Thought* (New York: Plenum, 1972).

Sombart, Werner, *Luxury and Capitalism*, intro. Philip Seligman (Ann Arbor, MI: University of Michigan Press, 1967).

Taylor, Charles, *The Explanation of Behaviour* (London: Routledge & Kegan Paul, 1964).

'Interpretation and the Sciences of Man', pp. 217–30 in *Understanding and Social Inquiry*, ed. Fred Dallmayr and Thomas McCarthy (Notre Dame: University of Indiana Press, 1977).

Taylor, Laurie, 'Vocabularies, Rhetorics and Grammar: Problems in the Sociology of Motivation' pp. 145–161 in David Downes and Paul Rock, eds., *Deviant Interpretations* (Oxford: Martin Robertson, 1979).

Taylor, Richard, *Action and Purpose* (Englewood Cliffs, NJ: Prentice-Hall, 1966).

Therborn, Goran, 'Social Practice, Social Action, Social Magic', *Acta Sociologica*, 16, 4 (1972), 157–74.

'Cultural Belonging, Structural Location and Human Action: Explanation in Sociology and in Social Science', *Acta Sociologica*, 34 (1991), 177–91.

Totman, Richard, *Social and Biological Roles of Language: The Psychology of Justification* (London: Academic Press, 1985).

Turner, Jonathan H. 'The Concept of "Action" in Sociological Analysis', pp. 61–88 in Gottfried Seebass and Raimo Tuomela, eds., *Social Action* (Dordrecht: D. Reidel Publishing Co., 1985).

'Toward a Sociological Theory of Motivation.' *American Sociological Review*, 52 (1987), 15–27.

A Theory of Social Interaction (Stanford: Stanford University Press, 1988).

Veblen, Thorstein, *The Instinct of Workmanship and the State of the Industrial Arts* (New York: Macmillan, 1914).

The Theory of the Leisure Class: An Economic Study of Institutions (London: Allen & Unwin, 1925).

Vygotsky, L. S., *Mind in Society: The Development of Higher Psychological Processes* (Cambridge, MA: Harvard University Press, 1978).

Wallis, Roy and Bruce, Steve, 'Accounting for Action, *Sociology*, 17, 1 (1983), 97–111.

Warriner, Charles K., 'Social Action, Behavior and *Verstehen*', *The Sociological Quarterly*, 10 (1969), 501–11.

Watson, Tony, *Sociology, Work & Industry* (2nd edn; London: Routledge & Kegan Paul, 1987).

Weber, Max, *The Protestant Ethic and the Spirit of Capitalism*, trans. Talcott Parsons, (London: Unwin University Books, 1930).

The Theory of Social and Economic Organization, trans. A. M. Henderson and Talcott Parsons, ed. and intro. Talcott Parsons (New York: Free Press, 1964).

The Sociology of Religion, trans. Ephraim Fischoff, intro. Talcott Parsons (London: Methuen, 1965).

Wertsch, J. V., ed., *Culture, Communication and Cognition: Vygotskian Perspectives* (Cambridge: Cambridge University Press, 1985).

White, Alan R., *Attention* (Oxford: Blackwell, 1964).

Winch, Peter, *The Idea of a Social Science and its Relation to Philosophy* (London: Routledge & Kegan Paul, 1958).

Wittgenstein, L., *Philosophical Investigations* (Oxford: Blackwell, 1963).

Wootton, Anthony, *Dilemmas of Discourse* (London: Allen & Unwin, 1975).

Yearley, Stephen, 'Settling Accounts: Action, Accounts and Sociological Explanation', *The British Journal of Sociology*, 39, 4 (1988), 578–99.

Znaniecki, Florian, *Social Actions* (New York: Russell and Russell, 1967).

Index